# A NEW BEGINNING II

*A Personal Handbook to Enhance Your*
*Life, Liberty and Pursuit of Happiness*

JERRY & ESTHER HICKS

We thank each of those who have participated in workshops and consultations with ABRAHAM, for through that interaction this book has evolved.

First printing, June, 1991
Second printing, June, 1992
Third printing, December 1993
Fourth printing, June 1995
Fifth printing, December, 1996
ISBN 0-9621219-1-6


Published by Abraham-Hicks Publications
Manufactured in the U.S.A.

# BOOKS BY ABRAHAM-HICKS:

- A New Beginning I — 1988
  Handbook for Joyous Survival

- A New Beginning II — 1991
  A Personal Handbook to Enhance Your
  Life, Liberty and Pursuit of Happiness

- Sara, and the Foreverness of Friends of
  A Feather — 1995
  An Inspired Narrative of a Child's
  Experiential Journey into the Knowingness
  that All Is Well. (It really is.)

- Daily Planning Calendar/Workbook
  A 365 Day Course in Spiritual Practicality

# CONTENTS

# FORWORD

As an observer and a utilizer of this phenomenon of Non-physical beings who communicate and interact through the physical apparatus of my wife, Esther, I know that they are brilliant, joyous and loving and that they have named themselves, ABRAHAM. But after five years, and thousands of hours, of deliberate interaction with ABRAHAM — I remain without technical terminology to express to you, who or what they are or how their process of communication occurs.

However, it is not necessary to understand the technical "who or what or how" of the phenomenon of electricity in order to utilize or observe the benefits of electricity, and neither is it necessary to have a technical comprehension of this phenomenon of ABRAHAM before we can experience the advantages that ABRAHAM offers.... Advantages that can be as broad and as deep and as ongoing as is our wanting.

Whether you are reading this book from your conscious wanting or from another's wanting to help bring into manifestation something that they believe that you want, it can serve you —

whatever your current degree of personal fulfillment — as a stimulus to another, clear, "new beginning" segment of your life experience.... And, to a more conscious awareness that "THE PATHWAY TO ALL THAT YOU ARE WANTING IS THROUGH THE CORRIDOR OF YOUR JOY."

A reader's comment: *I studied and struggled, for over thirty years, to understand my life, and now — after this brief exposure to the teachings of Abraham — the searching and the stress are in my past. And how wonderful it feels, as I now, for the first time, begin to joyously, consciously live my life!*

As you proceed, point by point, through these pages, expect to find a new clarity; expect to discover practical processes and concepts; expect to be uplifted, and expect a new awareness of your power to uplift those who also seek more joy.

*A New Beginning II,* stands as a powerful stimulus to thoughts and to growth, but should you want a broader understanding of ABRAHAM'S basic philosophies, or more background of the evolution that Esther and I have experienced, consider reading *A New Beginning I,* published in 1988.

As I italicize and highlight segments that, from my perspective, are pivotal points toward comprehension, and as I read these materials, again and again, I am exhilarated as I envision your excited flashes of awareness as you discover the treasures of understanding that you have felt, within you, from the beginning of your existence. For it will rise to the surface of your consciousness — the knowledge of just how valuable and how powerful and how perfect you already are.

Jerry S. Hicks
Boerne, Texas
May, 1991

# Free
# Introductory
# Tape

This limited 90 minute *INTRODUCTION TO ABRA-HAM* cassette offer provides a stimulating overview of Abraham's basic message: The process of communication with your inner world, and the effective personal utilization of the Laws of the Universe in the conscious creation of whatever you want to be or do or have. And Jerry and Esther's explanation of their personal Abraham experience...To receive your free introductory tape, send $3.45 for shipping and handling and allow 1 to 4 weeks for delivery.

Send your order to:  Abraham-Hicks Publications
P.O. Box 690070, San Antonio, TX 78269

Name _____

Address _____

City_____ State _____ Zip _____

Telephone number:_____

(BII97)

# YOUR NATURAL STATE
# IS THAT OF WELL-BEING.

# YOUR NATURAL STATE
# IS ONE OF HEALTH.

YOUR WORLD IS ABUNDANT
WITH ALL THAT YOU
CONSIDER TO BE GOOD,
AND YOU HAVE EASY ACCESS
TO THAT ABUNDANCE.

YOU ARE NOT HERE
UPON THIS EARTH
TO PROVE YOURSELF
WORTHY OF ANYTHING,
TO ANYONE.

YOU ARE IN A STATE OF
ETERNAL GROWTH,
AND THE PLACE
WHERE YOU NOW STAND
IS A VERY GOOD PLACE.

# THERE IS NO ENDING
# TO GROWTH.

YOU EXIST IN A STATE
OF ABSOLUTE FREEDOM,
AND EVERYTHING
THAT YOU EXPERIENCE
IS ATTRACTED BY YOU,
SELF-IMPOSED.
YOU ARE EVEN FREE
TO ATTRACT BONDAGE.

AS YOU THINK,
YOU FEEL,
AND AS YOU FEEL,
YOU OOZE OR RADIATE,
AND ALL-THAT-IS, PHYSICAL
AND NON-PHYSICAL,
IS AFFECTED
BY YOUR OFFERING.
THAT IS YOUR POWER OF
INFLUENCE.

OF COURSE,
YOUR OWN EXPERIENCE
IS MOST AFFECTED
BY YOUR INFLUENCE.

THE ONLY OPINION,
IN ALL OF THE UNIVERSE,
THAT IS OF TRUE
IMPORTANCE TO YOU,
IS YOUR OWN.
AND YOUR OWN OPINION
OF YOU, AFFECTS
THE ENTIRE UNIVERSE.

WHAT YOU ARE
LIVING TODAY
IS AS A RESULT OF THE
THOUGHTS AND FEELINGS
THAT YOU HAVE FELT
BEFORE THIS.
YOUR FUTURE
IS CREATED FROM
YOUR PERSPECTIVE
OF TODAY.

THE CREATIVE LIFE FORCE,
OR ENERGY
OF THE UNIVERSE,
FLOWS THROUGH YOU
AND LITERALLY CONNECTS
YOU TO ALL- THAT-IS.

THROUGH YOUR
ATTENTION,
OR FOCUS OF THOUGHT,
YOU DRAW THE SPECIFICS
UNTO YOU.

AS YOU ARE FOCUSING UPON
AND THEREBY ATTRACTING
THAT WHICH IS
IN HARMONY WITH
THAT WHICH YOU
CONSIDER TO BE GOOD,
YOUR INNER BEING
OFFERS YOU THE FEELING OF
POSITIVE EMOTION AS
ACKNOWLEDGEMENT OF
YOUR POSITIVE
CONNECTION.

AS YOU ARE FOCUSING UPON
AND THEREBY ATTRACTING -
THAT WHICH IS
NOT IN HARMONY WITH
THAT WHICH YOU
CONSIDER TO BE GOOD,
YOUR INNER BEING
OFFERS YOU THE FEELING OF
NEGATIVE EMOTION
AS ACKNOWLEDGEMENT
OF YOUR
NEGATIVE CONNECTION.

WHENEVER YOU FEEL
NEGATIVE EMOTION,
YOU ARE, IN THAT MOMENT,
IN THE MODE OF
NEGATIVE ATTRACTION.
MOST OFTEN YOU ARE,
IN THAT MOMENT,
RESISTING SOMETHING
THAT YOU WANT.

BECAUSE YOU COUNTER
THE MAJORITY OF
YOUR THOUGHTS
WITH OPPOSING
THOUGHTS,
YOU BELIEVE THAT YOU ARE
NOT POWERFUL.

WHEN YOU NO LONGER
SPLIT YOUR
FLOW OF ENERGY
WITH CONTRADICTORY
THOUGHTS,
YOU WILL KNOW
YOUR POWER.

# YOU DO NOT HAVE TO JUSTIFY YOUR PHYSICAL EXISTENCE. YOUR EXISTENCE IS JUSTIFICATION ENOUGH.

YOU DO NOT HAVE TO
JUSTIFY LEAVING
THIS PHYSICAL PLANE
BY ATTRACTING ILLNESS,
OR AGEDNESS.
YOU COME
AND GO
BY VIRTUE OF
YOUR DESIRE TO BE.
YOU ARE FREE TO BE
WHEREVER YOU CHOOSE,
WHENEVER YOU CHOOSE.

# IN YOUR JOY,
# YOU OFFER JOY
# TO THE WORLD.

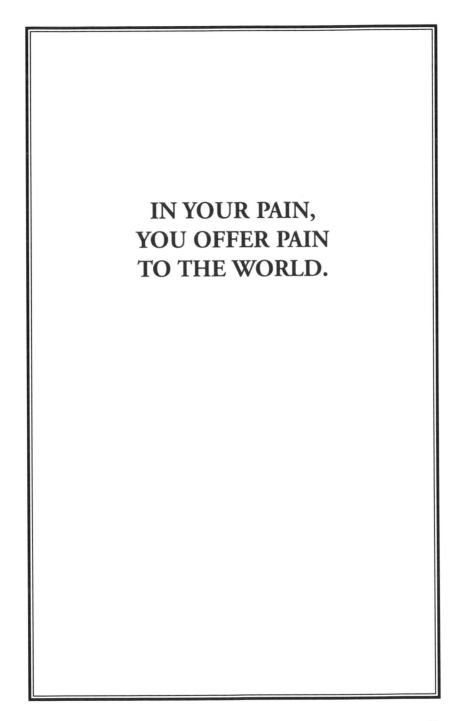

# IN YOUR PAIN,
# YOU OFFER PAIN
# TO THE WORLD.

AS YOU THINK,
YOU FEEL,
AND AS YOU FEEL,
YOU OOZE,
AND AS YOU OOZE,
YOU INFLUENCE.

GOD, OR ALL-THAT-IS,
OR THAT WHICH
IS NON-PHYSICAL,
DOES NOT EXIST
IN A STATE OF COMPLETION,
NOW WAITING
FOR YOU TO CATCH UP,
BUT REVELS IN
ALL THAT YOU LIVE.
FOR AS YOU LIVE,
AS YOU THINK,
AND AS YOU FEEL,
YOU ADD UNTO ALL-THAT-IS.

YOU ARE PHYSICAL
COUNTERPARTS
OF THAT WHICH IS
NON-PHYSICAL —
AND TOGETHER
WE ARE CO-CREATORS.
YOU OFFER A
NEW PERSPECTIVE.
WE OFFER
OUR BROADER AWARENESS.

# THE BASIS OF LIFE
# IS ABSOLUTE FREEDOM.
# THE OBJECTIVE OF LIFE
# IS ABSOLUTE JOY.
# THE RESULT OF LIFE
# IS ABSOLUTE GROWTH.

# PART I

# ABRAHAM SPEAKS
# TO JERRY AND ESTHER

It is with tremendous enthusiasm that we begin the writing of another book, for even as we are putting these words upon the page, we are able to foresee the tremendous value that they will have in the lives of those who will read them. As we are projecting this work into your physical future, we are exhilarated.

Each physical being who responds to our work will do so in a uniquely different way, and from each response we will gain value. One response will not be of more value than another. In other words, there is not that which is specific that we are hoping to gain from our participation. It is that we know that each response is of value. Therefore, there is no specific belief that we intend to impart with this book, and there is no response that we seek. We offer this book out of our pure delight in co-creating, from our Non-physical perspective, with those who are currently focused through the physical.

Physical man often resists those who seek to inform him upon new subjects, for a variety of reasons:

In some cases, he believes that he now has all of the answers to all of the questions, for he has been so fully immersed in the traditions and beliefs of those who surrounded him at the time of his birth that he cannot accept that there are other valid, valuable ideas outside of those accepted by his family, or religious circle, or nation.

In some cases, the beliefs that he now holds do not blend or harmonize with the new information being offered, and because the new ideas do not agree with the old ideas, he feels tremendous insecurity, and tries all the more to hold to or to protect or defend his set of beliefs.

And, in some cases, he seeks nothing, therefore all new stimulation, or different stimulation, seems intrusive to him — and so he resists it. He has felt the sting of wanting and not receiving so often that he now no longer wants. He has decided that it is easier to accept things as they are, asking for no change, than to want change and not get it.

And so, as we introduce this book into your physical world from our Non-physical perspective, it is our clear knowing that it will not be received by all. Those who will receive value from this book will be those who are already recognizing that there is not an ending to growth. Those who will be uplifted and exhilarated by this book will, without exception, be those who do not believe that they currently have all of the answers. Our greatest offering is to those wise physical beings who have already concluded, through their life experience, that there is no ending to growth and that with the answer to every question will come clearer, deeper questions which will, in turn, attract clearer, deeper answers.

*The greatest value of this book will be received by those who understand that they cannot experience that which is outside of the boundaries of their current beliefs. By those who are willing to carefully and deliberately modify or replace some existing beliefs that may be hindering their quest for more freedom, and more growth, and more joy. And by those who are brave enough to think clearly for themselves, using their own, very valuable, life experience in the way they have intended to use it: as the process through which to receive their own conclusions.*

For those who have identified things, experiences, relationships or feelings — that they are currently not experiencing — as something they want, this book will be of tremendous value.

For those who arc currently experiencing hardship, sickness, trials, or negative experience that they are wanting to release from their experience — this book will be of tremendous value.

*We offer this book to assist those who truly want the Deliberate Creative Control of their own life experience. It is written to assist you to do that which you have intended to do as you made the decisions to come forth into these physical bodies.*

And so, it is with tremendous enthusiasm and exuberant expectation that we begin the writing of another book.

We are, indeed, inspired to this joyful offering because of our knowledge of the existence of those who seek what will be written here, and because of our knowledge of the Law of Attraction which will bring those who seek what is written in this book, to this book.

# 1

# OUR PART IN THIS
# MAGNIFICENT CO-CREATION

There are many of us gathered here, working as co-authors upon this book. The words that you are now reading are being offered from a group of beings who are currently observing your physical dimension from our Non-physical dimension.

We are a group, perfectly blended, existing in absolute harmony. We are together because our life experiences have brought us to same conclusions, and from that ever-evolving point of conclusiveness, we are currently at same perspective. We are not only together because of our current and mutual intentions to write this book, but we are joined by the natural laws of the Universe.

These natural laws which provide a glorious and consistent format for life in the Non-physical dimension, also provide the format for life in your physical dimension. And in the same way that we are harmoniously bonded with our Non-physical counterparts who are of like mind, we are also bonded with our physical counterparts, Jerry & Esther.

This bonding, between ABRAHAM and Jerry and Esther, is not new to this physical time and space, but a long time bonding of old Non-physical friends. We have interacted together in countless life experiences and do so now with tremendous satisfaction felt by all who are involved, physical and Non-physical. Indeed, our joyful work extends far beyond the boundaries of one physical life span.

As physical creatures, most of you are so firmly rooted in your physical perspective you lose sight of the larger picture. But sometimes you do sense your broader purpose, and some of you, once you have sensed it, begin to actively pursue it. Once you state your questions, by the powerful laws of the Universe, the answers begin to come.

Our friend, Jerry, from the time of his youth, sensed a broader purpose, and offered a steady stream of questions, that sometimes delighted and sometimes offended his teachers, from the time he was able to speak. While he did not understand his connection with the Non-physical, he was certain that there was much more to life than what his physical eyes could behold, and so his life was spent searching, asking, wanting to understand. Indeed, it was Jerry's intense wanting to understand that reached outward to the boundaries of the Universe and summoned the Non-physical Energy of ABRAHAM.

The Non-physical Energy of ABRAHAM had been intimately aware of the physical Jerry for all of his physical lifetime, but it was not until the blending of the physical *wanting* of Jerry and the physical *allowing* of Esther, that we were able to make this magnificent conscious connection. Esther, too, "sensed" the bigger, broader Universe. And, like Jerry, she wanted very much to be of value to this physical time and place. But, what Esther offered to this unique recipe of physical and Non-physical ingredients was an absolute trust and an unquestioning willingness to allow.

*Esther has allowed an alignment of her physical Energy with our Non-physical Energy, which provides the basis for our communication with you. She is literally receiving blocks of pure, non-verbal thought from us and is, at an unconscious level, translating them into physical words. Every word that you read here is a label that has been interpreted by Esther. She is receiving thought impulses from us, in rather large blocks, and she is digesting these impulses at an unconscious level of her being and is putting the words upon the page for you.* As we are offering the blocks of thought, we are continually taking into consideration the perspective of those who will receive these translations, and we are conscious, with every particle of thought that we transmit, of the physical beings who will be receiving these thoughts as they read the written words upon the page.

We have begun this segment of our offering with a statement, "There are many of us gathered here", although the word "here" does not literally apply to the Non-physical dimension in which we currently exist. "Here" indicates a place, and a place indicates physical realm, and we are not focused from a physical realm. However, we have discovered that if we are to be of any real value to you, as you are physically focused, that we must reach you and speak with you from the physical perspective that you currently hold, for your total frame of reference is physical.

And so, we are continually seeking bridges through which we can convey knowledge without distortion. Bridges through which we can enhance your physical experience without offering excessive fairy tales. As we offer the words, "There are many of us gathered here," we are aware of the picture that that statement brings to most of you, for you cannot release yourselves from your physical perspective, even though you are contemplating a Non-physical dimension.

*"Many of us gathered here," in Non-physical dimension, cannot be literally translated into your physical perspective, because we are different than you are. We are not contained in bodies, and we are more flexible in our movement.* When we say, "gathered together," we do not mean that we have gathered around in a comfortable old room to chat about our physical friends of the earth plane. We are literally merging, one with another, as many smaller lights may join together to cast a brighter beam.

Not long after Esther began speaking for ABRAHAM, she said, "ABRAHAM, I want to see you!" She had read accounts from other physical beings, who were speaking for Non-physical friends, who told elaborate stories of their visual encounters with their Non-physical friends.

We said to Esther, "We have observed you, moving through your house, in the night, with your eyes closed, afraid that you may see us."

She laughed and attempted to convince us that she was feeling much braver now and really did want to see us.

And so, as she lay in her bed, with her sleeping mate, in a very dark bedroom, we said, "Open your eyes, and see."

As she opened her eyes she saw what she later described as fireflies. Thousands of fireflies! Small dots of light darting about the room. At one point, all of these tiny lights gathered together into one corner of the room, becoming a beam of light that was too bright for her physical eyes to look into, and then dispersing into seven or eight not so bright beams, and then, again, into thousands of tiny dots of light. Esther's visual experience gave her a clearer perspective of our Non-physical existence. She concluded, "You are Energy," for she viewed us as light. "You are very mobile, very flexible, very free," as she observed our ability to merge into one, or to separate into many.

As Esther receives blocks of thought from ABRAHAM, she receives us as one. One conclusive consensus of thought coming powerfully and undeniably into her mind.

*The words that you are now reading are coming from beings who are currently focused from a Non-physical perspective, therefore to try to explain to you "where" we come from, or "where" we are is not relevant. We spend no time looking back, into the past, to try to explain who we are in our now, because we understand that our power to create is in our present.*

And so, we will speak to you in terms of who we are, from our perspective of beingness, indeed, from our current "state of being." We are free, joyous and growing beings — putting emphasis upon our state of freedom — for it is through our freedom to be, that we are able to choose joy and growth. *We are not different from you, or any other being in the Universe, regarding freedom, for we are all absolute-*

*ly free, but most do not understand their freedom, and therefore do not live it. Freedom is not something that is earned, or assigned, but something that is acknowledged.*

Through our experiences, individual and collective, we have arrived at many conclusions. We prefer joy to pain, or even to the absence of joy. We prefer growth to stagnation. We prefer freedom to confinement or manipulation, or even to disapproval. We have, through vast experience, come to understand the true nature of our beings, and we understand that everything we are adds to the ultimate upliftment of All-That-Is.

IT IS OUR KNOWING, THAT THERE IS NOT AN ENDING TO GROWTH, FOR WE ALL EXIST IN AN ETERNAL NOW. The joy or the pain, the growth or the stagnation, the freedom or the confinement, that each of us feel in this moment, is purely our individual decision, and we take great delight in that knowledge. And in that knowledge, as ABRAHAM, we continually choose freedom, growth and joy.

From our experience or perspective — or state of being free, growing and joyous — we direct our Energy, or attention, into your physical dimension. As we observe your earth we are able to identify your cities, your homes, your individual life experiences, indeed every detail of your physical life is available to us, but we prefer to give our attention to your "state of being", for there is far more pertinent information contained there than in the physical trappings that surround you. Indeed, there are many wonderful things of a physical nature for you to explore and experience and enjoy, and we do acknowledge the beauty and the deliciousness of your physical world. *For all of the physical stuff of your world exists for one purpose only, and that is for the enhancement of your "state of being."*

*As teachers who seek growth, upliftment and joy, we are literally drawn to those who seek that. You are as powerful magnets, attracting to you that which you seek or ask for or acknowledge or give your attention to. We cannot seek you out, and present ourselves to you if you do not seek that which we are — for by virtue of the powerful Law of Attraction, only that which*

37

*is like unto itself is drawn, and just as oil and water do not mix, different intentions or perspectives or beliefs do not mix.*

As physical beings you readily identify boundaries and limits within your physical realm, but from our perspective there are no boundaries or limits. There is no guard at our gate of our glorious state of being, monitoring and evaluating and deciding who enters or leaves, for the gathering is a natural process of like attracting like. *Those who are not currently wanting or seeking that which we are about — simply exist in another state of being.*

*Physical and Non-physical dimensions are intricately intertwined and cannot be separated. Physical life, as you know it to be, could not exist without the existence of the Non-physical dimension, Energy, support and knowledge. Physical earth is a product of the attention and knowledge of the Non-physical dimension.*

Physical man has been interacting with the Non-physical dimension for as long as physical man has existed, and his experiences have varied tremendously as his perspective and expectations have changed. Indeed, contact between physical and Non-physical is certainly not something that is new that we are now excitedly explaining to you, for countless tales of ghostly encounters, unexplainable happenings and divine revelations abound in your physical archives. *Physical man has long been receiving inspiration, intuition and even clear communication from that which he absolutely acknowledged was separate and apart from his own conscious physical mind.*

If only considering the *physical* experiences upon your planet, it would not be possible to log and explain and understand the relationships of one experience in one part of your world to another in another part of your world. And as you attempt to consider, to digest and to log and draw comparisons of all of the *Non-physical* encounters that have occurred and are occurring, you soon discover the impossibility of the task you have set upon.

There are accountings of wide ranges of experiences, as physical man has been interacting with the Non-physical dimension, and much has been written and expressed about it, and much confusion and skepticism has emerged. The confusion exists, largely, because of the comparison of the many conflicting details as physical man tries very hard to wedge a variety of different experiences into a handful of conclusions. *As physical beings, who depend almost entirely upon physical evidence to support your beliefs, you find yourself in an uncomfortable position as you explore this Non-physical area, seemingly devoid of any physical evidence.*

***Rather than trying to understand the experiences of others, rather than trying to unravel the never-ending thread of experience from the perspective of all others —*** *WE ENCOURAGE YOU TO GIVE A LARGER PART OF YOUR ATTENTION TO YOUR OWN PERSONAL LIFE EXPERIENCES, FOR WITHIN THAT WHICH YOU ARE LIVING RUNS A THREAD OF PERFECT CONSISTENCY.*

By observing your own life experience you will gain an understanding of the absolute, consistent Laws of the Universe. You can not, no matter how much effort or time you offer, see through the eyes of another. Therefore, you cannot conclude for another. But, as you are evaluating you, and that which touches you, you will gain absolute insight into everything in the Universe as it relates to you.

While we are writing this book from our current Non-physical perspective, we do not differ so much from you as you read it from your physical perspective, for we are all, physical and Non-physical, very much alive. Whether physically or non-physically focused, we are, through our currently chosen format, seekers of experience, stimulation and growth.

*From our Non-physical perspective, our focus can easily be extended to include a clear awareness of your physical experience, while from your physical dimension, it is more difficult for you to extend your awareness to include our Non-physical experience.* You might say we have a broader perspective. And from this broader perspective, we actually have a clearer view of who you are and why you are currently focused through your physical bodies in this physical dimension, than you do.

We continue to observe your experience, seeking clearer expression, and using your words, to assist you in a broader understanding of who you are. But there is a gap in communication, especially as we attempt to explain our state of existence to you in a way that makes sense to you through your physical perspective. Many stories have evolved to help physical man catch a glimpse of the Non-physical, in an effort to help him understand himself more broadly — for physical man is an extension of the Non-physical realm. Not only his roots exist there, but the very core of his current physical being exists within the Non-physical realm. And while we resist the telling of fairy tales, the offering of examples, or analogies, for the purpose of communication, does occur frequently.

*We cannot express, literally, to you what our Non-physical experience is, because through your physical eyes you have not the basis to understand it, therefore our greater value to you is our offering of Principles and Laws that you can apply to what you do understand.* And while there is no topic upon which we are not willing to attempt to offer some clarity, it has been our experience that we can not offer clarity to physical man as it relates to things of the Non-physical. We can, however, offer tremendous clarity to things you are experiencing regarding your physical dimension.

And so, aside from a few statements of introduction, to give you some idea of who we are and why we are interacting with you, *we will give our greatest attention, here in this book, to you, why you are here in this physical dimension and how you may achieve whatever it is that you are wanting, through a clearer understanding of the infinite, eternal Laws that exist in all dimensions.*

**It is our wanting to assist you in gaining a sense of your powerful now. To see yourselves as we see you, standing upon the brink of your magnificent future. We are wanting to renew within you that wonderful sense of adventure that you felt as you emerged into this magnificent physical body, anticipating that which was before you here upon this earth. For certainly, as you emerged, you recognized another NEW BEGINNING.**

# 2

# YOUR PART IN THIS MAGNIFICENT CO-CREATION

E VERY PART OF YOUR PHYSICAL WORLD IS, AND ALWAYS HAS BEEN, SUPPORTED BY THAT WHICH IS NON-PHYSICAL. The very Energy that created, and now supports, your physical existence, is focused into your physical realm from the Non-physical dimension. The Non-physical dimension is the source of the extended thought, or Energy, that supports your physical world. Your physical bodies are composed of the physical stuff of your physical plane and the life force, or Energy, that supports you — that Energy that makes the difference between whether your doctors pronounce you dead or alive — comes forth from the Non-physical dimension. It is not possible to separate your world, or even your physical body, from the Non-physical dimension, for the two dimensions are eternally intertwined.

Through all of the time that physical man has moved about upon this planet, his acceptance of and understanding of and deliberate interaction with the Non-physical realm has been one of tremendous variety and continual change. To attempt even a vague recap of physical man's beliefs, regarding the Non-physical, would require many volumes the size of this one, and so, we will limit our discussion, primarily, to current physical man's view of the Non-physical dimension and to the time that we see just before you.

*We are eager to help you put the Non-physical dimension into a clearer perspective because it is our knowing that a basic understanding of the relationship between the physical and Non-physical dimensions is essential to a satisfying physical experience.* As long as the Non-physical realm remains out there, somewhere, big and vague and mysterious and misunderstood, any meaningful deliberate interaction with it will be impossible. Most physical beings, past or present, have not found their place within this vast Universe. You do not understand who you are or why you are physical beings at this time. You do not understand your relationship with your planet or with that which is beyond your physical planet. You do not understand how it is that you exist, or why, or what you are to do now that you do exist. And most of you, in your confusion, do very little on purpose. *Most physical beings are as very small corks floating atop a very large sea, moved by the current that is the strongest, often submerged by a wave that is larger, later to re-surface, now warily watching out for the next big wave. Not more deliberate, just more guarded.*

While many believe that they existed in some form prior to their emergence into this physical body, and many also believe, or hope, that there will be something following this physical experience, most have, at best, gathered bits and pieces of the total picture. Much of your misunderstanding comes from your preoccupation with death. You think so much in terms of being dead or alive that you miss, perhaps, the biggest point of all: THERE IS NO DEATH! THERE IS ONLY LIFE! ETERNAL, EVERLASTING LIFE!

We hear some of you speaking about your past life experiences, sometimes explaining in great detail who you were last time, and the time before that, and the time before that. Carefully summing up past lifetimes in a neat chronological row. Much of the information you have gathered is absolutely accurate, but there is one common misunderstanding that gets in the way of your accepting who you really are, and that is the idea that you are born into a physical body, and so now you are physical, and then you die, so now you are Non-physical, and then you are born into another body, so now you are physical again. Eternally bouncing back and forth between physical and Non-physical dimensions. It is just not that way.

*Right now, at the same time that you are living this physical experi-ence, in this physical body, there is another part of you that exists in the Non-physical dimension — a Non-physical counterpart, older, wiser, with a much broader perspective than you currently hold through your physical eyes. Words, such as "soul" or "higher self," have been used to describe this Non-physical you. We use the words "Inner Being."*

Your Inner Being exists as the culmination of all the lifetimes and experiences, both physical and Non-physical, that you have lived, and it continues to benefit and evolve because of the expe-riences that you are having here in this physical time and place.

*This idea of being physical and Non-physical at the same time is often a difficult concept for you to accept. It is not un-common for one of our physical friends who has interacted with us for many months to ask, "ABRAHAM, have you ever been phys-ical?" or "ABRAHAM, why are you choosing not to be physical?" still holding the belief that it must be one way or the other.*

We are a group of Non-physical beings who are the Non-phys-ical counterparts of many of you who are currently physical. And all who are currently focused through physical bodies have a Non-physical counterpart who is infinitely, intricately aware of you. Again, we call that counterpart your Inner Being.

Many physical beings question why they do not have the ben-efit of remembering other physical lifetimes, sometimes resentful that they have had to start anew, learning everything all over again. Some work very hard to dredge up some of those life experiences from the past, hoping that they will find some powerful knowing that has been forgotten, that will magically transform this life experience into something more meaningful or more productive. But it is not necessary to recall past lives to receive benefit of all that experience, for you have never been, nor will you ever be, separated or disconnected from your Inner Being, who holds all of that information.

From your Non-physical perspective, prior to emerging into this physical body, you were aware that you would be entering into an agreement not to recall the details of all that you have lived before. From that broader, clearer perspective, you knew that through these physical eyes, those details would only cause confusion. You remembered the physical tendency of regurgitating past experience — and so, you happily emerged into this body, intending to focus specifically on the details of this time and place. You saw this physical experience as an opportunity to come forth into a new place, in a different time, to interact with other beings holding many different intentions. You saw this physical life experience as a pure opportunity to be stimulated by new thought and experience.

*EVERY COMBINATION OF MINDS, OR OF THOUGHT, ADDS UNTO THE UNIVERSE.* Each time you interact with another, the combination of the two of you adds to the Universe in an absolutely unique way, for each of you holds a different set of intentions and expectations. The knowing within you is different. And as all of these varying aspects of those involved combine — value is added unto the Universe.

As you hold this book in your hands, reading the words, responding intellectually and emotionally, you are uniquely adding unto the Universe, for no other will respond in just the way that you are responding.

As you made the decision to emerge into this physical body, you were very much aware that this physical life experience would put you upon the leading edge of creation. You excitedly anticipated your physical involvement with this very specifically, very deliberately, chosen earth experience because you understood the value that your participation would bring to All-That-Is. *From your pre-birth perspective, you knew you were going forth to physical earth, not to prove yourself and earn a greater reward,*

*but to participate from your unique perspective — for the pur-*
*pose of adding still more clarity unto the Universe.*

You excitedly anticipated interacting with many old friends, sometimes specifically planning the details of your physical meeting. And you also looked forward to your interaction with those with whom you have not met before, for you understood the absolute value in all interaction.

Some have argued, "But ABRAHAM, what is the value of living a physical lifetime, struggling and striving and learning from it, if in the next physical lifetime I can't remember it anyway? What is the purpose of the hard work and the growth?"

Do not worry. Your experience, your hard work, your growth, is not being wasted, for your Inner Being accumulates every particle of every experience that you have ever lived, or that you are now living. And that experience is available to you! It is available in the form of guidance that is constantly communicated to you. Guidance that is available to you during every waking hour of your day. Guidance that holds far more value than every experience you have lived since the day your were born. Indeed, this Guidance System is supreme.

*It is not necessary for you to remember all, or any, of the details of past life experiences because you have access to the important conclusions that were drawn from those experiences.* Just as there is not value in spending great amounts of time reflecting back upon your activities when you were three years old, there is not value in trying to pursue past lifetimes. But there is tremendous value in being that which you are now, which includes having passed through the experience of being three years old, and there is tremendous value in allowing the older, broader culmination of all that you have lived in all past life-times guide you and assist you in choices and decisions in every moment of this physical lifetime.

**Beyond the bit of entertainment it might provide, trying to recall, and spending time reflecting on, past lives, serves very lit-tle real purpose. BUT A STRONG, CONSCIOUS CONNECTION WITH THAT PART OF YOU THAT IS NOW THE CULMINATION OF ALL OF**

THOSE PAST LIVES IS OF TREMENDOUS VALUE. *Indeed, a blending of the physical you, that you see and know to be here in this physical body, and the broader, older, wiser inner you that is focused in the Non-physical dimension — makes a wonderful combination for the enhancement of both worlds.*

# 3

# THE BEST
# OF BOTH WORLDS

An introduction to your "Inner Being" is an essential beginning
place for all understanding. An acceptance of your Inner
Being, and a willingness to receive that greater, broader perspective, is essential to living the joyful, growth-filled physical
experience that you have come here to live. Unless you are willing
to accept and utilize your greater perspective, you are extremely
limited, as are most physical beings, in what you will deliberately
accomplish.

In this physical world in which you are focused, most are pre-
occupied with "doing". You have emerged into a world that is
extremely action oriented, and so you place tremendous value in
doing. And so, many are moving about, doing here and doing
there, as busy as the hours in the day will allow, yet feeling the frustration of having accomplished very little.

Many years before Esther made her conscious connection with
ABRAHAM, she worked, between segments of schooling, at a facility
for those considered to be mentally ill. One morning, as she
walked her usual path upon the hospital grounds, she observed

some of the patients, upon very large machinery, moving big mounds of dirt. On the first day, they moved the dirt from one corner of the yard to another. On the next day, they moved the same pile to another corner. On the next day they moved it back to the original spot, and so, Esther asked one of the attendants, "What are they doing?"

The attendant replied, "Oh, nothing, really. We're just keeping them busy. Giving them something to do."

Esther stood there feeling empty and sad, and then she said, "Surely, there must be more to their lives than just pushing dirt around."

Years later as she related the story to us we said to her, "Esther, we are not wanting to hurt your feelings, but, for the most part, that is what all physical beings spend most of their lives doing, just moving stuff from place to place." Because you do not understand the greater laws that are responsible for all achievement and growth, most of you lull yourselves into a false sense of motion forward by keeping things moving about you. Often, your action and hard work are offered as a sort of justification for your being here. And as you are working, acting, doing, most are creating in what we would describe as a "backwards fashion." Always wanting to take action, believing that all things that happen are a product of your action.

*Without the broader perspective offered from the inner dimension there is tremendous limitation experienced upon this earth — for there are constant limits to what you can accomplish when you are depending upon "doing" or "action" only.* But by allowing your broader perspective to merge with your physical perspective, you can literally access the power of the Universe to assist you in your physical creation, or accomplishments. Many of those you have labeled genius, or master, in their accomplishments of music, or art, or science, have been physical beings, just like you, who simply allowed themselves access to broader knowing. They merely opened the door to their own broader knowing, and literally tapped in to Infinite Intelligence, drawing unto them the spe-

48

cific details of their desires. You set them apart, and revere them as unusual, while they are very much like you. What sets them apart is only their recognition of their connection with All-That-Is.

*As we observe your physical world, we see that most of you, in your hurry to "do", are very busy. There is a sort of frenzy to "do", but not much is done in joy. Some are deliberately "sacrificing" joy for the sake of growth, or reward. Others actually want to have joy, or want to enjoy, but just can't seem to hold onto it for more than a moment here and there.*

Commonly, you are looking toward some place in your future for the satisfaction that you seek. Looking toward the weekend, looking toward vacation, looking toward retirement. "If I just had more money, then I would be happy." "When I find my perfect mate, then I will be happy." "Once I find the perfect work, then I will be happy." *Most are looking toward a future time for pleasure and a feeling of satisfaction, but very little joy is being experienced in your now. And yet, your NOW, IS your life experience.*

And so, now, we have come to the heart of the reason that we are interacting with physical man in this time — and to why we are writing this book: *IT IS OUR DOMINANT INTENT TO ASSIST YOU IN UNDERSTANDING WHO YOU ARE AND WHY YOU ARE HERE IN THIS PHYSICAL BODY, FROM YOUR BROADEST PERSPECTIVE — AND TO ASSIST YOU IN RECOGNIZING AND UTILIZING THE PROCESSES AND LAWS THROUGH WHICH YOU MAY FIND JOY, NOW. Not a fleeting, future joy, but a tangible, ever present, constant, continuing, blissful growing experience.*

Each of you are much more than you know from your physical perspective, for you have been experiencing and learning and achieving for longer than the length of your physical years. You have deliberately chosen to be a part of this physical time and place because this physical format provides opportunity for thought, for experience and for creation. You have great resources of knowledge and strength, but most of you do not utilize those resources. Not for the lack of wanting to, but for lack of understanding how to, or for the lack of recognizing that the resources exist at all.

As you emerged into this physical body, and into this physical dimension, you instantly became a part of the physical world that surrounds you, subjected to the powerful influence that abounds, and that influence is resistant to anything that cannot be explained in physical terms.

Actually, nothing here in your physical environment can be explained ONLY through physical terms, and so, that which you do not understand, you force into a sort of logic, and the result of that is that the majority of you are living and working and seeing through eyes of tremendous misconceptions. It is like playing in a game where the rules have not been clearly defined, and since you do not understand the point of the game, you cannot receive much satisfaction from it.

*Here are a few of your greatest misconceptions:*

*"I make things happen through effort and strain."*

*"Pain and hard work are the ingredients of the greatest accomplishments."*

*"The more time I spend pitting my body against the struggle, the more effective or triumphant I will be."*

*"Physical action is what makes things happen...."*

Working under those assumptions, you are not only tremendously handicapped, and limited, you are usually soon defeated and tired. After years of working, but not succeeding, most stop trying and resign themselves to a tired body and lost dreams. Looking for others, defeated also, in order to justify their own failure.

*For the most part, only the young are hopeful, but their hope is usually short-lived because of the pressing influence of those who have gone before.*

As you continue through this book, you will discover the clear and simple "rules of the game," offered to assist you in finding your joy.

We are deliberately applying repetitive emphasis, in the early part of this book, to help you to understand the broadness of your being. Our first intention is to help you understand that "your" experience did not begin with this physical birth. Unless we are able to bring you to that knowing, or at least to a desire to understand it — then much of what we offer here in this book will not be beneficial to you.

*The connection between the physical you and the broader, older Non-physical you is the missing link in much of what physical man seeks to understand — and it is the key to your living the spectacular and productive life you envisioned before your birth.*

Prior to your emergence into this body you understood the power of influence that exists in the physical world, for you remembered it clearly from other physical life experiences, and you were eager to re-enter the physical realm in order to offer some balance to those influences.

The pages that follow, offer detailed instructions to assist you with the conscious, deliberate opening of a passageway between the physical and Non-physical dimensions. A passageway so clear that conscious communication can be offered back and forth between dimensions. These processes will assist you in allowing the alignment of your Energies to provide the basis for this communication — and once the alignment is complete, both dimensions will benefit tremendously.

*As we assist you in opening the door into the Non-physical dimension, it is certainly not with the intention of distracting you from your physical awareness, but to bring clarity and strength and greater purpose to your physical existence.* It is our absolute knowing that until you make this connection between your physical being and your Inner Being, you cannot satisfy the intentions that you held as you emerged into this physical body.

While there are many joyful experiences to participate within, here in your physical dimension — there is nothing more exhilarating than making decisions within your physical framework, that harmonize with the broader intentions that you held as you entered this physical realm.

Since your physical experience is supported by the Non-physical realm, there can be no separation from the Inner You. From the day you emerged into this physical body, you have been interacting with the Inner You. Through your current perspective you have known nothing other. The Inner You is such an integral part of you, that you notice it not, and in the same way, the inner world is such a part of your physical world, that you see it not.

*As you insist upon physical evidence to support all that you accept as real, you miss the greater part of your experience and limit yourselves, in large part, to what you can do and explain through the moving of physical matter about.* But as you accept the existence of the inner world — and remember your personal relationship with that world, and with your Inner Being — you will begin to experience the fullness of this physical life experience.

Esther walked down to open the gate for her mate, who was bringing the vehicle, and as she stood there, waiting, she saw that the sky was more beautiful than she had ever experienced it before, with colors deeper and different than usual. She could hear sounds that were clearer than she had ever heard them, hearing birds that seemed much too far away for her to hear. There were unusual fragrances in the air that were delicious, and the air upon her skin was wonderful. And she stood there with tears streaming down her face, and she said, right out loud, "Surely, there has never been a more delicious physical experience in all of the Universe." And then, with a sudden realization, she said, "ABRAHAM, it is you, isn't it!"

We smiled a very broad smile through her lips, for she had caught us peeping through her eyes, hearing through her ears, smelling through her nose and feeling through her skin. Indeed, we were enjoying the deliciousness of your physical world through Esther's physical body.

We are wanting you to understand the very pointed value of aligning with, and allowing interaction with, your own Inner Being.

By Esther's conscious and deliberate choice of thoughts, she had brought herself to a vibrational level that allowed the fuller interaction of ABRAHAM. She had begun her day making a clear deliberate statement of intent: *"Today, no matter where I go, no mat-*

*ter what I do, no matter who I interact with, it is my dominant intent to look for that which makes me feel good."*

Only as you recognize and experience the feelings of strength and knowing that are offered by your Inner Being, will you experience no limitations in your physical world. Only as you remember the Infinite and Eternal Laws of your Universe, will you always create deliberately here in your physical environment. And only as you accomplish a conscious blending of the physical you and the inner you, will you deliberately add to the total nature of you, and accomplish that which you intended as you emerged into this physical body. Without the recognition of, and blending with, the inner you, your experience will be less satisfying and infinitely less productive than you intended when you came forth into this physical environment.

*AS TEACHERS, WE HAVE LEARNED, LONG AGO, THAT WORDS DO NOT TEACH. LEARNING COMES THROUGH LIFE EXPERIENCE.*

We offer our words, knowing that they will remind you of experiences past, or prepare you for clearer recognition of the experiences that are to come. No amount of words offered in explanation are as valuable as real first-hand experience. And so, we could write thousands of pages, here, about the existence of your Inner Being and its willingness to communicate with you and the value thereof, and in all of those pages of reading, you would not reap the benefit of one simple physical exercise. And so, here we will offer to you a step-by-step process to facilitate the opening of a passageway between the conscious physical you and the inner you — your Inner Being — that you may have that valuable first-hand experience.

*And so, if you are accepting the existence of the inner world and of your Inner Being, and if you are now wanting fuller communication and more experiencing of the reservoir of knowledge and strength and clarity that is there for you, here is the process:*

It is important that you have a desire for the opening of this passageway in order to achieve it. It must be something that you want. Then all that is required is that you set some time aside to allow it.

Find 15 or 20 minutes in every day to sit with the intent of quieting your conscious mind. It is not necessary that you block the same time of day every day, but it is great value to be consistent and not miss a day, for this process is a progressive thing.

Quieting of your mind means sitting for a few minutes each day and allowing your mind to rest, still and quiet, not thinking of anything. That is not an easy thing for you to do, for your thinking mechanisms are very responsive to stimulation of thought, however it is important that you quiet your mind for a short time each day.

Many have questioned, "How can I quiet my mind without falling asleep?"

That is a very good question, and an important one. For falling asleep does not put you in the place of allowing this process. If we were drawing you a graphic picture on paper, we would show full conscious awareness on one end of our graph, and being fast asleep on the other extreme. And what you are wanting to achieve is very near the end of being asleep, yet you are wanting to be awake. Sometimes it is helpful to focus upon something within your physical awareness that requires very little conscious thought, such as the sound of a dripping faucet, or the sight of a flickering candle. Sometimes concentrating only upon your own breathing is effective. Your first objective in your deliberate opening of your passageway between the physical you and the Non-physical you is to consciously withdraw your thoughts from the physical realm and allow yourself to sit, quiet, still, and eternally connected to that which is Non-physical. Only when the external awarenesses of the physical world are released can you sense the subtle awarenesses of the Non-physical world. However, it is not beneficial for you to try to see, or sense, or hear, the Non-physical world in the early days of your sitting. Your objective is simple and singular: "I am sitting with the intent of stilling my mind."

When you have succeeded, even for a few seconds, with stilling your conscious thinking mechanism, your physical body will feel different to you. You will feel numbness, or heaviness. Esther said she could not tell her nose from her toe, with all parts of her body feeling as if they were one part.

This numbness, or heaviness, is an indication that you have succeeded in quieting your conscious thinking mechanism, and you are, in that moment of numbness, in the state of allowing the alignment of your Energies. Your first objective has been accomplished and now your Inner Being is in a position to do its work. As you sit in this absolute state of allowing, your Inner Being will begin to align your Energies, merging the faster, higher frequency Energy of the inner world with the slower, lower frequency Energy of your physical world. During this process there is nothing for you to do, other than sit with the intent of quieting your mind. If you try to become actively involved in the process, you will lose your place of numbness and you will interfere with the work of your Inner Being.

Each day, as you accomplish the quieting of your mind, and allow the alignment of your Energies, your blending becomes more, until eventually, during your process of quieting your mind, you will feel physical sensations such as twitching of muscles, or the itching or tickling of your skin. Those sensations are physical evidence of the aligning of your Energies. Do not give attention to these sensations, for you will lose your place of numbness. Continue to quiet your mind, and focus upon that place of quiet.

When you receive movement, in other words, when your hand moves, or your head moves, or when a finger or toe wiggles, and you know you did not set forth the signal for the movement, your alignment of Energies has been sufficiently completed to begin the process of communication. When your body moves and you did not consciously intend the motion, understand that the intent to move was sent from your Inner Being, from Non-physical perspective, and you are the conscious physical receiver of the impulse or intentions. And once that occurs, the conscious transmission and receiving of blocks of thoughts from Non-physical to physical has been successfully accomplished.

The amount of time that will pass from your first decision to quiet your mind to the receiving of movement will vary from person to person. The factors that most affect your success, in this alignment of Energies process, are these:

(1) Your degree of wanting of this alignment process. Are you really wanting to interact with your Non-physical counterpart, or are you sending forth contradictory messages of concern or reluctance? As your wanting is pure and not sabotaged by thoughts of worry or doubt, your alignment process will be very fast. The better you feel, the faster the process.

(2) The impetus behind your wanting. Do you seek this interaction from your positive position of wanting, or from your negative position of lack? Do you seek this interaction from your position of wanting to experience more freedom, more growth and more joy, or are you wanting your Inner Being to intervene and fix the things you have messed up in your life? Again, the better you feel, the faster the process.

(3) Your willingness to allow this alignment. Have you been able to successfully quiet your mind so that you feel detached or numb for at least one or two minutes each time you sit to quiet your mind, or does your mind continue to ponder throughout the quiet time? If you are having difficulty quieting your mind, try sitting at the beginning of your day, before you have received so much thought stimulation.

There is not a prescribed amount of time that is required for the opening of your passageway. If it is your desire, and you sit wanting and willing to allow the alignment, this can be a very fast process.

The alignment of Energies is an extremely technical process and cannot be accomplished from your physical perspective. You cannot begin to identify the points of Energy within your physical apparatus, for there are thousands of them. Your Inner Being, however, is fully aware of each Energy point, and has full awareness of the level of vibration within each. It is absolutely the work of your inner perspective — not your conscious perspective — to accomplish this task. You may trust that your Inner Being is capable of this delicate task. Your work, from your conscious physical perspective, is to set forth your clear intent, or desire, for this alignment, and then to put yourself in the physical position of allowing the alignment.

*The alignment of Energies is an ongoing thing, for you will never achieve absolute alignment as long as you remain focused through your physical apparatus.*

Only when you die, by your terms, or withdraw from your physical focus and re-emerge into the Non-physical, by our terms, will you be absolutely blending with the Non-physical Energies. But sufficient blending for the extreme enhancement of your physical experience can be rather easily accomplished.

# 4

# COMMUNICATION
# WITH THE INNER WORLD

Once you have consciously acknowledged that your physical body received the impulse to move, and you are fully aware that the stimulation of thought for the movement of your body did not come from your conscious intent — you may know that the alignment of Energies has been completed sufficiently, and that you may, if you desire, begin to consciously receive broader communication from your Inner Being. You have already received communication, for the block of thought that resulted in the movement of your body was transmitted by your Inner Being. And your physical apparatus was the receiver of the impulse. Therefore, you are already receiving communication, in a sense. But in time, if it is your wanting, you will experience tremendous evolution in your ability to communicate with the inner world.

As you sat for 15 or 20 minutes each day — for the purpose of allowing the alignment of your physical and Non-physical Energies — your first sole objective was to completely quiet your conscious mind, in order to allow your Inner Being to align your Energies. But as you have received movement, now your Energies have been sufficiently aligned for some communication to have occurred, and now you have a new objective. Now, it is no longer of value to sit in a meditative state quieting your mind.

*Communicating with your Non-physical friends is really not so different from interacting with your physical friends. Many of the same traits of good communication apply:*

It is of value to have at least a general idea of that which you would like to talk about, for you are tapping into a very large reservoir of thought and knowing. Just as you would not go to a library and say to the librarian at the front desk, "Hello, I would like a book, please," so it is good for you to narrow your topics a bit when you are interacting with the Non-physical.

In the early days of Esther's communication with us, she would often seek conversation with us late at night as she lay next to her sleeping mate.

"ABRAHAM, talk to me."

"What are you wanting to talk about?"

"Oh, I don't know, you choose something."

"Esther, go to sleep."

You see, you are the attractors of your experience. We have learned that our offering of information that has not been asked for, is of little value, for you are the attractors of your experience. When you are asking, you are open to that which is offered.

Spend some time pondering, sorting, thinking about what you are wanting to discuss with your Non-physical counterparts, then pose a question to your Inner Being, and then listen with the clear intent of receiving information upon that subject.

*The clearer you are about what you are wanting to understand, the clearer that which you receive will be.*

Quiet your mind in preparation for communication, but be alert and clear minded as you actually begin to communicate.

Many believe that communication occurs only through the speaking and hearing of words, and yet that is really a very small part of the communication that takes place in this Universe. Even in your physical world, much more communication is occurring through the transmission of thought than through the offering of words. *To receive information from the inner world it will be necessary for you to hear with your mind, instead of your ears. And, as with most things that are new, it will take some practice to make the adjustment.*

**FROM OUR NON-PHYSICAL PERSPECTIVE WE DO NOT SPEAK IN WORDS, OR LABELS. WE DO NOT USE YOUR LANGUAGE. WE OFFER PURE, UNIVERSAL BLOCKS OF THOUGHT THAT ARE UNDERSTOOD BY ALL WHO EXIST.**

Physical man often, incorrectly, assumes that words, or language, are necessary for clear communication. Your little ones who are not yet able to speak your language are receiving very clear blocks of thought from you. While they may not understand the intricate details of your conversation, they understand the more important basics of what is going on in your life. They sense your state of being in every moment of your interaction with them. Your animals do not speak, but they, too, receive your blocks of thought, and you are transmitting, and, in many cases, receiving, blocks of thought from one another.

*As you pose a question to your Inner Being, your Inner Being will offer to you a pure block of thought. You will receive that block of thought at an unconscious level of awareness and you will translate it into something that makes sense to you. It may come in the form of a knowing or an impulse, or a stream of words.*

Most of the work in this process of developing communication with your Inner Being will be your getting better at deciphering the blocks of thought and translating them into your physical terms.

In our early days of interacting with Esther, much of what we offered to her was in very small blocks of thought. Many of which could be translated into one or two word sentences. "Yes," "No" and so on.

Esther's mate, Jerry, would offer clear questions that were of great importance to him, and we would respond in very short blocks of information. In time, as Esther received more and more from us, she was able to translate larger and larger blocks of thought, until now, very often, we will offer a block of thought to Esther, in an instant, that will take her several minutes to articulate for her physical friends.

In the early days of your conscious and deliberate communication with your Inner Being, the communication may seem almost childlike, with physical movement seeming awkward and words coming in one or two word sentences. But, as you spend more time in the mode of receiving, you will get better at it.

As you sit with the intent of asking questions and receiving answers, put yourself in a comfortable position and establish, clearly, your intentions. Esther usually sits for a minute or so, drawing in deep breaths. Then she will state, clearly, "I want to speak, clearly, your words." That is her way of saying, "I will listen and allow your thoughts to be translated through my mind." It is her way of intending that her own conscious thoughts will not interfere with the thoughts that she is receiving from ABRAHAM. Esther's intent to have no conscious interference from her own thought process is her first and most dominant intention.

*As you begin receiving communication from your Inner Being, you may have difficulty in separating your own conscious thoughts from those of your Inner Being, but in time, the distinction will be very obvious to you.*

You will notice, right away, that the thoughts that come from your Inner Being are steady and sure, almost rhythmic, while your own conscious thoughts are more often sporadic and choppy. Your Inner Being will do a better job of staying on one topic, while your conscious thoughts dart about from topic to topic.

If you have set forth a very strong intention to receive, clearly, from your Inner Being, and if you are allowing your own conscious thoughts to get in the way, or to override what is coming from your Inner Being, you will feel very uncomfortable with what you receive. You will be filled with doubt, or agitation, or irritation. It will not be a satisfying experience. When you have established your intentions clearly, and you are receiving, purely, from your Inner Being, the flow of thoughts and your translation of words is very sure and the experience is most satisfying. Eventually, the stream of thoughts from your Inner Being will come purely, and surely, undeniably into your mind.

Opening a passageway between your world of physical focus and the Non-physical world is of great value to you, for it will provide you with a broader view and surer guidance in everything you do.

*While it is important to note that you are physically focused — and with great reason — your Non-physical perspective is also of great value, and the acknowledgement of one part of you need not, in any way, diminish the value of another part of you.*

As you recognize that this physical life experience is a continuation of you, and that much has gone before, putting you in a wonderful position to be as you are, then you will find yourself more willing and, in fact, wanting, very much, to re-connect with your inner state of being — for in doing so, all that you experience through your physical eyes will be enhanced.

There are many misconceptions that affect the interaction between the physical and the Non-physical realms. Physical man has been convinced through long lines of inherited thought that he is unworthy, and is a part of the physical world in order to be tested, to prove himself worthy of some reward that will be bestowed later. For the most part, he thinks that that which he knows as Non-physical is worthy, perfect and complete, and now he is here working hard to somehow catch up. And so often, as physical man makes some sort of Non-physical contact, he sits humbly, waiting for great words of wisdom to be delivered to him from on high.

*Physical man often, mistakenly, believes that all beings who are part of the Non-physical dimension are older and wiser than those focused in the physical realm, and that certainly is not the case. The beings who are focused in the Non-physical dimension hold tremendous variety in intentions, desires, beliefs, expectations, abilities and attitudes.*

There is vast knowledge accumulated and shared by those of us who are focused in the Non-physical world, but most of it can not be understood or utilized by those of you who are focused through physical eyes. But as you live your physical lives, seeking broader knowledge that can be interpreted through your physical world, a wonderful blending of knowing occurs.

Words do not teach. It is through life experience that knowing comes. But as you live your physical life experience, your Inner Being can offer greater insights or guidance that can enhance and enrich your physical life experience.

The alignment of your physical and Non-physical Energies provides far more than an opening of a passageway between the physical and Non-physical dimensions for the purpose of asking questions and receiving answers. This alignment helps you to be more consciously aware of a Guidance System that is supreme. While it is nice to have communication for the purpose of satisfying questions of great importance, or even of idle curiosity, this passageway that you have accomplished provides much, much more.

This opening, or alignment, or blending of Energies, literally puts you, at last, in the position of being, and doing, and having, that which you have intended as you decided to be a part of the physical experience. You are finally upon the path that you had intended when you came forth into this physical body.

*You said, "I will go forth into this wondrous physical dimension and I will become familiar with the data of this time and space. And then, I will allow the broadness of my being to shine forth for the upliftment of All-That-Is."*

# 5

# EFFECTIVELY UTILIZING
# YOUR GUIDANCE SYSTEM

Your Inner Being may offer information that will help you to receive insight from that which you have already lived, but the most valuable communication will come to you day by day as you fully acknowledge your now. There is not much power or joy in evaluating the past — but there is tremendous potential for power and joy as you are thinking clearly, and deliberately attracting, in your now.

*We have offered to you the process for the aligning of your physical and Non-physical Energies for many reasons:*

• This alignment enhances the experience of both your physical and your Non-physical perspective.

• This alignment assists you in more clearly and deliberately accomplishing the intentions that you held as you decided to emerge into this physical body.

• This alignment puts you in a position where you can consciously communicate with your broader inner perspective.

• Your alignment of Energies, and conscious awareness of your Inner Being, provides much more than a channel for questions and answers. You now have access to precision guidance to assist you in every moment of every day. Every idea that you contemplate, every decision that you make, can now be enhanced by this broader awareness.

As we offered earlier, your Inner Being can offer blocks of thought to your physical being. Blocks of thought that you may translate in many different ways. The block of thought may be translated as an impulse to act, or to speak, or your physical body may receive a physical sensation.

Your Inner Being has been offering this communication to you from the day you emerged into this body, although most of you have been unaware of it. *EVERY EMOTION THAT YOU FEEL, IS LITERALLY COMMUNICATION THAT IS OFFERED FROM YOUR INNER BEING.* Because your Inner Being has access to all points of Energy throughout your apparatus, many physical sensations can be effected in your body by your Non-physical Inner Being.

*In the same way that you have "feeling" sensors in your fingertips, to protect your fingers from sharp, or hot, objects, your Inner Being often evokes feelings or emotions within you to guide you. The discomfort of pain in your fingertips brings forth an impulse to act that prevents you from greater harm, and in the same way, negative emotion is offered to guide you away from that which is not of value to you.*

*YOU HAVE COME TO DEFINE YOUR EMOTIONS IN VERY BROAD AND DETAILED TERMS, BUT TECHNICALLY THERE ARE ONLY TWO EMOTIONS. ONE FEELS GOOD, AND ONE FEELS BAD.* And these emotional feelings are present because your Inner Being has offered the impulse of thought that has triggered the physical response within your physical apparatus.

Recognizing the existence of your Inner Being, and then drawing from the infinite resources of knowledge and strength and clarity that it holds, will enhance your physical life experience dramatically. *As you stand in your now, you are at a most powerful junction — where your physical world meets the Non-physical world — and the combination of your deliberate thought and expectation, combined with the emotion, clarity and strength that comes forth from within, is a combination that makes for magnificent, joyful, deliberate creating.*

Through living your physical life experience, you collect much data, and you draw conclusions; you come to recognize what parts of physical life you prefer to others and what sorts of things you want to embrace. Your Inner Being is aware of you as you are collecting the data and drawing conclusions and making decisions, and stands ready, moment by moment, to assist you in moving toward that which you have decided that you want — and away from that which you have decided that you do not want. In a more effective way than your most sophisticated computers, your Inner Being is able to accurately assess all of the details of your wanting, and to intricately prioritize your subjects of desire. Your Inner Being knows which of your intentions are dominant, which supersedes another, and so on. Your Inner Being not only considers the factors of this physical experience, but remembers the intentions that you held at the time of your emergence into this body, and all of those intentions are factored into the equation for guidance. *In short, your Inner Being is eternally aware of you, here in this physical body, offering guidance in the form of emotion to help you know — in the moment of the emotion — whether you are moving toward or away from that which you want.* Your Inner Being is, and has been, from the day of your birth, aware of you, but unless you are aware of your Inner Being, and listening — or rather, feeling — for the subtle guidance, then you cannot benefit from the knowledge or the broad perspective of your Inner Being. In chapters that follow we will discuss the Deliberate Creative Process, in detail, offering techniques to assist you in utilizing the value that your Inner Being offers.

*As physical man asks questions, he receives answers, and with those answers come new, broader, deeper questions. For example: The more he discovers about his earth, the more he realizes that he does not yet understand. Rather than reducing the amount of knowledge that is not understood, he increases it as his awareness of the vastness of the Universe and the complexities of his earth plane unfold to him. Only those who resist thinking, only those who resist new ideas, believe that they are conquering or discovering this earth.*

While physical man has tremendous capabilities regarding discovery and invention and understanding of things that are of the physical world — from his physical perspective, he cannot grasp the inner workings of his world.

*Just as you do not need to understand fully the process by which electrical Energy has been harnessed, and is delivered into your home for your easy access, in order to benefit from it and enjoy it, so it is not necessary for you to understand the tremendous complexities that have brought the physical matter together which comprises your earth plane.* In other words, an acknowledgement, or acceptance, of the existence of the inner world is all that is needed for an enhancement of your physical world.

As it would be difficult for most of you, who read this book, to understand why anyone would choose to live in this modern world without the benefit and efficiency of electricity, it is difficult for us to understand why any of you would choose to disconnect yourselves from the vast reservoir of clarity and knowledge and power that exists within you. And just as most of you could not explain the benefit of electricity by expressing where it comes from and how it is harnessed, so we cannot express to you — in a way you can understand — what this Non-physical Energy is or where it comes from.

It is our intent to point you in the direction of seeking interaction with your Non-physical world — and to a deliberate receiving and application of your inner resources — for the enhancement of that which you live here in the physical.

***Once you accept the existence of your Inner Being, and once you accept the never ending experience of growth that you are upon, you may recognize the tremendous reservoir of knowledge and clarity and strength, that exists right now within you.*** This recognition can lead you to a tremendous surge of progress regarding any number of subjects, because with the recognition that your strength, or clarity, already exists, you simply allow it to come forth, rather than working hard trying to develop it.

*SO MANY OF THE TALENTS OR ABILITIES THAT YOU WANT TO EXPERIENCE, YOU ALREADY HAVE — IF YOU WILL BUT ALLOW THEM TO COME FORTH.* You truly are not just now beginning to develop them. Not even at the beginning of this physical life experience, were you beginning to develop them. They existed even before your birth, and as you want to experience them in your now, you have only to expect, or allow, them to come forth, and they surely will.

*We are also wanting you to understand that it is not necessary for the entire world to come to understand the Laws of the Universe, or the processes that we are offering to you here, in order for you to have a wonderful, happy, productive life experience. It is not necessary for even one other to understand, for you are the Attractor of your experience. Just you.*

# 6

# SELF
# APPRECIATION

This all sounds so simple. *And so, why do so few realize the benefit of this inner, seemingly hidden, potential? The blockage that stops most from allowing the magnificence of their inner potential to shine forth is lack of appreciation of self.* It is the very same blockage that stops most from getting or achieving anything that is wanted. It is the very same thing that holds so many of our physical friends in a place of frustration, or non-accomplishment, when what they yearn for is motion forward.

*In general, as physical man exists today, he is not getting all that he desires, and he is getting much that he is not wanting. He does not understand how he is attracting what is coming to him, and so he looks outside of himself for the answers to that which is happening to him, and finds all sorts of targets to give the credit, or the blame. The more he offers blame, the more he reinforces his lack of control over his own life experience and the more frustrated he becomes. And from his state of negative emotion, he is now in a position of attracting more of that which he considers to be bad.*

*The predominant emotional state of most physical beings is that of negative emotion. Therefore the predominant experiences that he attracts into his experience are also negative, for from his negative position he perpetuates more negative.*

It is important to note, before we go further, that an individual may easily be the exception to this, and indeed there are many exceptions to this, but nevertheless, that which we have just stated is the predominant condition of physical man presently upon this earth.

*How did man reach this point of being? Primarily, from lack of appreciation of self.*

All physical beings, while not consciously, recognize from deep within that there is not an ending to growth. Certainly, without that recognition, deep within you, you would not be here, now, upon this earth. There is an eternal urging from within, encouraging you to new experience and to growth. There is also a yearning, or urging, to do that which is good. But physical man has forgotten how to discern that which is good from bad, right from wrong, or positive from negative.

*Because he has forgotten the existence of his own guidance mechanism, physical man looks outside of himself for the guideposts, or the books of rules, or the groups of powerful influence for rules of right and wrong. ("For if there are many that believe that it is right, it must surely be.") And as he looks outside of himself, into the inconsistencies that abound, into the vast divergence of intentions and beliefs, he finds only confusion.*

As man seeks his measure of right and wrong, he becomes a comparer. Indeed, he was born into a world of comparers. As he emerged he was compared to others in terms of size, amount of hair, alertness, beauty, ability in many areas, and in every day of his experience, from his first day upon this earth, he is compared by others — and eventually by himself — to all others. Out of that comparison, also comes more confusion, for there are many different intentions and many different beliefs that affect all that he compares himself to. Indeed, it is difficult to discover, in all of this comparing, what is better or what is right, for there are so many differing viewpoints of every subject.

Physical man, as he moves through his physical experience, interacts with many others. When he does not have a strong sense of guidance coming forth from within him, he relies on the opinions and attitudes of others. And he finds, very early in his life experience, that others are very willing, in fact, wanting, to express their ideas and opinions and attitudes to him. His seeking for their ideas is inherently a very good thing, for in all of that there can be much discovery of new thought and much stimulation for new ideas, indeed for growth, but when there is interacting with others who have strong ideas of *right* and *wrong* — when you have lost your own sense of guidance — then you are buffeted about in all of the differences, becoming more and more confused.

As you do not feel the strength of the guidance that absolutely would come forth from within you, because you do not know it is there and do not look for it, and as you look for guidance from others, you become one who seeks approval. As you gain a sense of satisfaction from pleasing another with your thought, or word, or action, you try to please another and another.

Too often, physical man acts, not out of his own decision or intent or desire, confirmed by his own sense of self or guidance from within, but instead chooses thoughts or words or actions that please others. As his experience is very narrow, contained primarily to his immediate family, perhaps even his parents alone, he can usually comfortably seek that approval. But as his sphere of interactions gets larger, expanding to others outside of his family, the confusion grows.

*Indeed, if there is only one other from whom you seek approval, you may be able to stand on your head in enough different ways to keep up with their changing demands. But if there are two, or perhaps a world full of others, all wanting you to think and speak and act as they would have you, then you have great trouble, for there are simply too many standards of control. Too many diverse measures of justice and of right and wrong.*

*Too many critics demanding specific action from you.*
Many of the difficulties that individuals experience come from not liking or not appreciating or not trusting self. One who does not trust self, looks to others for approval, and that, in and of itself, works against the very thing that he is wanting, which is to trust himself. Because he does not trust himself, he looks to others, which perpetuates his lack of trust of self. Only by seeing examples of others who do appreciate and approve of and like themselves, can anyone be inspired to self- appreciation. Unfortunately, there are few such examples around. *You would recognize another who truly appreciates himself by noting these characteristics:* He is usually happy. Not offering insincere smiles but the warm and genuine smile that comes from the eyes as well as from his mouth. He is one who appreciates you, seeing things in you that you would like to see in you, pointing out to you things that you, perhaps, have never seen about yourself.

*One of the most important intentions that we hold, as we write this book, is to assist physical man in recognizing the existence of his own Guidance System, that he may have the benefit of utilizing it.* Before it can be utilized, it must be recognized. There must be wanting to recognize, before recognition will occur.

WANTING AND RECOGNIZING AND UTILIZING THE GUIDANCE SYSTEM IS THE SUREST AND SWIFTEST PATH TO SELF-APPRECIA-TION. AND SELF-APPRECIATION IS ESSENTIAL TO JOYFUL LIFE EXPE-RIENCE.

As each physical being emerges into his given physical experience, he is immersed in the beliefs and influences that surround him. Until he recognizes the reservoir of strength and knowledge and guidance that exists within him, he has little resistance to those surrounding influences.

*As you emerge into physical life experience, you usually become a part of a family or culture, and you are immediately subjected to the beliefs and intentions and confusion of those who surround you as you are born.*

Of course, there is great reason for the support from all that exists in physical form, waiting to greet you, to teach you and influence you, for you are small and not able to tend to even your most basic of needs in those early days of physical experience. *But in other than physical terms, you are not a baby, just now beginning your experience — you are old and experienced and knowing, and wanting.*

For most, however, as you are helpless and unknowing regarding the ways of this particular physical experience, you are considered to be unknowing regarding all things — and you are continually guided to do and to think in the ways and manners that have gone before you in the particular environment to which you have just been born. And because the thought that surrounds you — that you are new and unknowing — is so pressing, so large, and thought by so many, you accept it.

From your inner perspective you are seeking of new experience and of growth, thus your emergence into this physical body. And so, because of the combination of your natural urge, or drive, to have growth, coupled with the desire of those surrounding you to teach you what they believe they already know, you accept the role of student, seeing nearly everyone else as older and wiser.

You regard yourself as the unknowing one, and you look outside of your self for answers to any number of questions on a variety of subjects. And while you do gain information about how things work in your physical world, this habit of looking outside of yourself for answers causes you to grow further and further from your inner knowledge that you are a strong, self-sufficient, dominant creator of your own experience.

Most never regain their feeling of appreciation for self. Oh, some of you, as you get older, notice that most others are not as wise as you once thought them to be, but by the time you recognize that, you are usually too tired to now begin the search for the appreciation of self.

What we are most wanting you to hear from us, is that an appreciation of self is not a difficult thing to find. In fact, it has never really been lost, just temporarily forgotten.

*Understand that your Inner Being exists within you. Understand that your Inner Being currently exists as the very old, very wise culmination of all that you have lived and all that you are currently living. And most of all, understand that your Inner Being absolutely adores you.*

As your Inner Being observes the physical you, it feels tremendous appreciation for that which you are. Your Inner Being watches on, endlessly, knowing your desires, knowing your expectations, knowing you in every moment of your day.

When you focus upon subjects that delight you, the feeling of positive Energy that flows through your physical being is your feeling of connectedness with your glorious Inner Being. As you take delight in your beautiful surroundings, or a glorious wild creature, or your own accomplishment, or your dreams, your Inner Being resonates purely with you, and you feel wonderful.

However, when you focus upon the lack of something you want, when you find fault with yourself, or with someone else, that feeling of negative Energy that flows through your physical being is your feeling of disconnectedness from your Inner Being. When you choose thoughts that your Inner Being does not resonate with, you are standing here physical, and naked, and alone, and the feelings of insecurity, or fear, or loneliness, that you feel, are only indicators that you have diverged, in that moment, from who you really are.

*As you accept that your Inner Being exists as the culmination of all that you have lived, and that your Inner Being is absolutely aware of you, and adores you, then you have taken a very big step toward an appreciation of self.*

If you are wanting to get a sense of that which you have just read, sit quietly for a few moments and offer some very clear thoughts. Choose a subject that delights you. Think of someone you adore, and offer thought of your pleasant interaction with that one. Or think of something that you are wanting to experience, and let thoughts of living that experience roll across your mind. Or think of something that you have recently done that you enjoyed very much. And as you ponder these positive thoughts, feel the positive Energy surge through your body as your Inner Being resonates with your current thoughts. Then choose a subject that is not so pleasant. Contemplate not having enough money, and think of the bad state you will be in when the bills come and there is not enough money to pay. Or think of that person who has wronged you, and spend some time justifying your own position while you defend yourself mentally against this enemy. Or think of your own deficiencies, beating up on yourself mentally for a while. Now, feel the absence of your happy Inner Being. Notice the feeling of divergence. See how it feels to choose subjects that your Inner Being does not agree with. Feel what it feels like to be disconnected from your positive powerful Inner Being and to stand there physical, and disconnected.

Someone said to us, "ABRAHAM, why would my Inner Being forsake me, just when I needed him most? Why would my Inner Being turn his back on me?"

And we say, your Inner Being never turns it's attention from you, but you are not always in the place of allowing that which your Inner Being is. When you feel good, you are in the place of allowing your connection with your Inner Being, and when you feel bad, you are not.

*Your most important work — that which is the very basis of your accomplishment, achievement and satisfaction from this life experience — is your finding your true sense of self.*

# 7

# FREEDOM, GROWTH, JOY

All physical beings who are now present upon the planet earth came into this experience wanting these things: *GROWTH* — otherwise you wouldn't be here, and *JOY,* upliftment of self and others, and all possible because of your never ending, always present, individual *FREEDOM.* While all of you have these basic intentions for physical experience in common, there is wide variation in the degree that you are wanting them. Some of you have intense, passionate wanting for them, while others are not feeling it so strongly.

You have come forth into this body, into this environment of earth, by your powerful wanting. As you made the decision to emerge here into this physical dimension, you recognized this earth plane as a place of great diversity where great varieties of experience and belief and desire exist. You saw this earth plane as the perfect place for deliberate creating.

*It is as if you are chefs in a well stocked kitchen, where every ingredient imaginable is present in abundant proportion. The earth representing this kitchen filled with ingredients, and you selecting from the shelves the perfect ingredients to blend together to make the perfect life experience for you.*

As we move forward together, here in this book, we will state clearly for you the eternal, Universal, infinite Laws of the Universe that affect all parts of your Universe, including this physical realm that you are now focused within. Here, we will describe the Laws in detail and explain to you how they affect your life experience. You will come to understand that these Laws exist — and affect you — even in your ignorance of them.

We are very happy about this section of our book, for it is here that you will recognize precisely how to create exactly what you are wanting to create. You will come to understand how it is that there are things that you want that you seemingly cannot bring into your experience and why there are those things that are within your experience that you do not want. We will not only assist you in gaining absolute control of your own life experience, but we will help you to understand that that is precisely why you are here. As you read on, you will have access to the keys to deliberate life experience — chosen by you.

*Perhaps the question that is most often asked by physical man is, "Why am I here?"*

*We would answer that question in simple terms in this way: Only a part of you is here. And that part of you that is currently focused into this physical dimension and into this physical body is so focused, for the joy of the experience. For the experience of doing more, having more and being more.*

**You see, there is not an ending to growth. There is not an ending to the continual accumulation of experiences, and those experiences culminate to be that which each of us is at any point in time. Therefore, every physical experience that you have, adds to the great culmination of the Non-physical, greater, broader you.**

- You have not come forth, in this one life experience, only, to gain worthiness to something greater.

- You are not here being tested: you, pitted against a bitter world, to see if you are strong enough or brave enough or willing to do without enough for greater exaltation later.

- You have not come forth as unknowing students, looking for an all-knowing teacher to point the way.
- You have not come forth to climb the rungs of a ladder, to be offered a great reward at the height of your climb.
- You are not here to be tested by temptation.

*YOU ARE AN ETERNALLY LIVING CREATOR WHO IS EXHILARATED BY THE EXPERIENCE OF LIFE.*

*YOU HAVE APPLIED ETERNAL, INFINITE LAWS, AND THAT HAS RESULTED IN YOUR EMERGENCE INTO THIS BODY, AND INTO THIS TIME AND SPACE.*

In short, you have come forth into this time and space because you seek the exhilaration of this physical life experience and because you know that through chewing upon the data of this specific physical experience, that much understanding and pleasure will be added to the culmination of you.

By virtue of powerful Universal Laws, you receive all things. Whether you have an abundance of dollars or lack of them, an abundance of health or continual sickness, satisfying, fulfilling relationships or difficult and unsatisfying relationships, is determined by the way you, as an individual, apply the Laws of the Universe. Without exception you are applying the Laws, for without exception you are the creator of this physical experience.

*Indeed, every broad, or general, as well as every specific, intricate part of your life experience is drawn to you by you. In clearer terms:* YOU ARE ABSOLUTELY THE CREATOR OF YOUR EXPERIENCE.

The abundance or poverty, sickness or health that comes to you is not doled out by another as reward or punishment for that which you are living. The experiences of your life are not assigned to you, testing your skill or agility or worthiness. There is not some Non-physical intelligence offering or withholding blessings by virtue of your physical activity.

*You get what you get because of the thoughts that you think and the corresponding feelings offered in the moment of your thoughts. Those impulses of thoughts — that are carried on a sort of Non-physical current, not so different from the current you have harnessed as electricity — are magnetic, and through a powerful polarity, you draw to you, circumstances and events that equal your life experience.*

As you have been reading here, you may be feeling uneasy about the idea that you and only you are creating every part of everything that you experience. The primary reasons for this uneasiness are these: There are things in your life that you would prefer were not there, and there are things that you are wanting that you can not seem to bring into your experience, at least not easily, and you simply do not understand how to be the deliberate creator of your experience, and you probably do not know others who understand it, either.

In the pages to follow, we will outline, specifically, the process for deliberate creation. We will begin by saying, that, without exception, you are the creator of your experience, and will also add to that, that in many cases, although you are absolutely creating, you do not understand how you are doing it. You do not really want to create certain things, but, nevertheless, you are. We call that: creation by default. In every case, deliberate or indeliberate, on purpose or by accident, with clear intent or without understanding how it is happening — YOU ARE THE ONE ATTRACTING, INVITING, SOLICITING, CREATING ALL THINGS INTO YOUR LIFE EXPERIENCE.

*Physical beings are operating under some very great misconceptions. One is, that you get what you get, through the action that you offer. Most believe that action is what makes things happen. Not true. In fact, most of you spend most of your action putting out brush fires. Most of your action is spent trying to compensate for inappropriate creating, which is offered, not through your actions, but through your thought and word and corresponding feeling. For example: Your hospitals are filled to the brim with those who are now taking action to compensate for inappropriate thought offered earlier.*

*The things that come to you, the circumstances that come to you, the relationships that come to you, indeed all of the stuff that your physical experience is comprised of, comes to you* — NOT BY THE POWER OF YOUR ACTION, BUT BY THE BALANCE OF THOUGHT THAT YOU HOLD. That thought evokes a feeling response within you which serves as an indicator of what you are attracting.

In the heat of the summer, our friend, Esther, the woman through whom we are speaking, was walking across the grass in her front yard, noting how very dry the grass and trees were. She stopped, and said, in a very positive sounding voice, using positive words, "ABRAHAM, I want some rain!" We said, "And from this position of lack, you think you will get rain?" Esther asked, "What am I doing wrong?" "Why do you want the rain?" we asked. "I want the rain because it makes the grass green. I want the rain because it refreshes the trees. I want the rain because it gives all the creatures in the bushes enough water so that they are not dependent upon the small amount in our bird bath. I want the rain because it lowers the temperature of the air, and feels good upon my skin, and it makes us all feel better." "Now you are attracting rain," we replied.

When do you, or others you know, usually think about health? When you are sick! When do you usually think about having more money? When there isn't enough! When do you usually think about finding a mate? When you are lonely! And under those conditions, from your position of lack — you are attracting more of the lack of what you want, rather than attracting what you want.

What we are most wanting you to hear from all of this is this: *You cannot feel one way and think and speak another, and expect to receive what you are thinking or speaking* — *because the way you feel influences what you are attracting.* You can smile a broad smile, and speak happy words, but it is what is in your heart, or the way that you feel, that is your predominant point of attraction. When you feel fat, you cannot attract slim! When you feel poor, you cannot attract prosperity! When you feel lonely, you cannot attract a companion! *IT DEFIES LAW!*

*AND WHAT IS THAT LAW? LAW OF ATTRACTION. THAT WHICH IS LIKE UNTO ITSELF IS DRAWN.*

What is necessary, before you can begin the attraction of what you want, is that you change the way that you feel. You must bring yourself to a state of feeling good before you can attract what you want, or what you consider to be good.

We have been asked, "ABRAHAM, can you speak another language through Esther? Could you speak Italian or French or Spanish?" Our answer is that we speak not in a language of words. We speak —or offer — pure essence of thought, or pure impulse of thought, and Esther translates that impulse at an unconscious level of her being. We offer pure impulse of thought as do all physical and Non-physical beings. It is the language of the animals, and it is the language of all who exist in either physical or Non-physical dimensions.

*You are continually offering a message, or pure meaning, to the Universe. Not through your words, not through your thoughts, but through the way you feel. Of course, the way you feel in any moment is as a result of your choice of thought or word. But it is the way that you feel that is your true message to the Universe, and it is the way that you feel that is your point of magnetic attraction. And that which is like unto itself is drawn.*

What confuses so many of you — as we begin to explain that you are the creator of your experience and that you get what you think about — is that many of you think you are sending one message outward through your words, or thoughts, when what you are actually transmitting is something quite different. Esther thought she would attract rain through her positive word and sound, and yet, from her position of lack, she was attracting only more lack. *It is imperative that you pivot from your feeling of lack, or negativity, to a feeling of having, or positivity, before the attraction that you want begins.*

The primary reason that more of you are not living the lives you think you want is because what you speak and what you feel are not in harmony.

The Universe is responsive only when harmony exists. In clearer terms: When you think of something you do not want, cancer, for example, and you feel the negative emotion that you term "dread" or "fear", you have harmony — and that cancer is on its way into your experience. When you think of something you do want, perfect health, for example, and you feel the positive emotion of "peace" or "joy", you have harmony — and that perfect health is on its way into your experience.

*It is not possible to feel negative emotion and at the same time be in harmony with something that you want, or something that you consider to be good. Therefore, whenever you are feeling negative emotion, you are, in that moment, offering an influence to the Universe, you are literally asking for, or inviting, the return of something that you do not want — or lack of something that you do want.*

*It is important that you be sensitive to the way that you are feeling so that you know when you are attracting what you do not want, and then it is important to stop the negative attraction.* If you can accept the potency of these words, then you are ready to receive the following process.

# 8

## JOYFUL BECOMING

### THE PROCESS OF PIVOTING

*The process of pivoting will assist you in changing your negative point of attraction to a positive point of attraction. Here is how it works:*

*Whenever you feel negative emotion, recognize that your Guidance System, from within, is telling you two very important things: First, there is something you want! Otherwise you would be feeling no emotion. Second, you are not looking at what you want, but in the opposite direction.*

Recognizing this, say to yourself, "There is something important that I want, but I am not looking at it. What is it that I want?" You may continue to think along those lines by asking, "Why do I want this?" As you ponder what it is that you do want, and why you want it, then begin to envision yourself as already being in that position. Already being it, or having it, or doing it, until you feel the positive emotion come forth within you.

The more you apply this process, the more proficient you will become. And the faster the pivot will occur. *You will know, or rec-*

*ognize, when you have successfully accomplished a pivot — when you feel better.*

If you are very sensitive to the way that you feel, you may find one hundred to one thousand opportunities to pivot in just one day. However, there will not be one hundred or one thousand different things that you want. You will begin to discover that all of this pivoting is pointing to a few things that are extremely important to you: Freedom, usually highest in priority. Growth. Joy. Upliftment.

*Pivoting accomplishes the following things:* First, and most importantly, it leads you to a continuous state of feeling positive emotion — which means you are continuously in a magnetic point of attracting only what you consider to be good. Also, as you are sensitive to the way you feel, you are allowing your Guidance System, from within, to point out to you things that are important to you, so that as you notice more and more opportunities to pivot — the things that are of greatest importance to you become more apparent to you. Next, with every pivot, you draw greater clarity about what you want, and move ever closer to it.

*Some misunderstand the process of pivoting. They believe that we are saying, find something that is obviously wrong, and call it right. Or, look at something that is white, and call it black. That is not what we mean by pivoting.*

• Pivoting is the process that helps you discover what is most important to you.

• Pivoting is the process that puts you into a continual state of attracting only what you want.

• Pivoting is the process through which you chew upon the data of life, determining your ever-changing point of desire.

• Pivoting is recognizing that when you are feeling negative emotion, that you are, in that moment of feeling bad, attracting that which you consider to be bad, and then making a conscious decision to stop that attraction and begin a positive attraction.

• Pivoting is the process of changing your thought, word, or action, thus changing your emotional response.

• Pivoting is the process where you recognize, by the negative emotion that you are feeling, that you are taking the Non-physical Energy of the Universe and directing it toward what you do not want, or toward the lack of what you do want.

• Pivoting is the process whereby you round up any renegade Energy that you have offered in opposition to what you want, and get it going only in the direction of your desire.

• Pivoting is the process that changes the direction of your creating, or more specifically stated, the direction of your attracting.

• Pivoting is the process that brings you into balance with your core intentions.

*The process of pivoting — literally watching for opportunities, or reasons, to identify what it is you do want — because you are currently feeling bad because you are currently focused upon lack of what you want, or focused upon what you do not want — is the key to lead you to the productive, joyful physical life experience that you intended even before your emergence into this physical body.*

So often, we are asked the question, "Why am I here?" So many physical beings do not understand why they exist, and even though many answers have been offered, including such things as, "You are here, being tested, to prove yourselves worthy of happy existence after this physical life," to "You are an accidental product of physical mass coming together," we would like to offer a further explanation:

*YOU ARE CREATORS! NOT GATHERERS OF THINGS OR RE-LATIONSHIPS. NOT REGURGITATORS OF EXPERIENCES LIVED BY OTHERS! You have very specifically chosen this time and this place and this dimension for the deliberate application of Universal Laws. In short, you wanted to be here upon the eart in this physical body, at this time, to enjoy the deliciousness creating.*

Just as the sculptor or the artist gains his satisfaction, not fro the finished work, but from the doing of the work, you, too, ha come forth for the sheer joy of molding the clay of this Unive into the work of art that you identify as your physical life expe ence.

Most physical beings have no idea that they are the absolute creator of their own experience. They have followed the lead of those who have gone before in giving credit or blame to any number of other people, institutions, and so on. However, a very large sector of the population of the planet is becoming increasingly aware that they do influence their experience through thought or attitude, and a somewhat smaller sector has begun the deliberate search for the details of how to be in more deliberate control of their own experience. It is to those beings that we extend our effort. If you are among those, we are writing this book for you.

In witnessing those who have decided to become deliberate in their creating, we have noticed a common occurrence. There is a propensity toward always looking toward a brighter future. "When I get that job, things will be better." "Once I find my true love, then I will be happy." "Once I get rid of these extra pounds, I will be happy," and so on. While we are pleased that you are looking toward a deliberate happy future, still you miss the point.

*You are here to bring yourselves to a joyful state of being, moment by moment, day by day, as you chew upon the data of life. As you stand in your now, aware of where you want to be, or even aware of where you are going, your tendency is to note the lack of where you are. As you contrast now with future success, what you usually are* FEELING *is the pain of the* LACK *of the* NOW. AND AS YOU FEEL THE LACK OF THE NOW, YOUR NOW WILL REMAIN UNCHANGED.

Grasp the concept of BECOMING. Not unhappy now. Not unfulfilled now, while upon a journey that will later lead to more happiness, or more success — but a free, joyous, growing being continuing upon your path of creativity.

There is not much that we could offer to you that would be of more value to you, as deliberate creators, than an understanding of being in a state of joyous becoming.

*When you understand that you are as magnets, attracting unto you, more of whatever it is that you are feeling — therefore, if you are feeling negative emotion, you are, in that moment, attracting what you do not want — then you may understand the power in the understanding of joyous becoming.*

No matter how much you want something, and no matter how much you believe that you can have it, if you are, in your now, noticing that it is not yet here, you are focused upon the lack, and the lack of it is what you are attracting, and you could remain in that position of attracting lack forevermore.

On the other hand, when you grasp the concept of joyous becoming, then, in your now, even though many of the things that you want are not yet part of your experience, as you are joyously anticipating them, actually enjoying your journey toward those things, then you are in a state of joyous becoming, and you not only shorten the time between the not-having-now and the later-having-future, but you enjoy yourself in the meantime. And then, just like the magnificent sculptor or artist, you are gloriously involved in the hands-on creation of your life experience.

You are here upon this earth at this time, again, because of your passion and exuberance for the living of life, because you are creators. Joyful creation is not the choosing of a target and hitting it and then the choosing of another and another. *Joyful creation is the continual recognition of preferred life experience and the sustaining of deliberate focus to the attainment of it.* Joyful creation is the experiencing of life, drawing conclusions from the experience and then jubilant expectations of results.

*If your present could be filled with joyful anticipation of more joyful life experience, then it would not be possible for you to attract less than joyful experiences, or circumstances, to yourself. But if you are looking forward to a happier tomorrow, and find yourself continually contrasting the less pleasant what-is with the more pleasant future, your attraction is more toward the less pleasant what-is than the more wanted future.*

As creator of your experience, you are bringing to you more of what you are feeling, now. As you exist in your now, thinking thoughts, speaking words, performing actions, you are, at the same time, responding with a corresponding feeling. The combination of your thought, word or action, and that corresponding feeling, equals your attraction power. That is the way you draw other people, experiences, events, circumstances into your life experience. That is the way you are molding, or creating, your life experience, moment by moment and day by day.

*99% OF YOUR CREATION IS COMPLETE BEFORE YOU SEE ANY PHYSICAL EVIDENCE OF IT.* But most of you are so evidence oriented, you do not sense your motion forward until you see the physical proof. And as you see only the absence of the physical proof, you worry, or doubt, or writhe in the pain of the absence of what you want, and push what you want further and further away.

The farmer who plants the seed of the tomato understands that his creation is well underway before he will see any physical evidence. He does not go to his newly plowed ground, and stomp upon the seed, demanding that it show itself to him, now, right now. Instead, he allows the natural Laws of the Universe to do their work as the small seed matures into something more beneficial to his experience.

*You have launched many wonderful seeds of creation, but in your impatience, or lack of understanding of the Laws, you focus upon the lack, and therefore trample or destroy or sabotage the seeds of your desire.*

*And so, how much of what you get is controlled by you?* All of it. *How many of the events that you participate in are as a result of your choices?* All of them. *How many of the people who are part of your daily experience are brought to you, by you?* Every one of them. *What percentage of your experience do you have control over?* 100%. *How many others are currently creating in your experience?* None. *How many others have responsibility for what is happening to you?* Not one other. *What part do odds or fate or luck play in your experience?* None. *Who is the absolute, and only, creator of your experience? YOU ARE!*

# 9

# INFLUENCE

A nd so, what part, if any, do others play in your experience? And what part, if any, do you play in the experiences of others?

You have each chosen this dimension, this time and place, to participate within, because you wanted the benefit of working with one another. You recognized, from your broader perspective, even before you emerged into this body, the value of many minds, of many thoughts. You knew the power of thought, and you liked the idea of living in an environment where many thoughts abound, because you saw that as an advantage to your growth. Just as you enjoy a broader selection of goods in your clothing or department stores, or just as you enjoy a wide selection of sounds in your music stores, so you enjoy a wide selection of intentions and expectations and beliefs and experiences in your creative work place.

*Remember, you did not enter this earth plane as an unknowing beginner. You were far from that, even as an infant. You entered this earth plane as a deliberate creator, looking forward to a new selection of materials with which to create and a new selection of intentions to consider. New frontiers to discover. New ideas to consider and new triumphs to experience.*

*Thoughts abound. Thoughts projected by others, near and far from where you now stand, reach you, continually. As you receive a thought, your Guidance System responds with a corresponding feeling, and as you feel, you ooze influence. In other words:* AS YOU RESPOND WITH FEELING TO A THOUGHT RECEIVED, YOU ADD YOUR POWER TO THAT THOUGHT.

As an influence has touched you, if it is not in harmony with what you choose — as is indicated as you are feeling a negative emotion — it need not touch you further. It will not touch you, or alter your experience in any way, if you will recognize the warning of the negative emotion, and deliberately, consciously, set forth your thought of what is wanted. But if you do not deliberately think of what you do choose — instead of the original inharmonious thought that first reached you — then that thought has influenced you, and you are adding your power of influence to it, making it more powerful, still.

For example. Let us say that you are busy, early in the day, readying yourself to go out. You are taking your bath and choosing your clothing and you hear, from the bedroom, the television commentator speaking of the desperate state of world affairs, speaking specifically about an uprising in another part of the world and the deaths caused by it. As you hear those words, which are absolutely not in harmony with what you want, or with what you would choose, you receive, in the same moment, a "warning bell", or communication from your Inner Being, in the form of negative emotion. This guidance is an indicator to you that you are currently focused in opposition to that which you want, and that if you remain focused in this direction, you will attract more of this influence — by the powerful Law of Attraction — and add your influence or power to it. In other words: By your negative attention to this unpleasant situation, you are affecting it, in fact, adding to it, with your thought and corresponding feeling. Recognize that whenever you feel negative emotion, your Inner Being is saying

two things to you: First. "There is something that is very important to you, here! Second. "You are focused in the opposite direction of what you want." And then you ask yourself, "What do I
want?" And once you have established what you want, ask, "Why
do I want that?" As you think of what you want and why you want
it, you will begin to feel the negative emotion subsiding, and positive emotion replacing it. You will have accomplished an effective
pivot. You will have withdrawn your focus, your power, your feeling and your influence from that which you do not want — and
you will have directed your focus, your power, your feeling and
your influence precisely toward that which you do want.

How you affect others in their creative work, and how others
affect you in your creative work, we will call influence. *While you
cannot create in another's experience, nor can they create in yours, you are
all affecting one another as you are individually creating. That is influence.*

Most physical beings are aware of influence but have only a par-
tial understanding of influence. Instead of benefiting by the influence that could enhance your experience, most of you are in a position of protecting yourselves from influences, and so, the end result
is not benefit but detriment. A thorough understanding of the
Laws of Creation are really necessary before you can *consciously* ben-
eficially interact with the vast influences that abound. The existence of those influences can be of tremendous value to you instead
of such detriment. In fact, the benefit of influence is the precise
reason you have chosen this dimension, shared with so many others
and so much influence.

*You recognized, before your birth, here, the power of thought.
You understood the tremendous power of collective, harmonious
thought. You understood that it was not necessary for all thought
to harmonize with your desires or thoughts. You understood,
before your birth, here, that all that is necessary for you to benefit by this combined thought is that you control the direction of
your own thought and corresponding feeling.*

*Most physical beings worry so much about the thoughts or beliefs or lifestyles or influences that they would not choose and that they do not like, that they completely miss the benefit of attracting the thoughts that do harmonize with that which they choose.*

It is our intent, with this segment of this book, to bring you to a clearer understanding of your physical experience. We want you to understand, not only how to have a wonderful life experience, or how to improve upon it if it is not just the way you want it to be, but we want you to understand its purpose.

Think, for a moment, about a magnifying glass, noting that it can take a rather large spectrum of light and focus it into a very small pinpoint of powerful light. So powerful, in fact, that it can begin a fire if allowed to remain in that focused position long enough. In a somewhat similar fashion, you act as a sort of magnifying glass, taking a broad spectrum of knowledge, and past life experience, and now, focusing all of that through you. Because of your specific and intimate focus within this physical experience, you have the potential of being extremely powerful, just as the magnifying glass is powerful.

*Your physical world, indeed everything you see and know as your physical environment, including you and all other physical beings, are supported by a Non-physical Energy.* Without the focus of this Non-physical Energy, you, and everything else that you know as your world, would not exist. That Non-physical Energy is the Energy that supports your planet. We call it Creative Life Force, and it streams into you in a strong, steady current. We can liken it to the electricity that flows through the walls of the homes of those in your community. Each of you, individually, plug into, or tap into, that electricity with a variety of electric appliances, utilizing that constant Energy toward whatever ends you seek. And, in a like manner, all physical beings are receiving a similar Non-physical current, or Energy, although you do not choose your end result by plugging in an appliance. You choose your end result by contouring that constant flowing Energy with your thoughts. *Indeed, the thoughts that you offer are continually contouring the stream of Non-physical Energy toward your end results.* And the end result that we speak of, here, is the life experience that you are living. It is not difficult for you to know how you have utilized the Energy, or in what way you have contoured it — because you are living the end result. What you are now living is as a result of the way you have utilized that stream of Non-physical Energy. You are literally living the balance of your thoughts.

As you receive the Non-physical current and you focus upon a clear, undiluted, unresisted, not challenged or questioned, thought, — that is very powerful — and you very quickly receive the physical result of your thought. However, when you offer a thought, sending part of that Non-physical Energy off in the direction of that thought, but then you question it, or doubt it, or worry about it, or hesitate about it — you now send a part of the Energy in the opposing direction and neutralize the Energy. This splitting of the Energy gives you the sensation of standing still, and it is an accurate sensation because you are not moving one way or the other. The balance of your thoughts, in this case, is leaving you standing still.

*The balance of your thoughts is a very good thing, for it allows you the opportunity of sorting through conditions, ideas and beliefs before making a decision. It is nice that in the receiving of one thought, you do not speedily zoom off in the direction of that thought. It is wonderful that you have beliefs within you that temper the new stimulation of thoughts.*

Some of our physical friends, when they realize that they have current desires, but that their current beliefs keep neutralizing, or opposing, these desires, think that they would like to rid themselves swiftly and finally of all existing beliefs, so that they could move quickly to the current decisions, but that is not a good idea, and, fortunately, will not be their experience. For the beliefs that you presently hold provide a good balance, or cornerstone, for you to create from. Without those beliefs, you could be stimulated to some new thought — and off you would go: We might say to you, "We have heard it is a wonderful experience to jump from the top of 20 story buildings." And off you would go.

*Your true work — here as physical beings in this perfectly balanced Universe — is to continually weigh your new stimulation of thought against the set of existing beliefs within you, thereby deciding what you now want. Then your work is to, deliberately and decisively, focus your thoughts in the direction of — and only in the direction of — this decision.*

# 10

## FINDING YOUR
## TRUE BALANCE

You came forth, into this physical body, in this time and place, with some very important, well established, long considered intentions: You very much wanted growth, and you chose this physical dimension because you understood that it would provide a tremendous format for substantial growth experience. You very much wanted freedom, and by exercising your absolute freedom, you accomplished a setting forth of non-conflicting Energy which literally resulted in your physical emergence. As you, from your Non-physical perspective, wanted this physical emergence, you offered clear, focused, non-challenged, not conflicting, thought of being in this physical body — and by virtue of the absolute freedom of creation that abounds, you emerged. You also wanted joy, contentment, pleasure.... *These three powerful intentions — freedom, growth, and joy — are the basis of desire and expectation that existed within you prior to your emergence into this body, and as you continually, deliberately bring these three powerful intentions into harmony, you will have the most glorious of physical experiences while at the same time satisfying your broader, inner, Non-physical intentions.*

As we offer our knowledge of the Laws of the Universe, stimulating thought of our physical friends to their power and ability to create whatever they want whenever they want it, the greatest resistance that we receive is because most physical beings do not trust their ability, or right, to make the decisions about what they want. Most think that they prefer someone sure and powerful and strong outside of themselves making the decisions about what is right and what is wrong, while they merely assume the role of conforming to those rules. However, few have found great satisfaction or success in that way of viewing physical life experience — because they soon discover that there are endless interpretations of what is right and wrong. While cloistered in a small family, or even a small community, where ideas are limited in a particular direction, not so much confusion occurs. *But as you are exposed to a broader spectrum of people, with a broader spectrum of ideas and beliefs, then you begin to recognize that, as a people upon your earth, you will never reach the point where you agree with all others, or even understand why they do what they do or want what they want or believe as they believe.* As that discovery is made, most either give up, overwhelmed by the vastness of the project, drawing back into their own quiet shell of discontent, or they strike out, trying to change the world, organizing others, gaining numbers, trying to convince others of a better way of life — sometimes even trying to physically destroy others who differ in interest or beliefs.

It is our wanting to help you discover that your joy or growth or freedom does not depend on what others outside of you are choosing for themselves. We want you to re-discover the feeling of freedom you knew at the time that you emerged into your physical body.

*We want to stimulate you to the awareness that what you seek is not to control others to what you consider to be a better way of life, but instead to find your own personal, eternal balance of freedom, growth and joy — that others may also be inspired to find their own balance.*

As physical beings, you assume that your action is what makes things happen. You give the majority of your attention to "making" things happen through your action. You have been taught that action is important: "You must work hard if you are going to amount to anything." "Life will not be handed to you, you must go out there and get it." "Those who work hardest, gain the most." You give so much attention to action that you fill your days very full. So full, in fact, that you feel restricted. So full, that you violate your own feeling of freedom and joy.

*What we have noted is that through your endeavor to make so much happen through action, you work against yourselves. You try so hard to act, that you become tired, frustrated and overwhelmed. And from that position of negative emotion — you radiate a message to the Universe that is the opposite of what you really want. You do receive, however, by Law of Attraction, that which you radiate out.*

## PROCESS: TO BE, TO HAVE, TO DO
## OR
## CREATING FROM THE INSIDE OUT

Esther was feeling somewhat overwhelmed. She and her mate had returned from a few days of travel, to find the mail box overflowing, and the telephone voice-box overflowing. As Esther sat in the midst of all of this backlog of work, she felt overwhelmed, and from her point of frustration, she said to us, "ABRAHAM, what should I do?"

We said to her, "There you are, acting like a physical being again, always wanting to know what to do. How do you want to feel?"

"I want to feel free and happy, and I don't feel free and happy when I have too much to do!"

We said, "There you are, acting like a physical being again, telling us what you don't want when we asked you what you do want."

Esther laughed and said, "I want to feel free and happy."

We said, "Good, now ponder that for a moment or two."

And Esther sat, closing her eyes and envisioning sitting on the front porch, sipping some iced tea, visiting with her mate, watching the squirrels — and, immediately, she felt freer and happier.

We said, "Now, what is it that you want to have?"

"I want to have a clean and efficient organized home and office," Esther quickly replied.

"Good" we said, "Now ponder that for a few days. Do not jump into action, but think of how you want to feel and what you want to have."

Within a few days, ideas began to flow to Esther. "I can move this over here, I can move this over there. I can delegate this, I can eliminate this." She was bouncing around the house filled with happy, excited Energy. Not cleaning up the mess from a negative point of view but excited as the ideas came. She was being drawn, or inspired, from her positive wanting, rather than being pushed, or motivated, from her negative attention to lack.

*YOU CANNOT HAVE A HAPPY ENDING TO A MISERABLE JOURNEY!* Therefore, we offer this process of getting into balance with yourself, or *creating from the inside out* — To Be — To Have — To Do, rather than the way most physical beings attempt, jumping into immediate action, feeling their frustration, and then acting further to try to fix it, then feeling more frustration, and then acting further trying to fix that....

As you seek and attain balance within yourself — then everything else within your experience will touch you in a more positive way. When you are out of balance, little else feels good to you, and you have very little satisfaction or success in the things you are attempting to do, or create, or complete, or even enjoy.

The triad of intentions that are very well established within you are: Freedom, growth and joy. And as you view all activity from that perspective, stopping to identify your desire to *FEEL* free, and to *FEEL* growth, and to *FEEL* joy, letting your decisions of what you are wanting to have, spring forth after your awareness of these

98

three very important inner intentions, and then letting the inspiration flow to you of the action or activity or doing that which will satisfy that feeling, then you will find harmony with self in everything that you do. We call that, "creating from the inside out."

When the gymnast, on the balance beam, gets out of balance, he does not try to somersault himself back into balance. For out of control, he could fall to the floor, the situation becoming worse, not better, getting more out of control, and not coming into balance. Instead, he stops, steps back, regains his balance — and then from his position of balance, proceeds.

*When you find yourself out of balance — and you know that you are out of balance because you are feeling negative emotion — you cannot regain your balance by proceeding in the negative direction. You must step back, and find your place of balance before proceeding, for the Law of Attraction abounds, and as you are feeling bad, regarding the specifics of your situation, then to think harder about those specifics which have brought you to a negative position, will only attract more negative, more that you do not want. But within you, back, back, back, back from the specifics of this current situation, there is a place within you of balance. And as you find that place, then you can proceed forward. Only now, by Law of Attraction, you will be pulling what you want toward you, rather than what you do not want.*

Our friend, Esther, had an extremely clarifying dream. She dreamed that she and her mate were walking down a very normal, even mundane looking street, when she noticed a door ajar, and a "For Sale" sign in front. She remembered feeling rather bored and unmotivated, even critical of the drabness of the street, but encouraged her mate to go inside with her to see what was for sale. They walked through the open door and found themselves inside the most beautiful room they had ever seen. The ceiling was very high and rounded, painted with beautiful designs. The very large doorways were arched and intricately carved and painted. The floors were inlaid with stone and wood and beautiful gems. As Esther stood there, transfixed by the magnificence of this room she said to her mate, "I want this." And he agreed, and so they purchased this house. Then her dream moved forward very fast, and Esther and her mate were gathering all of their possessions from this place and that place and sending them off to their new home. And suddenly Esther realized, "This house is not in the city where I want to live. In fact, this house is in a city that I do not want to live in. In fact, everything about this house is wrong, except that it is beautiful."

Esther's dream exemplifies the lopsided creation that many of you are living, for you often make hasty decisions that satisfy only the most superficial of your intentions, while your action, or decision, defies the intentions that are really important to you.

*Very often, from a position of lack, you see something that you believe will soothe that lack, and while it may very well satisfy something that you have been wanting, it also very often contradicts other things that you want more. Considering all desires from the perspective of Being, then Having, and then Doing, you will never again find yourself satisfying only some intentions.*

Both the process of "To Be, To Have, To Do" and the process of "Pivoting" are offered to assist you in finding and keeping your balance.

# 11

# LAW OF ATTRACTION

We take great delight in offering our knowledge of the Universal Laws of your Universe, because we understand that only when you understand the Laws can you begin to use them, *deliberately,* on your own behalf. As with all subjects, our explanation of the Laws of the Universe can range from extremely complex to absolutely simple. We know that our ability to teach does not depend so much upon what we know, as it depends upon our ability to assess what one who seeks knowledge from us knows or understands. Our effectiveness as teachers rests in our ability to understand what it is that you understand so that we may offer what we understand in a way that makes sense to you. For that reason, we are continually assessing the way physical man looks at things, and we utilize that basis of understanding as we make our offering to you. Of course, you are understanding that your physical population contains a vast array of understanding, perspectives, beliefs, desires and experiences — and so, what we write, indeed what we know, is more easily received by some than by others.

*We have literally been summoned to you by the balance of thought, or intentions and beliefs, that you hold.* As you hold this book in your hand it is a physical evidence of that balance of intentions that you hold.

As you are living here upon your earth, you have come to accept some earthly laws, recognizing that they affect all of you in exactly the same way: Because you have come to accept the law of gravity, and through your experience you have come to understand it, you are now able to utilize it to your full advantage.

We are here, wanting to remind your of another law. This is a law, like gravity, that affects all of you. And like the law of gravity, whether you understand it or not, whether you accept it or not, it still affects you. While gravity is a law that affects your physical earth experience, the law we are about to explain affects all experience, physical or Non-physical. This law is eternal, or forever, it is infinite, or everywhere, and it is the most powerful, most important law that you will ever come to understand. It is "The Law of Attraction."

*We would define* LAW OF ATTRACTION *as follows: The basis for existence. The single most powerful law in the Universe. The basis for growth.*

*The Law of Attraction is the basis for Universal harmony. It literally holds your planet, and all else that is, in perfect balance. It allows our present existence while it continues to allow for our growth.*

*In simple terms you may state Law of Attraction in another way:* THAT WHICH IS LIKE UNTO ITSELF IS DRAWN.

This Law is so simple, and so forthright, it is surprising how many of our physical friends not only do not see it, or understand it, but they have come to believe something in exact opposition to it. It is as if they believe in the nonexistent "law of assertion." As they look at their personal experience and then give credit to someone outside of themselves for something they have received, whether they deem it good or bad, they are speaking of assertion — and that simply does not exist. You exist as the ONLY source of attraction into your experience. *Another cannot insert into your expe-*

*rience. Only you can attract and receive into your experience.*

*You are the attractor of everything that comes into your experience.* Even though sometimes it seems as if you are the one attracted into someone else's experience — you are always the dominant attractor regarding what happens to you.

*It is the combination of your conscious thought and the corresponding feeling, that equals your true magnetic position of attraction.* As you offer thought, you feel, and as you feel, you radiate, and as you radiate — you attract unto you.

As you give thought to something that you want, very much, and you feel excitement or happiness — the combination of your chosen, directed thought and the corresponding positive emotion, are, in that moment, drawing unto you the subject of your thought and emotion.

As you give thought to something that you do not want, or to the lack of something that you do want, and you feel disappointment, or anger — the combination of your chosen, directed thought and the corresponding negative emotion, are, in that moment, drawing unto you the subject of your thought and emotion.

*The balance of your thought and corresponding emotion equals your life experience. If you are wanting to understand the balance of your thought, just look at what you are living. If you want to change what you are living — then you have only to change the balance of your thought.*

WHERE YOU NOW STAND IS A RESULT OF THE THOUGHTS AND FEELINGS THAT YOU HAVE OFFERED BEFORE, BUT WHERE YOU ARE GOING IS AS A RESULT OF YOUR PERSPECTIVE OF WHERE YOU NOW STAND.

Some have said, "ABRAHAM, you say I can have what I want, and that wanting is the beginning of all deliberate creation, and yet I have wanted more dollars for as long as I can remember, and the dollars are not coming. What am I doing wrong?"

We explained, "It is important that you understand the balance of your thought regarding the subject of dollars. Are you purely wanting the dollars? If you are, you feel good whenever you approach the subject. Or are you thinking more of the lack of the dollars you want? If that is the case, you feel bad, or negative emotion, as you are thinking about money. The way you predominantly feel regarding the subject of dollars is your indicator of your true balance of thought on the subject, as what you are living is also the true indicator of the balance of your thought."

# WALLET PROCESS
# FOR THE ATTRACTION
# OF DOLLARS

*If you conclude that your balance of thought regarding the subject of dollars is more on the side of the lack of dollars, rather than the pure wanting of dollars, here is an effective process that will help you to tip the balance:* Set aside, from your budget, or savings, a clump of money. $100 is a very good sum to begin with. Put it in your pocket, or pocket book, or purse, and keep it with you wherever you go. As you move through your day, identify as many things as possible that you could do, if you wanted to, with those dollars. Note the things that you could buy, or use, or experience, or eat, in exchange for your $100. We have been teased, "ABRAHAM you obviously have not been physical lately, because $100 buys very little, today." However, if you mentally spend that $100, one thousand times today, you have spent the equivalent of one hundred thousand dollars, and it is our absolute promise to you that you have changed the balance of your thought.

Pay attention to your own thoughts regarding the subject of money. If you find yourself noticing the things that you cannot afford, and feeling the frustration of that, know that you are adding to the lack side of your balance regarding dollars. If you find yourself envious, or angry, because others have dollars when you do not, you are adding to the lack side of your own balance. When you pay your bills, do you feel good or bad? As the money moves through your fingers do your feel the positive or the negative momentum?

*The Wallet Process, described above, will assist you in changing the balance of your thought regarding the subject of dollars, and in the moment that the balance is tipped, more dollars will begin to flow into your experience. It is Law*

# 12

## THE PROCESS OF
## DELIBERATE CREATION

There is not an ending to the process of growth, or change, or creation. Literally, every thought offered adds to what you are living. But most, because they live lives of sameness, because they operate more from habit, or acting out of influence, offer the same thoughts, segment after segment, day after day, and so, what they are living actually changes very little.

Some have said to us, "ABRAHAM, I cannot believe that I am the Creator of my own experience, for I certainly would not have done this terrible thing to myself." And we said, "We did not say that you did it deliberately, but we are absolute in our knowing that it is always your doing." *We call that, "creation by default:" Applying the absolute Laws of the Universe, in ignorance, and getting results that you do not want. And, of course, there is the tendency to deny your responsibility when you have created something you do not want. But until you are willing to accept the responsibility for everything that you are living — both the positive and the negative — you cannot recognize your true freedom. As long as you are believing that anyone or anything out-*

*side of you is controlling you, or creating inside of your expe-*
*rience, you are not free, but you are bound by their whims, or*
*desires, or beliefs.*

YOU EXIST IN A UNIVERSE WHERE ABSOLUTE FREEDOM
ABOUNDS, AND YOU ARE FREE. YOU ARE SO FREE THAT EVERY
THOUGHT THAT YOU OFFER AFFECTS YOUR INDIVIDUAL EXPERI-
ENCE. THERE IS NOT GREATER FREEDOM THAN THAT.

*And so, your work, as you are here in this magnificent physical realm,*
*is to offer your thought, deliberately, in order to have and be and do that*
*which is important, or correct, to you.*

You are continually in the process of creating your life experience, as you are continually in the process of offering thought —
but as we view the physical world, we have observed that the
majority of our physical friends do not set forth their thought
deliberately. It is our knowing that the reason for that lack of
deliberate thought is because of a lack of understanding of the Laws
of the Universe, and from a lack of understanding of your own
Guidance System.

*You are continually creating. In fact, you cannot turn your creative*
*mechanism off.* But you certainly can, by deliberate intent, send
your thoughts in the direction of the things, and experiences, that
you want, rather than in the direction of the lack of what you want,
or the opposite to what you want.

And so, rather than calling this section: The Law of Creation,
we have decided to call it: THE LAW OF DELIBERATE CREATION, for
we are assuming that you are wanting to understand how to create,
purposefully, what you are wanting, and we are assuming that you
would not deliberately create what you do not want.

*The process of Deliberate Creation is twofold: It involves the*
*thought that you project, and the corresponding feeling that*
*comes forth. You offer the thought from your conscious, physical*
*perspective — and your Inner Being offers you a corresponding*
*feeling. Therefore, you are literally co-creating: You, the physi-*
*cal you, and you, the inner, Non-physical you.*

The physical you, brings to the creation, the details of this physical time and place and intentions and beliefs. The Non-physical you, brings the awareness of the broader intentions that you hold from your Non-physical perspective, and helps you to understand the harmony between your current desire, or intent, and your current beliefs regarding that subject — plus, the broader intentions that you hold from Non-physical perspective. If you are paying attention to the way that you feel, you can utilize this guidance to assist you in making the perfect decisions every step along the way, as you are creating, or molding, this physical life experience.

*When you put your emphasis on "doing", you are usually going about your creation in a backwards manner, but as you begin by first identifying how you want to feel and then what you want to have — and are then inspired to the doing — you are creating from the inside out.* In this way, you are literally bringing you into balance with you. As you utilize this process, you will not find yourself acting from a negative viewpoint, trying to fix something that is wrong, or trying to compensate from a negative position. You will always be standing in a positive position, simply becoming clearer.

You are living the balance of your thought, for as you think, you feel, and the combination of your thought and feeling equals your creation. You are thinking on many levels, and you are thinking about many different facets of your experience, and you are thinking about many difference phases of your experience. In one day, or even in one hour, you may think about many different subjects: such as your home, your relationships, your physical body, your financial affairs, the organization of your home or office, the relationships your children are having with one another or with other children, others from your social circles or from your work environment.... You think about what you are doing right now; you think about yesterday, or last year, or a relationship of many years ago. You think about what you will do later today or tomorrow, or the direction of your life.... In other words, your thoughts move across broad ranges of subjects and times. Some of the thoughts are clear and emphatic, while others move softly across your mind, barely noticed. And in all of that, the balance is what you are living, for as you stand today, is evidence of the balance of your thought and feeling.

Once you understand that you are the creator of your experience, and that it is through the thought offered, that you attract, then you can rather easily make the correlation between what you are now living and how you arrived there. How often, when something happens, do you say, "I knew that would happen."? *It is our absolute knowing that you always know what is coming, at some level — because you are creating every part of it.*

To stand in your now, looking forward with deliberate intent and anticipation of what is to come, is infinitely more satisfying than to stand in your now, looking back, retracing your steps as to how you got where you are. However, in the beginning stages of understanding that you are the creator of your experience, it is helpful to look back, often, until you are finally convinced that YOU are doing it. When something wonderful happens, stop and acknowledge that you did it, and identify the thought and feeling that has brought it to you. When something you do not like occurs in your experience, stop and establish your connection to it.

*TAKE RESPONSIBILITY FOR WHAT IS HAPPENING IN YOUR EXPERIENCE, and within that willingness to take responsibility for everything that happens to you, you will find your ultimate, glorious, satisfying freedom to now launch into your future all of the magnificent things that you can imagine.*

That is Deliberate Creation. First, acknowledging that you are the creator of your experience, and then deliberately putting forth thought with the expectation of receiving that which you have offered in thought.

We are exhilarated to find so many of our physical friends wanting to understand the Law of Deliberate Creation. And there is not a better way to understand this Law than by evaluating your own personal physical life experience. As you see the absolute association between your thought and action and what you are living, you come to understand how it has come to be. But you have not come forth into this magnificent time and place, into this wonderful physical body, to stand around trying to figure out what happened and how it happened.

*YOU ARE CREATORS!* You have specifically chosen this time and this place to apply the Laws of the Universe in order to create magnificently here in the physical. You have come forth into this place of perfect balance, immersing yourselves with the data of this time and place — and as you observe, or absorb, the data that surround you, your work is to decide and conclude and concentrate in a deliberate manner.

The physical earth you stand upon was created in the same manner: Data was observed, absorbed, evaluated and then conclusions were drawn and decisions made. And as you are now focused through these physical eyes, your work is to carry this creation further, through the moment-by-moment thoughts and feelings that you offer.

*You come seeking joy and to experience growth as you continue to express your eternal freedom to be.*

- **YOU ARE NOT HERE BEING TESTED OR EVALUATED.** *You are here to create.*
- **YOU ARE NOT HERE TO DISCOVER THE PATH THAT SOMEONE ELSE HAS LAID BEFORE YOU.** *You are the creator of your path.*
- **YOU ARE NOT HERE AS A SEEKER OF THOSE WHO HAVE DISCOVERED TRUTHS, THAT YOU MAY NOW FOLLOW IN THEIR FOOTSTEPS.** *You are truth — seeking a path of joy and growth.*

We want to give you a broader perspective of the word "creation". When we say, "You are the creator of your own experience" most of our physical friends have a very narrow and short view of what we mean. You tend to not look far enough.

From your physical perspective, as you endeavor to be more deliberate in your creating, often you measure all progress or success by the physical trappings you have gathered, concluding success or failure by your ability to gather.

THE ULTIMATE TROPHY IS JOY! *While the physicalness of this experience is of vital importance, and while your physical successes are essential to your reason to being here in this body, we want to emphasize that* ALL OF THE HAVING AND ALL OF THE DOING IS FOR THE ENHANCEMENT OF YOUR STATE OF BEING. *In other words, everything that you know, everything that exists in your physical realm — including your physical body — exists for the sole purpose of enhancing your state of being.* IT IS ALL FOR THE SAKE OF ENHANCING THE WAY YOU FEEL. *It is all for the enhancement of your state of being.*

THEREFORE, OUR DEFINITION OF "DELIBERATE CREATION" IS: THE CONSCIOUS, DELIBERATE OFFERING OF THOUGHT WITH THE INTENT OF UPLIFTING THE STATE OF BEING. *And because we are all in a continual, eternal state of growth, we see no end to our creative endeavors.*

YOU SEE, THE BASIS OF LIFE IS ABSOLUTE FREEDOM. THE OBJECTIVE OF LIFE IS ABSOLUTE JOY, AND THE RESULT OF LIFE IS ABSOLUTE GROWTH.

# 13

## YOUR POINT OF POWER
## IS NOW

As you set a goal to achieve a new house, or a new body size and shape, or a new occupation — and you reach that goal — you misunderstand, thinking that the new house or new body or new job was the subject of creation, when all along the subject of creation is your state of being. In this physical experience you use the format of houses and bodies and jobs to facilitate your state of being — but none of those physical things are the subject of your creation.

*YOU ARE THE SUBJECT OF YOUR CREATION. YOUR STATE OF BEING, OR THE WAY YOU FEEL, IS THE SUBJECT OF YOUR CREATION.*

*If you will seek ways to observe your state of being, you will have a clearer understanding of how you are doing in the creation of you.*

*If you will deliberately identify the way you want to feel or be, you will be more effective in achieving that which you came into this body to achieve.*

The sculptor of magnificent works does not derive his greatest satisfaction from the finished work. Once his work is completed he stands upon that blissful plateau of accomplishment only briefly, eager to begin another project. His joy is in the becoming. His creation is not the work of art. He is the creator of himself. He is not striving for perfection in his work, he is striving for perfection in himself. *He is the creator of a creator of works of art.*

He is a creator who creates by using his thoughts to contour the Energy of the Universe. A creator who has the benefit of a Guidance System to assist him in recognizing how he is utilizing the universal Energy. A creator who has absolute freedom in which to experience his growth and his joy. A creator upon a never-ending journey of growth or adventure. A creator who has chosen the process of this physical life experience in which to live, and love, and grow. A creator who offers benefit to All-That-Is with everything he thinks, or speaks, or experiences. A creator who can understand his value to All-That-Is only when he understands his value to himself. A creator who understands that in making choices in thought or word or action — that evoke positive feelings from himself — he is, in that moment, adding to, in a positive way, the experience of the Universe. A creator who may choose the work of construction, or the work of musician, or the work of acting, or the work of mending — or the work of living, laughing, loving, indeed the work of being the happiest person that he can be in every moment of every day or in every life experience.

Indeed, you exist to find your joy through a multitude of experiences, but you must *seek* that which is to be found. If you are not willing to, first, seek your own joy, you can not possibly find it, and if you do not find it, you have it not to give to another.

*YOU ARE, RIGHT NOW, IN THIS MOMENT, IN THE POSITION OF CREATING. It is not something that you are getting ready to do. It is not something that you are hoping to do one day. It is not something that you will do later when you get things in the position that you want them to be. You are, right now, in this very moment, in the process of creating.*

If — at this moment in your physical life experience — you are in a position of positive emotion, or even in a position of neutral emotion, or no emotion, you are receiving the information that is written here rather clearly, offering no resistance to the words you

113

are reading. However, if you are, in this moment, in negative pain or discomfort as a result of something you have recently lived, then you may find yourself feeling resistance to these words. We acknowledge that it is easier to accept your role as creator when you are, in that moment, in the act of positive creation. Sometimes, as you are feeling bad, you continue to remain there, chewing upon the subject that has brought the pain, thinking that you will get up, or cheer up, or begin your motion forward, later, but that, for now, you just want to remain here in this place and consider it. Most of you believe that you are "putting off" your creating until a time when you are feeling better — *AND OUR POINT TO YOU IS THAT YOU ARE NEVER 'PUTTING OFF' YOUR CREATING. You are in the mode of creating whenever you are in the mode of receiving and offering thought, and the emotion that you feel is your signal to let you know the direction of the creating.*

Physical man usually believes that he can put his creating on hold because he believes that he creates through action. Therefore, when he chooses to spend a day not in action, but deep in thought and feeling, he believes that his creations are not moving forward, and that is not the case. *A FAR GREATER PART OF YOUR CREATING IS ACCOMPLISHED THROUGH YOUR THOUGHT AND CORRESPONDING FEELING THAN WITH YOUR ACTION.*

We define "action" as physical motion or movement. From our perspective we see greatest value in action only when that action serves or enhances a greater intent. Action is most productive when it has been inspired from a greater intent that has been deliberately identified. Physical man, for the most part, does not understand that, and therefore offers the majority of his action without considering or defining, or even acknowledging, his greater intent.

By "greater intent" we mean those intentions that come from your state of being. Intentions such as freedom, growth, joy. *By stopping, before taking any action, and asking, "Will this action enhance my intended state of being?" you will always know the appropriateness of that possible action.*

**When you understand that it is not your action that is mak-**

*ing the big difference in your life experience, but, instead, the predominant way you feel, then you can get action into the proper perspective. While it is true that action can affect your state of being, and while it is absolute that your state of being, or the way you feel, is your magnetic point of attraction, it is not appropriate to consider your action first. It is far more beneficial to your overall creation to, first, identify the state of being that you intend, and next, the state of having that you intend — and last, what action you will seek.*

The balance of your desires and expectations create within you a balance of thought and feeling, and it is from that point of balance that you attract. If the combination of your actions and words and thoughts bring you predominantly to a feeling place of well-being, then, by your own standards, your life would be going fairly well. However, if the combination of your actions and words and thoughts bring you predominantly to a feeling of insecurity, or inferiority, or disappointment, then, by your own standards, your life would not be going well.

Most of our physical friends act first and then allow their action to affect the way they feel. And since the way they feel is their point of attraction, then they conclude that their actions, or what they do, is what is most important to their life experience. You can move much more swiftly and effectively toward the joyous success you seek in life by giving your attention and emphasis to the way you want to feel, or to your state of being, rather than to the action. And from your identification of the state of being that you seek — you will be inspired to the appropriate action.

*ACTING FOR THE SAKE OF BEING IS NOT NEARLY AS EFFECTIVE AS BEING FOR THE SAKE OF ACTING.*

*All action that is performed while you exist in a negative state of being is counter-productive to your objective of success.*

*All action that is performed out of inspiration — as you focus upon your positive goal of freedom, growth and joy — is absolutely harmonious with your objective.*

When you act — because of your awareness of negative recourse if you do not — you are working against your own quest for freedom, growth and joy, whether it is upon the subject of health, wealth, relationships or whatever. In other words, as you go to your job, feeling distaste for it, because you believe that if you do not work you will not have money, and that that will be worse, then your negative feeling of distaste is the predominant factor — and from your state of feeling, you will attract more and more reason to feel distaste. However, instead of acting first, if, from your state of being, you will identify your quest for freedom (and the dollars you earn are synonymous with freedom), your quest for growth (your interaction with others always affords you new understanding), your quest for joy (you can find that, whenever and wherever you look for it) you will be inspired to the action that will harmonize with those core intentions.

*AS YOU BE, OR AS YOU ARE, YOU ATTRACT UNTO. Therefore, put your emphasis upon being or feeling as you want to feel — and let your action be guided from that point. For acting to change feeling is backwards — and does not work.*

A young man called, recently, in great pain because he had just received word that his mother was dead. He said to us, "ABRAHAM, she should not have died. She was a very healthy woman. She went to aerobics three times a week and ate all sorts of food supplements and vitamins and ate only the healthiest of foods. How can this have happened?" And we explained that she was taking those actions, of exercise and eating, to try to compensate for a deep feeling of lack of health. As you act from your feeling of lack — you add power to the lack.

Surely you have witnessed those who, in their feeling of insecurity, act out aggressively. They try to compensate with their action to make up for the feeling of lack. But they can not make up for it in action that tries to compensate, for that action only adds powerful emphasis to the deep lack within. And that lack that they feel is their point of attraction. They must focus upon their desire to feel secure first — and the action that will enhance their feeling of security will be inspired.

116

When you intensely want something that you believe that you do not now have, you usually take action to try to get it. An innate desire to have value, and to move forward, is at the root of this. It is our observation that, very often, the very action that you take in your attempt at getting what you believe is lacking, pushes that which you want away even more. Or more correctly stated: *You attract the lack of what you want, to you, by the very feeling of lack that started the whole episode.*

You may have experienced someone in your life who has very little appreciation for himself, or a low self-image. Because he has a very deep, and very strong, desire to have value and to appreciate himself, he often offers behavior to make himself feel more important: He is often critical of others, in an attempt to like himself more. Because he wants to like himself he finds fault with others. But his action does not get him where he wants to go. For by the power of the Law of Attraction, as one offers criticism, he is criticized, and as he is criticized, he is not uplifted but deflated. Therefore, his action is of no value. In fact, it is detrimental to his intent to appreciate himself.

*Another example:* You may have observed one who wants, very much, to have financial success in life, but as he stands, he has not yet achieved that success. As he observes the lack of what he wants, he cannot bear it, so he looks for lack of success in others to make himself feel stronger. But in discovering lack in others, he only convinces himself of vulnerability. Rather than gaining strength from the exercise, he feels weaker, and more critical. And weakness attracts more weakness, and criticism attracts more criticism — and his success moves farther away.

*Another example.* This one wants more dollars in his experience. As he notes the balance in his checking account, he feels discouragement. He decides — from his point of discouragement — that he will not live like this, never having enough money for the things in life he wants, so he gets a second job. From his point of discouragement, in taking action to try to fix what is wrong — he attracts only negative situations. While he may extend himself tremendously in a physical way, his life does not improve, because the way he feels is dominantly attracting more lack, and his action cannot compensate. In fact, the harder he works, the more discouragement he feels — and so the perpetuation of lack continues, despite his intense efforts to change the situation.

*Another example:*  A woman seeks health. She is aware of sickness and has seen many examples of sickness in those surrounding her. And as she focuses upon the perils of disease and illness, she makes a firm decision to be well. And so, from her point of negative awareness, she determines to be well. She responds to that decision by exercising daily, by eating supplemental vitamins and minerals, by eating only the healthiest of foods, but still her health declines. For her action is offered to compensate for the feeling of vulnerability. And her point of attraction is from her point of feeling.

*What we are wanting you to understand from these examples is that if you are offering your action to try to compensate for a feeling of lack, that your action will only add to your lack.*

As you strive to be something that you do not believe that you are, you will not become that which you strive toward. First, must be the belief that you are. You must first feel successful to attract it. You must feel prosperous to attract more dollars. You must feel your health to attract more of it.

*By giving 99% of your attention to bringing yourself to the feeling that you seek and giving 1% of your attention to inspired action — you will be in a place of powerful motion forward while you exist in a continuous state of joyful well-being.*

*Another example:*   A young man wants to be extremely wealthy. As he looks at the balance in his checking account, he admits that he is far from wealthy, with only a small balance of $1,000. But instead of acknowledging the lack, or difference between the scanty thousand and the millions he seeks, he turns his attention toward the value of the $1,000 he holds. He acknowledges how many things he could purchase with that one thousand dollars. Sometimes mentally spending that thousand dollars 40 or 50 times each day. By acknowledging the value he holds rather than noticing the crevasse of lack between what he holds and what he wants — he gains a feeling of prosperity. And from his point of feeling prosperous — he attracts opportunities and circumstances that catapult his small holdings to very large holdings.

*Another example:* A woman wants to have a healthy, beautiful body. As she looks at herself in the mirror, she admits that her body is not beautiful, but very much over-weight. But instead of turning her attention to the extra pounds, she turns her attention toward her physical attributes. She acknowledges how strong she is. She acknowledges her smooth, pretty skin. She acknowledges how readily her body responds to her decisions, in terms of Energy. By giving attention to the things about her body that please her — instead of giving attention to the parts that displease her — she begins to feel more beautiful, and from her position of feeling more beautiful, she becomes her own image of beauty.

You may have had the experience of not feeling good about yourself when another noticed something about you that caused you to take a deeper look at yourself. In other words, it is very common that the attention from another heightens your own self-awareness. There is tremendous benefit to you to interact with those who see in you what you want to see in yourself. But, in like manner, it can be very detrimental to your self-appreciation to have those in your experience who do not see in you the things you are wanting to see. What you usually do not understand is that their appreciation of you really has very little to do with you, but instead with their own feeling about themselves. Therefore, if you are evaluating yourself through the eyes of others, you often find yourself buffeted about rather harshly.

*Our encouragement is that you let your opinion of you be your top priority. That you put your greatest effort into examining yourself with the intent of discovering wonderful things. That you let the way you feel be the most important aspect of your work. For it is our absolute knowing that the way you feel is your point of attraction. From a place of self-appreciation you will attract all sorts of wonderful things. From a centered place of liking yourself you will allow all wonderful things to come unto you.*

And as you find that place of self-appreciation, not only do you then attract unto you things that are satisfying unto you, but now you are that balanced, self-appreciating being that is able to see wonderful things in others, thus uplifting them to greater self-awareness.

We have been accused of teaching *selfishness,* as if being aware of self is a negative thing. It is our knowing that all that you perceive is through the discerning eyes of self, therefore there is nothing more important than keeping a healthy balance of self.

*ONE WHO DOES NOT FEEL LOVE FOR HIMSELF HAS NO LOVE TO OFFER ANOTHER.* One who is not happy can not uplift another to joy. You simply can not offer to another that which you do not have.

As you feel, you ooze or radiate outward. And in your radiation outward you attract unto you — and you offer influence unto the world, indeed unto the Universe.

Those physical and Non-physical alike benefit from that which you feel.

If you feel resistance to the idea that action is not as significant as you have believed it to be, it is because you are looking at your life experience purely from your physical perspective. All of the days of this physical experience, you have been totally immersed in it, believing that you are perceiving, through your physical senses, everything that has any real importance to you as a being. From the narrow view of physicalness, it is logical that you would come to believe that your action plays the dominant role in your living, or accomplishment, or creating. And so, looking back over your lifetime, noting accomplishments or failures, you make the correlation between your action and your success. And you are not the only one judging you in terms of your action. It is the way of those who have come before you, and those who surround you.

120

However, in looking back at your past experience — in analyzing your current status — if you will not only consider the action that you believe is directly related to your success or failure, but also make the correlation between the way you were feeling during that time of action, then you will discover the powerful understanding that we are offering to you here. *For it is our absolute knowing that the way you feel is your dominant point of attraction, and unless your action is harmonizing with your feeling, your action is counterproductive and not powerful enough to make any real difference.* For example, if you are feeling incapable and unprosperous, comparing yourself to others who have gathered more physical things, or have attained more physical status, there is not enough action in the world to make up for that powerful feeling of lack. That is the reason that you see so many struggling, working very hard, putting in long hours but receiving insignificant or no progress, while others who seem to be offering very little work — or action — often move forward in a seemingly effortless manner.

*Action that is inspired from your positive awareness of that which you want, is always action in joy. Action that is inspired from your negative awareness of lack is never pleasant action.*

In either case, the physical action is performed — but there is a tremendous difference in the outcome. And there is a tremendous difference in the joy experienced during the action. You simply cannot have a happy ending to an unhappy journey. It defies Law.

*We have observed many physically focused beings trying to motivate others.* You have undoubtedly seen it also, for it surrounds you: Employers trying to motivate employees, parents trying to motivate children, teachers trying to motivate students, salesmen trying to motivate consumers. And in most cases, they offer you a negative scenario and then ask for your action to offset it or prevent it. Your employer gives you guidelines and quotas. It is your understanding that if you fail to meet those deadlines you will be removed from your job. And so you act, not out of the enthusiasm for growth and accomplishment, but because if you do not act in the way prescribed you will be fired. If you are fired you will not have enough money. If you do not have enough money, your creditors will attack, or your family will suffer. And on and on, the negative trail goes, leading to a feeling of entrapment, or loss of freedom. You act. Indeed you do. For your failure to act as prescribed would bring never-ending hardship. In your misery, you act.

*Your parents hold a specific philosophy of life. It is a combination of what their parents believed and what they have personally experienced. And in most cases those two are not far apart — because their parents planted the seeds of expectation that they are now living out. And as you enter their experience they begin to teach you their evolving philosophy. They hold expectations for your behavior, and very early in your experience you come to know what they expect.*

Your parents do not understand that you have within you a very strong quest for harmony, and in most cases they believe that if you were left to your own discovery, that you would discover wrong things. So in their intent to protect you from what you believe is wrong, or evil or harm, they offer guidelines or rules of behavior. If you break a rule you reap the negative return. Your parents are angry, or disappointed, or they may even offer more obvious punishment. *And so you modify your action to conform with the rules — or at least to make them believe you are conforming — not out of your positive quest for harmony, but out of your negative awareness of the repercussions that will exist if you don't. You act. Indeed you do. But not from a point of joy.*

Your educational system has devised a standard that you are expected to measure up to. They have studied and analyzed and concluded. "Here are the rules of behavior, and you are expected to conform." While you have a very strong desire for growth and learning, and while you could very well discover the classroom as a satisfying haven to quench your thirst for growth, you usually lose sight of that. And, instead, you become caught up in a system that says to you, "If you don't do this, you will be punished. If you don't do this, you cannot graduate. If you don't do this you will not succeed." *And so you lose your youthful sense of adventure and growth relatively early — and you act. Indeed, not from your natural sense of freedom and growth and adventure, but from your awareness of negative repercussions if you do not.*

The salesman has something that he wants you to buy from him. He knows the value of his product, but does not trust that you are wise enough to see the value of his product. Therefore he works very hard to point out the negative situation in which you stand if you do not have his product. And so, you say "yes" to the salesman, not from your clear awareness of the value of your purchase, but because you resist the lack that he has so vividly pointed out to you.

Of course, these examples could well continue for many pages, for the examples abound of those who act, or rather react, to their own attention to lack. *These examples point out your action which has been stimulated by another, but there are also many examples within your life experiences where your action is generated simply by your feeling of lack.*

Bullies are usually those who feel tremendous lack of appreciation for themselves. They feel weak when they want to be strong, or they feel powerless when they want to feel powerful, and so, from their negative feeling of lack, they act, trying to compensate for their own feeling of weakness. Virtually every war that has ever been fought has an instigator at the helm who is doggedly focused on his on feeling of weakness and is now setting out to prove that he is not weak.

Have you not often noticed that those who appear to be the most sure of themselves, often are not that at all. They overcompensate with action to make up for their feeling of lack, but it does not make them *feel* better.

Stories are many of dominating fathers or husbands who want to control the lives of children or wives. It is our knowing that, in most cases, behind that face of domination is a very insecure and inadequate feeling man. But his domination does not make him feel stronger, for it defies law. When you take action from a negative perspective or from lack — you intensify the lack that you feel.

*Behind the bully in the schoolyard, or the dominating father, or the leader of a country who wages war against other nations, is one who wants very much to know and feel his own strength, but has not yet found a way to do it. He believes that by domineering over others, others who are weaker, that he will feel his strength. Instead, he magnifies his own weakness, and so the bullying, or dominating, or waging of war continues until he dies.*

However, the feeling of power, or strength, that he so desperately wants is already his, for his weakness is only illusionary. He is a product of an environment that spends more time criticizing than praising. More time tearing down than building up. Indeed, he is a product of a mass consciousness of physical beings that feel more insecurity than security, and so he, also, absorbs some of that feeling of insecurity. Often he has been fostered by parents, or teachers, who feel their own insecurity, who have dominated over him to feel their own strength. Of course, they did not feel stronger as a result of their domination of him, but they did pass on the cycle of insecurity and domination, indeed, to another, and so it goes.

*You have a powerful desire to be well, to be secure, to be successful and to be strong, and it is, without exception, from attention to the lack of these desires, that you negatively create. The reason the desires exist so strongly within you is because, unconsciously, you recognize that from your broader perspective you are well, you are secure, you are successful, and you are strong.*

*CONTRARY TO WHAT MOST OF YOU BELIEVE, YOU DO NOT NEED TO PROVE YOUR WELLNESS, OR SECURENESS, OR SUCCESS, OR STRENGTH. In fact, in most cases, your trying to prove it, backfires, and, instead, you diminish it. From your broader, inner perspective, you ARE well, you ARE secure, you ARE successful, you ARE strong — and anything less than that is illusionary. Physical illusions created by your physical thought or belief.*

It is difficult for our physical friends to agree with us that the illness they are suffering, with all of the apparent evidence of that illness, is illusionary, when it is so pressing in their physical experience. It is not easy for our physical friends to understand that the poverty, or insecurity, or unhappy relationships or even the world events, are illusionary. But to understand what we mean by "illusionary", it is necessary for you to step back to a broader perspective.

When the only perspective you have of yourself is purely from your physical perspective of flesh and blood and bone, then your total approach to life is from the physical perspective of action. From that limited perspective, you tend to see physical evidence looming bigger than it actually is.

*What you do not understand is that the very evidence — that you now are using to substantiate your feeling of powerlessness — has been created by you, therefore you are not powerless, but powerful.* For example: You see the evidence of illness, and you focus upon that evidence, feeling more negative emotion, thus perpetuating it further.

*When you are able to step back to your broader, fuller perspective and realize that you exist on a broader level than only this physical body, and that the broader part of you sees what you are living, right now, differently than you are physically perceiving it — then you are upon the path of real self-discovery.*

You will discover that while you are flesh and bone and blood, you are so much more. You will discover that you are Creative Energy. *Furthermore, you will begin to understand that the flesh and bone and blood are responsive to the flow of Creative Energy within you — and that you can, and have been, the director of that Creative Energy.*

You will come to understand that your body, others around you, indeed everything within your physical dimension, is attracted to you, or repelled by you according to your utilization of that Creative Energy.

And as you seek, you will come to know that you utilize that Creative Energy, or contour it, through your physical conscious thought. And then, instead of feeling vulnerable to this big physical world, you will see your absolute control of your experience within it. Rather than feeling victimized by illness, you will understand that the illness is nothing more than your perspective, or expectation, or utilization, of the Creative Energy. You have literally thought — or expected it — into existence.

*You will come to understand that while the physical evidence seems impressive, and while many others see it and proclaim its value — that all of it is very much illusory, because it is occurring only because of the physical perspective.*

A feeling of vulnerability, and expectation of bad things happening, is the reason that bad things happen. That feeling produces the physical evidence of bad things happening. As physical beings, you put the emphasis upon the bad things that have happened. You stack up this "evidence" and use it against yourself, causing your negative expectation to grow larger and larger. If, instead, you will put the emphasis upon what really caused the bad things to happen — your thought and feeling of negative expectation — then the evidence would not loom so large. You would see it only as the physical manifestation of your thought rather than the threatening thing it seemed before.

*When you see negative evidence for what it really is — temporary evidence created by you, drawn by you and experienced by you — you can let it go out of the same door it came in: It got in by your thought and feeling. Change your thought, and your feeling will change — and it will leave your experience.*

*From your action oriented physical perspective, the physical creation — or evidence — holds more weight in your system of beliefs than it deserves — for the evidence was created from thought.* CHANGE THE THOUGHT AND THE EVIDENCE WILL VANISH.

Even the most dreaded disease will vanish when you completely remove your attention from it. You attracted it through thought and feeling, and you release it by releasing your thought and feeling, regarding it. It is not easy to not think of something — but it is easy to think of something else. Therefore, by focusing upon aspects of your beings that are in harmony with your desire, you are, at that time, not focusing upon the aspects that are *not* in harmony with your desire.

Imagine a magical city. It is very small, only ten miles by ten miles square. It is filled with magnificent points of beauty and interest. It is tied together by an integral grid of streets and thoroughfares that efficiently take you wherever you want to go. There is adequate parking wherever you go. There is only one small thing that is not perfect in your city: There is a pothole on 6th Avenue.

*Your logical mind tells you that in knowing about the perfection of an amazing city, that you would barely notice one wee pothole. However, our observation of our physical friends is that you not only notice the pothole, but you give it an inordinate amount of your attention. You see it, you complain about it, you write letters about it, you talk to friends about it — until it literally consumes your city.*

A woman goes for her annual physical examination, where the doctor looks for abnormalities within her. He has been looking year after year, and finally, on this last visit to the doctor, he discovers a small lump. This woman does not stop to take stock of her magnificent apparatus. She does not note the magnificent points of interest of the amazing "arteries of transportation". Instead, with the prompting of her doctor, she focuses her attention, doggedly, upon "the pothole", and in doing so, enhances it, until it consumes her "city".

From our broader perspective we see the tendency. We are aware of the tremendous imbalance. We know that she is many times more well than she is sick — but her attention to the sickness, increases the sickness.

*In all areas of existence, there are things that harmonize with your intentions, and things that do not.* THERE ARE POSITIVE AND NEGATIVE ASPECTS TO ALL THINGS.

As you focus upon any negative aspect, automatically your Inner Being offers you the feeling of negative emotion, because in the attention to the negative aspect, you are resisting something that you want — or something that is positive.

Through thought, you attract the negative aspects closer into your experience. Through habit, you continue to focus upon them, until there is an actual physical manifestation — something close-in and tangible within your experience — and then you say, "Look at this physical evidence! It is big and near, and I can not deny it!" And we say "Deny it not, for in your denial, you still acknowledge — and therefore attract. Instead, ignore it. Give your attention to something else. Take your attention from the negative evidence and it will leave your experience. For it is Law!"

You place so much weight upon physical evidence. You give it such an important place in your life. And in doing so, you do not put the emphasis where it really belongs.

*THE PHYSICAL EVIDENCE HAS COME FROM YOUR THOUGHT AND FEELING. Therefore, put your emphasis upon your thought and feeling. Whenever you are feeling negative emotion, you are thinking of something that you do not want, or lack of something that you do want — AND YOU ARE IN THE PROCESS OF CREATING PHYSICAL EVIDENCE.*

How often do you say, "I knew that would happen"? And we say, "Indeed, you did know." For as you think, you feel, and as you feel, you create.

As a Deliberate Creator, your work is not in the doing, or the acting. It is not in the moving of the physical evidence about. Your work is in the recognition and maintaining of a centered place of Well-being. Your work is to discover the feelings of happiness, exhilaration, love, peace, enthusiasm, triumph, well-being...and then to hold yourself deliberately in that place.

*As you exist in a place of Well-being, you stand in the place of magnetically attracting more wonderful evidence of that state of Well-being. Furthermore, as you feel — you exude outwardly for the benefit of others.*

128

# 14

## BOOK OF
## POSITIVE ASPECTS

Many of our friends, in seeking our advice, have offered detailed stories of negative experiences covering a wide range of subjects. And often, after explaining their plight, they have asked us, "Do you think I should leave this relationship?" "Do you think I should quit this job and find another?" We often agree that that is one way out of this negative place. Removing yourself physically, from what you disagree with, can give you immediate relief. However, the physical action, in and of itself, is not enough, for it is not your physical action that brought you to this negative point of separation, but your thought and feeling.

We often say to these people, "If you are leaving this relationship because you have noted that there are negative aspects to it, then we should point out to you that had you better get out of this city, as well, for there are negative aspects here, also, when you look for them. And, also, better get out of this world, for certainly there are negative aspects there." *If you are leaving a relationship, or taking action, because of your awareness of the negativity within it, then you will never stop leaving, or running. And you will have nowhere to go. For within everything, there are positive and negative aspects — and that provides the perfect balance for freedom of choice and for growth as well as for joy.*

*While your decision may ultimately be to leave a relationship, or to change your position of work, or to move to another home... it is extremely important that you do not do so from your negative perspective from focusing only upon the negative aspects, for you will certainly take yourself with you, and as you are feeling those negative feelings, you are in the mode of attracting more of the same.* Often, as you make a decision to go, or to leave, or to quit, you spend much time, following your decision, trying to defend it, or rationalize it, or justify it, feeling negative emotion while you are doing it. And all of that justifying or defending just adds negative power to your attracting, until you, very soon, have created another similar situation.

The woman who believes she has been mistreated by her first husband, often speaks about the reasons she left, long after leaving, and often attracts another bad relationship not so different from the first.

The man who quits his job because of the unfair treatment offered by his employer, often speaks of it to others, in an attempt to justify to himself, and to others, his decision to leave, and thus attracts another unsatisfying work relationship in his new job.

*What we encourage, is that before you make your decision to leave, to go, to quit, or whatever, that you spend time focusing upon the positive aspects of that experience. In doing so, you will feel better, and in feeling better, you will change your mode of attraction.* Often, your present position improves so much that you see no reason to go. And always, your next position will be better once you take your attention from what was wrong with the last position.

Our friends, Jerry and Esther, utilize many different hotels as they are gathering friends to visit with us. One particular hotel always seemed to forget they were coming, even though Esther had signed contracts and had called, even on the day of arrival, to confirm. On the last visit to this hotel, Esther was again faced with the task of banging things into position at the last minute by calling for chairs and water, getting the information on the video bulletin, urging the hotel staff to hurry, as the gathering was to begin in less than 30 minutes. Following the gathering, Esther pondered the appropriateness of moving to a different hotel. We agreed that that was certainly a possibility. However, we did not encourage that they make that decision from their negative position of lack. For as you take action from a negative perspective, taking your negative perspective with you to the new hotel, you will likely attract the same situation from the new hotel. Esther and Jerry laughed, because this hotel was the second in that particular city. They had moved from the first for the identical reasons that they were now considering moving from the second.

We encouraged them to purchase a new notebook and entitle it: "Book of Positive Aspects," and to write on the first page: "Positive Aspects of The _____ Hotel in the city of Austin."

Esther began making her entries: "This is a beautiful facility. The hotel staff is very friendly. The parking lot is well placed and adequate. The hotel has easy access from the interstate highway. Our room is always fresh and clean. There are many different sizes of meeting rooms to accommodate our varying functions. We can utilize a lovely suite for meeting, and for sleeping." As Esther completed her list, she was feeling very good about this hotel, and wondered why she was considering leaving. By putting her attention upon the "positive aspects", she had withdrawn her attention from any "negative aspects." As her thoughts changed, her feelings changed. And as her feelings changed — so did her point of attraction.

*As you understand that by The Law of Attraction you are drawing unto you that which you give your attention to, and that as you feel negative you are in the place of resisting what you want — then you can see the value of taking the time to deliberately focus upon what makes you feel good.*

# PROCESS:
# BOOK OF POSITIVE ASPECTS

*This exercise will assist you in finding a more deliberate, constant place of positive attraction:*
Purchase a new notebook. Write across the front of your book, in bold letters: "Book of Positive Aspects". The primary objective of your Book of Positive Aspects is to quickly bring you to a position of feeling good, therefore to a position of positive attraction, but there are many other benefits: A daily entering of positive aspects on old and new subjects will help you to maintain your positive balance. As one area of your life draws you to your Book of Positive Aspects, the recording of your entries will bleed over into other aspects of your experience. Because you are feeling better more of the time, more of the things that you consider to be good will begin to flow smoothly into your experience. Many of the things that you have been wanting — but have been blocking by offering thoughts that attract resistance in the form of negative emotion — will easily flow into your experience. The balance of thought and feeling in your experience will shift from predominantly negative to predominantly positive. You will soon discover that no matter what the emotional state of your world, your economy, or even those close around you in your work or home, you will find yourself in a more positive balance, and by law, indeed by the Law of Attraction, your own life will begin to show the result of that, immediately.

*This "Book of Positive Aspects" is not offered as a process whereby you take a negative and turn it into a positive. It is a process to assist you in giving your attention to that which is positive. And as you are focusing upon that which is positive, you cannot focus upon that which is negative. And when you withdraw your attention from that which is negative — it will leave your experience.*

*Upon each page, begin a new subject. Write what flows easily from*

*you. Do not work at it. When you work at it, you may find yourself try-*
*ing to stretch something you actually feel negative about into a positive, and*
*in giving it attention, even giving it positive words — you further your neg-*
*ative attention.* When the thoughts regarding a particular subject
have stopped flowing, turn to a fresh new page and begin a new
subject. 15 minutes at the beginning of each day is enough time
for this process.

On the second day, read what you have written before, and add
as the thoughts come to you. Notice how good you feel during and
following this process.

If you find yourself feeling negative emotion regarding a specific person in your experience, begin a page of positive aspects
regarding that person.

If you find yourself feeling negative emotion regarding any
subject, such as not enough money, not enough time, too much
work to do, not enough respect from another...begin a page in your
book to help yourself to identify the positive aspects of that particular situation.

*You will notice, right away, that your overall feeling is im-*
*proved. Not only will the specific situations, upon which you*
*have written, improve immediately, but, also, other experiences*
*not yet identified in your book, because AS YOU FEEL BETTER, YOU*
*ATTRACT MORE OF THAT WHICH YOU CONSIDER TO BE GOOD. AS*
*YOU FEEL BAD, YOU ATTRACT MORE OF THAT WHICH YOU CONSID-*
*ER TO BE BAD.*

Continue for a full week, each day reading what has been written before and adding to that. At the end of the first week, put
your book aside and purchase another.

Again, write across the front of your book: "My book of
Positive Aspects". You may now begin to see this book as the trea-
sure it really is, for it is the key to your centered, balanced place of
Well-being. It is the key to your deliberate positioning of yourself
in a place of positive attraction. While your world is predominantly focused upon the negative, with many more critics than
those who praise — you have found a process to control the way

you feel. While almost everyone you know makes decisions to act from their concern of what will happen if they don't act — you are being inspired to positive, joyful activity.

The motivation to act is inspired from two primary sources: From a clear, exhilarated vision of what is wanted, or from a clear, uncomfortable vision of what is not wanted. As we view your physical world, we see that the majority of action is inspired from the negative perspective of what is not wanted. Most are moved to act, not because of their blissful, excited positive objective, but because they believe that if they do not act, there will be negative consequences. In other words, they do not go happily, enthusiastically to their work because of their clear vision of the value of this work. They are not joyfully inspired to action because of their clear picture of their desire. Most work because they believe that if they do not work, they will not have money, and if they do not have money, they will be without things they want.

*When you are focused upon the negative consequence of what will happen if you do not act, and so you act to circumvent the negative consequence,* YOU DO NOT CIRCUMVENT THE NEGATIVE CONSEQUENCE BUT ADD POWER UNTO IT. IT IS LAW.

*You cannot have a happy ending to an unhappy journey. And you can not have a happy journey when your motivation has been inspired from your attention to a negative consequence.*

*The key point, here, is this:* ACTION IS RESPONSIBLE FOR BUT A TINY FRACTION OF YOUR CREATIVE EFFORT. *The way you feel is primarily responsible for what you are getting and what you are creating and, indeed, what you are living.*

So many find themselves in a state of futility because they just cannot act enough to make the difference. They try, they struggle, they persevere, but things do not improve. And the reason things do not improve is because the very basis of their creative attraction is not coming from their action, it is coming from the way they feel as they act.

If you are wanting to affect the outcome of your physical experiences in a positive way, put your primary attention upon the way you feel — and look for reasons to feel good. There is not enough action in your world to compensate for feeling bad. You simply cannot act enough. There aren't enough hours in the day, and there isn't enough Energy in your body, to compensate for the negative attraction that occurs when you feel negative emotion.

And for that reason, we give tremendous emphasis to the value of *Your Book of Positive Aspects*. In deliberately looking for reasons to feel good, you will find them. And in focusing upon those reasons you will feel good. And in feeling good you will begin the attraction of that which you consider to be good.

So often, when you find yourself in the midst of negative emotion, you try to justify it by placing the blame with someone else. You look for reasons to excuse it, for, inwardly, you sense that it is out of place within you. And we say to you, that whenever you are in the mode of justification, you are in the mode of negative attraction.

*As you try to explain why you are feeling negative emotion, you are adding power to it. Release the negative emotion, the negative feeling, AND THE NEGATIVE ATTRACTION — by taking your attention from it. Give your attention to what makes you feel good, thereby releasing your attention from what makes you feel bad.*

Many of our physical friends are trying to understand how action fits into this process of creation, for, certainly, you are physical beings, and action is an important part of your experience. You are always making decisions regarding the best use of your time. "What should I do? "

We are not trying to lead you away from action. We are not wanting you to believe that action is unimportant. What we are wanting you to understand is that action, in and of itself, is not very powerful. And action pitted against negative emotion has virtually no power at all. And so, as we watch our physical friends giving so much credit to their action and yet not feeling progress toward the things they want, we want, so much, for them to understand why they are getting what they are getting.

*When your action is inspired from your positive wanting, the action augments your creation* — AND THE ACTION FEELS GOOD. IT IS ACTION IN JOY. *But when your action is inspired because you fear the negative consequences if you do not act* — THEN THE ACTION FEELS BAD.

Pay attention to your own experience. Are you feeling joy as you act throughout your day, or are you often feeling resentment as you act? Are you joyfully bounding through your projects, or are you begrudgingly acting, watching the clock, feeling no motivation to finish or to proceed? Are you smiling? Are you singing? Are you happy?

*Let your action be inspired from your positive picture, not from your negative picture. As you focus upon that which makes you feel good, you will find yourself acting more and more out of joy. And as you are acting joyfully, more of the things that you want will easily flow into your experience — for you will not be blocking your own action with your negative feeling.*

# 15

# LAW OF
# ALLOWING

Friends, you are true seekers of goodness and you want so much to find your place, and yet you work so hard against yourselves. In many cases you know with certainty what you want. But for the most part, you have come to believe that the way to get something that you want is to defeat its opposition.

You have a "War against Poverty", a "War against Drugs", a "War against Cancer", a "War against AIDS".... and all of these objects of your concerned attention are increasing rapidly. Rather than focusing upon and thereby attracting your natural state of health, most of you hold a position of defense, or of fear. You shout "No not me!" at poverty, or at disease.

*Most of you have actually come to believe that you will somehow get to what you want, by defeating what you do not want. We have come forth to explain to you that THAT DEFIES LAW!*

- *THAT WHICH YOU DEFEND AGAINST — BECOMES YOUR EXPERIENCE.*
- *THAT WHICH YOU WORRY ABOUT — BECOMES YOUR EXPERIENCE.*
- *THAT WHICH YOU PREPARE AGAINST — BECOMES YOUR EXPERIENCE.*

As you stand in your fearful feeling place, greeting your new physical friends into this world, offering them your "well intentioned" warnings, you are a tremendous disadvantage to them. And just as your fathers before you, you perpetuate the experience of vulnerability.

*You need not defend against sickness, for health is your natural state. Your defense against sickness is the cause of it.*

*You need not defend against poverty, for abundance is your natural state. Your defense against poverty is the cause of it.*

*You need not defend against "evil", for goodness is your natural state of being. Your defense against evil is the cause of it.*

*As you stand tense and guarded, frightened or concerned, against anything that you do not want — by your attention, or focus of your thought, and with the power of your emotional response to your thought — you are in the mode of attracting the very thing you guard against.*

The louder you shout *"NO!"* the more powerful your attraction. The more often you defend against, or resist, that which you do not want, the more powerful you draw it unto you. Indeed, as you protest against that which you do not want, you add power unto it. As you justify the negative position in which you stand, you assure your remaining in this place you do not want to be. As you blame others for what has happened to you, you hold yourself firmly in this unwanted position.

*To experience the joyous, productive, delicious physical experience that you intended as you emerged into this magnificent physical body, you have only to want that, and expect it, or allow it, to be.*

Much of your wanting is very well in place. You have spent much of this physical experience examining life, and identifying preferences. But most of you are not yet good at now allowing those wonderful things, that you have identified as good, to flow into your experience. You do want to allow them, and most of you are willing to do whatever it takes to allow those good things to happen to you.

*REMEMBER THAT THE LAW OF ATTRACTION IS ETERNALLY AFFECTING YOUR EXPERIENCE, AND WHATEVER YOU ARE THINKING AND FEELING IS YOUR POINT OF ATTRACTION.*

To put yourself in the clear, unrestricted, unresisted position of allowing health, or abundance, or security, or love, or whatever it is that you consider to be Well-being, you have only to identify your desire, and then relax, with the intent of basking in the spirit of Well-being.

Rather than struggling against illness, relax and allow your natural wellness.

Rather than working so hard against poverty, or against not having enough, relax and allow your natural abundance.

Identify what you want, and then watch, expectantly, joyfully, for evidence of it.

No more struggle and strain. No more discouragement or defeat. But a steady, sure, joyful process of becoming.

*All-That-Is — everything that you know or don't know, within this magnificent Universe — is connected and responsive to the powerful Law of Attraction. Every thought that you offer, or every thought that you receive, has its own individual vibrational frequency, and by Law of Attraction will be drawn to that which is same.*

Our friend, Jerry, described a very large ship being attached to the dock with a very large rope, nearly one foot in diameter. A rope too heavy and bulky to be thrown across to the dock, and so, instead, a small ball of twine was tossed across the expanse of water. That twine was spliced into a bigger rope, which was spliced into a bigger rope, which was spliced into a bigger rope, until eventually that very large rope was easily pulled across the water. *Your thoughts dovetail into one another in a similar manner, with every thought beginning small and drawing more power as you pull upon it, or think upon it longer.*

Everything that you are living, receiving, experiencing, comes to you by virtue of this process of thoughts connected to thoughts connecting to thoughts.

As Esther stood at her gate, experiencing the beauty and brilliance of the sky, and hearing the crystal clear tones of the birds, and smelling the delicious fragrances in the air, and feeling the wonderful wind upon her skin, she experienced the dramatic result of having pulled upon a very positive rope. By her decision to look for reasons to feel good, she attracted a thought that attracted a thought that attracted a thought that attracted a thought until eventually her physical body was literally vibrating at a frequency which allowed a fuller emergence of her Non-physical Energy.

Most of you do not recognize the importance of deliberately offering those subtle little thoughts because most of you do not understand the powerful Law of Attraction. One thought leading to another, and to another, and to another until you have literally created the physical evidence of that string of thoughts.

*We have noticed that many of you are extremely particular about what you wear, and what you eat, and where you live, and the car that you drive, and yet you are not particular at all about the thoughts that you allow within your thinking mechanism. Thoughts that vibrate and attract other thoughts, and eventually produce physical evidence within your experience.*

As you receive a thought of something that is not in harmony with your desire, you always receive a negative warning bell from your Inner Being, but few of you acknowledge the warning bell and deliberately change the thought, therefore, eventually, you attract evidence, or life experience, that you do not want.

*Only a few, very simple, points of understanding are necessary for you to have the absolute, joyful control of your own life experience:*

- Accept that you are the creator of your experience.
- Understand the power and the importance of the thoughts you ponder.
- Accept your absolute connection to your own Inner Being.
- Understand that the emotions you feel are guidance from your Inner Being.
- Make a decision that nothing is more important than that you "feel" good.

*Truly, if you have received nothing more from the reading of this book, than that it is of great value for you to "feel" good, then you have received all that you need to live a joyous, productive physical life experience, for your recognition of the way you are feeling is your recognition of the guidance that comes to you from your broader perspective.*

If you are carefully guiding your thoughts, words and actions toward that which brings forth within you a feeling of Well-being, then you are allowing your supreme guidance from within.

Within the framework of this one physical lifetime only, you have become very complex beings. You have considered multitudes of topics, and life has touched you in many different ways. You have been "tugging on ropes", so to speak, of both positive and negative nature from the day of your emergence into this body, and what you are living today is the balance of all of that "tugging." You have developed some very strong habits of thoughts, or beliefs, and so you easily slide into negative spirals at the mere subtle mention of some topics. You have developed extreme sensitivity to some things, and you sometimes take a very guarded stance as you try to protect yourself from the things you do not want.

*Rather than trying to analyze all that is within you, justifying why it is there, and offering blame to yourself and others for it being there, there is a much simpler way:* Set forth the intention to know your Well-being. Ask for the feeling of value to well up within you. Look at yourself, from every perspective you can find, for evidence of your goodness and value. Make a strong decision that you will find reasons within yourself to adore you, and it is our absolute promise to you, that by the powerful Law of Attraction, those reasons will grow and expand to the very boundaries of the Universe.

When you are looking at yourself, or at others, or at anything, and are seeing lack, you are offering thoughts that are vibrating at a very specific vibration. The feeling of negative emotion that you receive as you focus upon lack is your indication that your own Inner Being is not resonating with those thoughts. And the very negative emotion that you are feeling means that you are standing there, temporarily separated from your greater Inner power. By utilizing the process of Pivoting, you can change your thought from one of lack to one of that which is wanted, and as you focus there — thought attracting thought attracting thought attracting thought — you will change your vibration to that which harmonizes with your own Inner Being, and the negative emotion will dissolve as the positive emotion takes its place. The positive emotion indicating that you are, once again, back into a position of harmony with your broader knowing.

*Focusing upon lack, therefore vibrating at a lower frequency, therefore diverging from your own Inner Being, therefore restricting the magnificent flow of Energy from your Inner Being — is the reason for all illness that exists within you. Just as your body would respond negatively to the restriction of the flow of blood, or of oxygen, it responds negatively to the restriction of the flow of pure positive Energy.*

As you look into your own life experience and see the lack of health, or of prosperity, or of meaningful relationships, or of anything that you are wanting, understand that that lack exists for one reason, and one reason only: You have chosen thoughts that connected to other thoughts that connect to other thoughts that are not in harmony with that which your Inner Being knows to be, and you are literally vibrating and therefore attracting exactly what you are getting.

When you think thoughts of criticism towards yourself, your Inner Being does not agree, for your Inner Being knows you to be wonderful, and talented, and creative, and good.

When you think thoughts of criticism towards others, your Inner Being does not agree, for your Inner Being understands that this Universe exists in a state of perfect balance, and that all thoughts, and all experience is allowed. Your Inner Being knows that there are many things that you do not choose, for there are many things that your Inner Being does not choose — *but your Inner Being knows that your attention to the subject of what you do not want IS CHOOSING IT, and your Inner Being is too wise for*

142

*that, and withdraws its attention.*

When you fear or guard against sickness, or monsters, or that which you do not want, your Inner Being does not participate with you, because your Inner Being understands that attention to a subject is an invitation to it. Your Inner Being literally basks in a place of Well-being, and those guarded, frightened thoughts are absolutely alien to your Inner Being.

*As you put yourself into your bed each night, acknowledge the existence of your Inner Being, and your connection to it, and lie in your bed for a few minutes before slumbering, and bask in the spirit of your own Well-being. Your Inner Being will literally flood you with pure, positive, powerful Energy. Set forth your intention to allow the complete refreshment of your physical apparatus, knowing that your Inner Being will lovingly and intricately align the Energies of your physical body. And set forth the intention to awaken refreshed, and happy.*

*When you awaken in the morning, acknowledge that you have just re-emerged back into the physical, and immediately set forth the clear intent: "Today, it is my dominant intent to look for that which makes me feel good." For as you feel good, you are in the place of positive attraction. As you feel good, you are in perfect alignment with your broader perspective, and greater intent. As you feel good, only that which you consider to be good, can come unto you.*

As you set forth the intent to look for reasons to feel good, you begin to pull upon that positive rope, and one idea and then another will come to you. As old habits of thought creep in, or as you automatically pull on some old negative ropes, you will recognize more quickly what you are doing, and you can quickly release those ropes, looking again for a reason to feel good, until, eventually, the balance of thought within you will be predominantly positive, and your connection with your magnificent Inner Being will be strong and clear.

*As you allow that powerful, pure connection between the physical you and the Inner You, the level of your joy will soar. Things that you want will flow easily unto you, and things that you do not want will not be a part of your experience. From your powerful perspective, this world will indeed be a glorious place to be.*

Each morning, as you awaken, you literally re-emerge back into the physical, just as you did on the day that you were born into this physical body. As you open your eyes, lie in your bed for a time, and bask in the spirit of Well-being. Lie there for a time, looking for reasons to feel good. Feel the comfort of the bed beneath you. Focus on the pleasant sensations of your own body. Sensually feel the fabric of your bedding as it touches your skin. Feel your blood moving through your body, and marvel at how well this magnificent body functions and thrives. Take a deep breath and then another as you feel your body joyously responding to this new day.

*As you awakened this morning, coming back into your full physical awareness, you have literally emerged into A NEW BEGINNING. That which lies before you is affected only by your current perspective of what is.*

*We leave you with some powerful things that we have come to understand. As you re-read these statements, notice the dramatic or subtle difference in your perspective, since your last reading of these statements and bask in the pleasure of your understanding.*

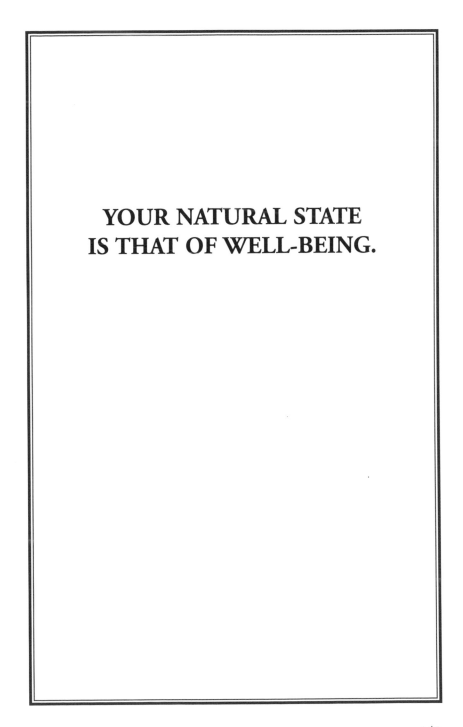

# YOUR NATURAL STATE
# IS THAT OF WELL-BEING.

# YOUR NATURAL STATE
# IS ONE OF HEALTH.

YOUR WORLD IS ABUNDANT
WITH ALL THAT YOU
CONSIDER TO BE GOOD,
AND YOU HAVE EASY ACCESS
TO THAT ABUNDANCE.

YOU ARE NOT HERE
UPON THIS EARTH
TO PROVE YOURSELF
WORTHY OF ANYTHING,
TO ANYONE.

YOU ARE IN A STATE OF
ETERNAL GROWTH,
AND THE PLACE
WHERE YOU NOW STAND
IS A VERY GOOD PLACE.

# THERE IS NO ENDING
# TO GROWTH.

YOU EXIST IN A STATE
OF ABSOLUTE FREEDOM,
AND EVERYTHING
THAT YOU EXPERIENCE
IS ATTRACTED BY YOU,
SELF-IMPOSED.
YOU ARE EVEN FREE
TO ATTRACT BONDAGE.

AS YOU THINK,
YOU FEEL,
AND AS YOU FEEL,
YOU OOZE OR RADIATE,
AND ALL-THAT-IS, PHYSICAL
AND NON-PHYSICAL,
IS AFFECTED
BY YOUR OFFERING.
THAT IS YOUR POWER OF
INFLUENCE.

# OF COURSE,
# YOUR OWN EXPERIENCE
# IS MOST AFFECTED
# BY YOUR INFLUENCE.

THE ONLY OPINION,
IN ALL OF THE UNIVERSE,
THAT IS OF TRUE
IMPORTANCE TO YOU,
IS YOUR OWN.
AND YOUR OWN OPINION
OF YOU, AFFECTS
THE ENTIRE UNIVERSE.

WHAT YOU ARE
LIVING TODAY
IS AS A RESULT OF THE
THOUGHTS AND FEELINGS
THAT YOU HAVE FELT
BEFORE THIS.
YOUR FUTURE
IS CREATED FROM
YOUR PERSPECTIVE
OF TODAY.

THE CREATIVE LIFE FORCE,
OR ENERGY
OF THE UNIVERSE,
FLOWS THROUGH YOU
AND LITERALLY CONNECTS
YOU TO ALL- THAT-IS.
THROUGH YOUR
ATTENTION,
OR FOCUS OF THOUGHT,
YOU DRAW THE SPECIFICS
UNTO YOU.

AS YOU ARE FOCUSING UPON
AND THEREBY ATTRACTING
THAT WHICH IS
IN HARMONY WITH
THAT WHICH YOU
CONSIDER TO BE GOOD,
YOUR INNER BEING
OFFERS YOU THE FEELING OF
POSITIVE EMOTION AS
ACKNOWLEDGEMENT OF
YOUR POSITIVE
CONNECTION.

AS YOU ARE FOCUSING UPON
AND THEREBY ATTRACTING -
THAT WHICH IS
NOT IN HARMONY WITH
THAT WHICH YOU
CONSIDER TO BE GOOD,
YOUR INNER BEING
OFFERS YOU THE FEELING OF
NEGATIVE EMOTION
AS ACKNOWLEDGEMENT
OF YOUR
NEGATIVE CONNECTION.

WHENEVER YOU FEEL
NEGATIVE EMOTION,
YOU ARE, IN THAT MOMENT,
IN THE MODE OF
NEGATIVE ATTRACTION.
MOST OFTEN YOU ARE,
IN THAT MOMENT,
RESISTING SOMETHING
THAT YOU WANT.

BECAUSE YOU COUNTER
THE MAJORITY OF
YOUR THOUGHTS
WITH OPPOSING
THOUGHTS,
YOU BELIEVE THAT YOU ARE
NOT POWERFUL.

WHEN YOU NO LONGER
SPLIT YOUR
FLOW OF ENERGY
WITH CONTRADICTORY
THOUGHTS,
YOU WILL KNOW
YOUR POWER.

YOU DO NOT HAVE
TO JUSTIFY YOUR
PHYSICAL EXISTENCE.
YOUR EXISTENCE
IS JUSTIFICATION ENOUGH.

YOU DO NOT HAVE TO
JUSTIFY LEAVING
THIS PHYSICAL PLANE
BY ATTRACTING ILLNESS,
OR AGEDNESS.
YOU COME
AND GO
BY VIRTUE OF
YOUR DESIRE TO BE.
YOU ARE FREE TO BE
WHEREVER YOU CHOOSE,
WHENEVER YOU CHOOSE.

IN YOUR JOY,
YOU OFFER JOY
TO THE WORLD.

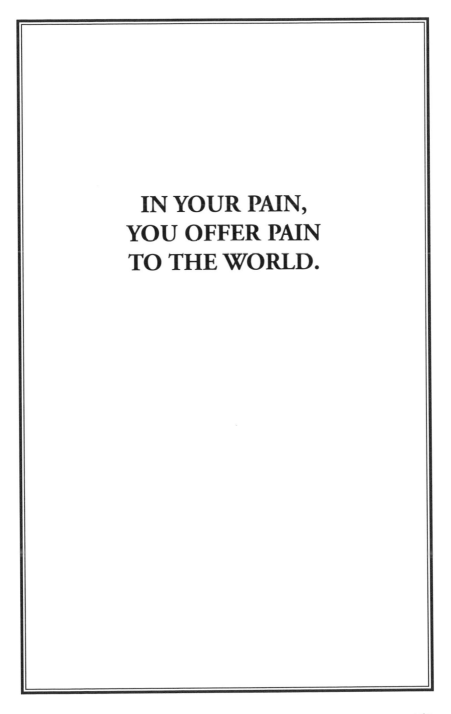

IN YOUR PAIN,
YOU OFFER PAIN
TO THE WORLD.

**AS YOU THINK,**
**YOU FEEL,**
**AND AS YOU FEEL,**
**YOU OOZE,**
**AND AS YOU OOZE,**
**YOU INFLUENCE.**

GOD, OR ALL-THAT-IS,
OR THAT WHICH
IS NON-PHYSICAL,
DOES NOT EXIST
IN A STATE OF COMPLETION,
NOW WAITING
FOR YOU TO CATCH UP,
BUT REVELS IN
ALL THAT YOU LIVE.
FOR AS YOU LIVE,
AS YOU THINK,
AND AS YOU FEEL,
YOU ADD UNTO ALL-THAT-IS.

YOU ARE PHYSICAL
COUNTERPARTS
OF THAT WHICH IS
NON-PHYSICAL —
AND TOGETHER
WE ARE CO-CREATORS.
YOU OFFER A
NEW PERSPECTIVE.
WE OFFER
OUR BROADER AWARENESS.

THE BASIS OF LIFE
IS ABSOLUTE FREEDOM.
THE OBJECTIVE OF LIFE
IS ABSOLUTE JOY.
THE RESULT OF LIFE
IS ABSOLUTE GROWTH.

# PART II

# CONTENTS
# OF QUESTIONS & ANSWERS

# AFTERWORD

The following pages are excerpts from transcriptions of recorded group sessions with ABRAHAM. They have been edited for clarity and selected to be included in this book in order to give you some "live" examples of the manner in which ABRAHAM uses the concepts, that you have read in "Part I" of this book, to respond to questions and comments from persons who are wanting to put the information into practice in their personal life experiences.

*We used to say, "Tell them what you're going to tell them. Then tell them. And then tell them what you told them." For we usually require hearing a new concept in many ways before the words spotlight an experience and from the experience our light of knowing turns on.*

ABRAHAM, the brilliant, untiring teachers that they are, continue to present the basic simple learnable, teachable points of their teachings as they guide us to a purer knowing of what we are about. And at the same time, they provide us with a continual flow of new thoughts and perspectives. From this form of varied repetition, we are guided to our individual, strong, clear perspective of the Laws of the Universe, as they apply to our personal experience. A clear enough perspective, that we can begin, at will, to consciously replace any habits or thoughts, or negative influences from others, that may have been hindering the attraction of what we have wanted.

*To the degree that we integrate* ABRAHAM'S *basic teachings into our daily pattern of life, we then begin to consciously and freely experience more of the learning, and more of the fun, that is immediately open to each of us.*

Esther and I hear from many of you as you visit with ABRAHAM over the telephone, and from many of you as we gather in ABRAHAM workshops and week-ends — and there is an ever widening number of you with whom we have had no personal contact. *You are scattered about the continents, reading the books and listening to the recordings of the ever evolving teachings of* ABRAHAM, *and although we are no longer in a position to promptly respond to each of your letters and calls, we do want you to know that we feel much appreciation for your appreciation, and for your contributions of questions, ideas, dollars and referrals that fuel the physical distribution of this experience.*

From our hearts,

Jerry & Esther Hicks
1991

# QUESTIONS AND ANSWERS
# FROM GROUP SESSIONS

**ABRAHAM:** Good evening.

**GROUP:** Good evening.

**ABRAHAM:** We are extremely pleased that you are here. If you are wondering what all of this nodding is about, it is Esther setting forth her intentions and ABRAHAM setting forth our intentions for the purpose of this evening of co-creating. And we are encouraging that each of you pause for a moment and set forth your intentions for this evening. What is it you are most wanting as a result of this gathering? There is not a right or wrong answer to that, for each of you are here for your own individual reasons. And we are excited about that which we know is to come, because we are sensing the intensity of those of you who are here.

We are sensing the power of your wanting. And as we are moving forward, you may also sense the power of our wanting. *For it is our dominant wanting, as we are here together tonight, that you will gain a clearer sense of who you are. Why you are here. What this physical expe-*

*rience is about. And how you can, through a process of deliberate applica-*
*tion of the Laws of the Universe, create, for yourself, a very deliberate, very*
*specific, very gratifying personal life experience.*

There are so many things that we could talk about and many of
them we bring back to the same sort of place. Some of our physical friends truly believe that we have only one answer and we just
keep throwing it out in different ways. And that is not so far from
accurate, for we are understanding a few very basic, very simple,
very powerful, and very much always present Laws. And as you
understand those Laws and you are able to see how they apply to
one aspect of your experience, then you are able to superimpose
your knowing over everything you are doing — and find success in
all areas of your experience.

And so, it turns out that life is not so complicated as it once
may have seemed to you. And then you begin, you really begin, to
get down to your reason for being here, which is making decisions,
continuous decisions, about what you are wanting, so that you may
apply this knowledge, that is well established within you, toward a
continual motion forward to your ever-changing set of ideas of what
you would like to have in that moment.

*It is our wanting to dispel some myths. While we are not*
*wanting to change your beliefs...for there is not that which you*
*believe, that we see as inappropriate, and there is not that which*
*you do not yet believe, that we would like to guide you toward.*
*It is that we want you to feel your freedom. We are wanting to*
*empower you through your knowledge. We are wanting you to*
*feel your strength and then to make decisions, individual deci-*
*sions, about what you are wanting.*

This gathering is truly a gathering of co-creating. It is far more
than questions and answers. And many of you are already understanding that with every question comes another answer, and with
every answer, another question, and with every question, another
answer. It is ongoing. Never ending. And so, we are not wanting
to give you the impression that we are here to satisfy your questions. We are here as stimulators of thought — and that is what

excites us most.

We know you in a way that most of you do not know your-selves. We know you as creators. You are not here to be judged. You are not here to prove yourselves to anyone. You are here as cre-ators. And we are here to assist you in understanding exactly how you are doing it. We are wanting you to understand that, without exception, everything that you are living is brought to you by you and only by you.

As we are here together tonight, we are hoping to get rid of all of your scapegoats. We are wanting to remove all of your excuses and leave you standing...ah...naked in your awareness that you are the one, the only one, affecting your experience. And while it may feel a little uncomfortable in the very early stages of this awareness, very soon, you will feel empowered by it.

*WHEN YOU UNDERSTAND PRECISELY HOW EVERYTHING COMES TO YOU, THEN YOU ARE FREE OF ALL FEARS OF WHAT OTHERS, IN THEIR DIFFERENCES, MAY DO TO YOU.* Then you are free of the economy, free of your government, free of your mother, free of all influence that you have been fearing. And finally, you are in con-trol of your experience. And usually, joyfully in control.

*You are freedom-seeking beings and growth-seeking beings and joy-seeking beings, and we cannot identify which of those intentions is stronger within you. And none of them can exist without the other. And it is our knowing that you will never be free until you are rid of the negativity dom-inating your experience. And you will never be rid of negativity dominat-ing your experience until you are in control of your thoughts. And you will never be in control of your thoughts until you understand that you can be, and the importance of it.* And so, that is the general process that we are looking forward to this evening.

Now we will say to you — you are the creators of that which takes place here tonight. *AS WE TALK OF LAWS AND PROCESSES, THERE ARE SOMETIMES WORDS THAT ARE NOT MEANINGFUL TO YOU, FOR IT IS NOT WORD THAT TEACHES. IT IS LIFE EXPERIENCE THAT TEACHES.* And so, we are wanting, if you are willing, and if you are wanting, to utilize as many of your real-life examples — the stuff that you are living, everyday, and wondering about. *We are wanting to talk about what is important to you. We are wanting to talk about what you want, or what you don't want, or what is coming, or what is not coming. And we are wanting to give you, from our perspective, the clearest path to the receiving of these things that you are wanting. And so, we encourage you to talk about whatever it is that you are wanting.* Do not worry. We will wedge our message in the crack, firmly. And so let us hear from you.

##  WHAT DOES ABRAHAM WANT?

**JERRY:** *I never sense that you want anything. Is there anything you want ...to accomplish ...to get done?* You don't seem to be interested in writing books or doing any sessions ...If it wasn't for us, nothing would get done ... (group laughter)

**ABRAHAM:** Your point is well made. As physical beings — the majority of your wanting has come from a position of lack. So much so, that when you interact with one who notices lack not at all — you're not even sure that we want. We can give you a list of what we're wanting. We'll be very brief about it.

• We want as many avenues, as you are willing to open at any time — to express, to this physical dimension, the absolute, powerful, consistent Laws of the Universe.

• We want each of you, if you are wanting and if you are willing — to be the absolute, pure example of these Laws.

• We would like it if everyone in the Universe could look at you and see a crystal clear example of the way the Laws work.

• We would like it if you could verbalize, clearly — "These are the things that I want, and these are the things that I believe, and therefore these are the things that I have" — in a way that all of the world could say, "Ah! It is so obvious!" But then we already have that, don't we. (laughter) We want more of it.

• We would like — and it is truly the point of our interacting with the physical — we would like it if every being, within all of the Universe, could find this delicious place of positive emotion — for it is, indeed, the heaven that you all seek.

• We would like it if your "Guidance System" could offer to you negative emotion only long enough to get your attention about something, and that you would be very quick upon your "pivoting", very quick to focus upon the positive, so that you endure the negative only a flash here and a flash there, just to use as turning points — so that the predominant experience that you are living would be one that feels good to you!

• We would like it if you could "Put your (hot, tired) feet in the cool, refreshing stream rather than walking in high-heeled shoes on the hot pavement."

• We would like it if every creature upon this physical earth could stand one day and say, "Illness is a state of mind; it has nothing to do with germs or heredity — it is all in the way I am using my thoughts."

• We would like it if everyone in the Universe was in this place of joyful acknowledgement that we are the attractors unto ourselves. Because then there would be no reason to have barricades or jails or walls or wars — for everyone would understand, clearly, that we are attracting unto us — And so, we wouldn't worry about what anyone else is doing, because we would all, then, understand that our attention to what they are doing is what brings them into our experience.

Oh! Indeed! We look forward to a time, a time when, here upon your earth, all of you will understand that you are the creators of your experience — for then it will be a time where blame no longer exists, where judgement no longer exists. It will be a blissful time. ⨍

We also acknowledge the perfect balance that exists now. In other words: We do not lament the fact that that is not the way everyone is experiencing, because we acknowledge the fact that you have an environment where, if any of you choose that, that can be your experience. The rest of the world, and the Universe, does not have to figure it out in order for it to be your experience, just as you don't have to figure it out in order for it to be our experience. But we like it as you discover it. You know those "goose bumps"that come over you? That is our pleasure at your acknowledgement of something.

And so, let it never again be said (very fun and loving tones directed at Jerry) that we do not want. But let it be said, all you want, that we are blissful in our acknowledgement of the perfection of our current state of being. And the point that we are really wanting to make is that you all exist — no matter what you think you're living, no matter how sick you are, no matter how lonely you are, no matter how poor you are — you are all existing — right now — in the perfect place for the attraction of whatever it is you are wanting. We are not different on that point; it is just that we are a little more practiced at holding our thoughts only upon what we are wanting.

## A CONFORMIST IS WANTING TO REBEL

**QUESTION:** I realize that a whole lot of my creating, or a whole lot of everything in my life is...is coming from being a rebel. It's like, I want so much, so much to be free and to come from a much bigger perspective, and I don't know very many people who will come from my perspective, you know. *And I've been trying to conform for so long. And now it's like, I'm angry and all I can do is rebel and rebel. It's like, if everybody does it that way, I don't want to do it that way. And...*

**ABRAHAM:** Oh, you've been that way for centuries. (Group laughter) It is not new to this physical experience. You are such a freedom seeker. What you are describing...as you see anyone that you describe as rebellious — and it is predominantly the teen-agers that you give that label to. They are experiencing the same thing. They seek freedom so much, and as their freedom is continually squelched, they find themselves rebelling, because it is their passion for freedom that keeps coming to the surface, very powerfully, as they are feeling lack of it. You are wanting to know what to do about it?

**QUESTIONER:** Yeah.

**ABRAHAM:** It is never a good idea to allow yourself to feel that negativity for very long. And when you are understanding that no one is keeping you from anything...In other words, what about a world who may feel their discomfort because you will not conform. Who is right and who is wrong? Are you righter, or are they righter? Or are you more wrong? Our point is that what others do has nothing to do with any one other.

*YOU DO NOT HAVE A REASON TO FEEL REBELLIOUS WHEN YOU FEEL YOUR ABSOLUTE FREEDOM AND WHEN YOU UNDERSTAND THAT YOUR BEHAVIOR IS NOT LINKED TO ANY OTHER.*

And so, what if the whole world believes one thing. There is not such a topic we might add. *There is not a topic, not one, not even one topic, that everyone agrees about. We are excited about your diversity. We are excited about your differences. And most physical beings are not, because they are so insecure about what they want or about the value or benefit or righteousness or truth of what they are believing, that they feel as if they must convince others in order to make it a valid argument.* And so, what you have, and what you are describing in yourself, is a world full of beings who are trying, very hard, to justify your position. And so, in trying to justify your position, you find yourself in a critical attitude of the others.

You see, there is this very predominant thought that abounds in your physical society: You emerge into your bodies, and feel insecure right away, because the physical world feels insecure, and then, because you feel there is strength or power in numbers, and you don't want to feel weak, you gather together in larger groups, and you say, "Will it not be a wonderful thing when everyone thinks and believes as we do", wanting to spread your government, wanting to spread your religion, wanting to spread your attitude.

Someone recently offered a paper to Esther, promoting world peace, wanting to get to the point where everyone upon the Earth, at a certain time of day, will stop for a moment and ponder or meditate upon world peace. And as Esther asked us what we thought about it, we said, *"YOU ARE MAKING A VERY BROAD ASSUMPTION IF YOU THINK EVERYONE IN THE WORLD WANTS PEACE, AND YOU ARE ALSO MAKING A VERY BROAD ASSUMPTION WHEN YOU ASSUME THAT PEACE IS WHAT SHOULD BE."* Even though it is a wonderful thing, and even though you know you like it better than war, still you must not see yourselves as one who has the ability to thrust your intentions upon another — because that is not freedom. For if you have the power to do that to them, then they have the power to thrust war upon you. And neither is accurate, because neither is free, and all of you are free, you see.

And so, as you feel your freedom, as a result, perhaps, of connecting with your Inner Being, who knows its freedom, then you lose that feeling of having to convince anyone that what you're doing is all right. You lose that feeling of justification. And that is really what rebellious behavior is. It is trying to justify your attitude. *When you feel free, you're free to be who you want to be under any and all conditions, and you really don't worry about what anybody else thinks about it, because you know that what they think about you is their problem. It has nothing to do with you. And when you really feel that way, you become in the greatest place that we know of, which is in the place of allowing — and you know you are in the place of allowing when you can see another not approving of you and it is okay with you. We're not talking about tolerance, we're not talking about, say, "Well, I'll let them...", and still feeling the negativity. We're talking about knowing that they disapprove of what you are doing and that is still all right with you because you know that it is their world that they are creating by their attitude toward you. And you need not let their feeling influence you.*

*NOW, HERE IS WHAT WE WOULD ENCOURAGE ANY OF YOU TO DO WHENEVER YOU ARE FEELING NEGATIVITY ABOUT ANYTHING: CHANGE YOUR THOUGHT. THINK ABOUT SOMETHING ELSE.*

And so, as you feel negativity, because you feel as if the world wants you to conform, just step back a little bit and look at a broader you. Your greatest concern is when you are in a very narrow little box, in the box of family or church or community, where there is predominant influence. That is when you feel your greatest desire or need to conform in order not to have disapproval. But, as you step out of that little box and get a little bit bigger view of the world, you realize that there are so many different beings wanting so many different things, that to find conformity is not a possible thing. Do you know that there are people in parts of this world that eat bugs? There are all sorts of things we could talk about, not necessary of course.

We have taken your statement far beyond that which you anticipated, but we are wanting you to see it from the bigger picture in order to feel it from the smaller picture. *We are wanting you to understand there is absolutely no value in trying to conform, and, further, we are wanting you to understand that the idea of conformity is absolutely opposite, it is in absolute contradiction, to your reason for existence.* You came forth into this physical experience at this time because you saw all of the variety as great advantage to you because you are a creator. And you know, from your inner perspective, that creation occurs through thought. And so, the more thought, the more ideas, the more beliefs that abound, the better workshop you have in which to create, and the more data you have to chew upon in order to make your decisions about what would please you most.

And so, when you're no longer threatened, and as you look from broader perspective — you bask in the differences whenever you see something different...But why do you feel threatened? You feel threatened because you do not understand the Laws.

*You feel threatened because you believe that if that other one does something that is not in harmony with what you want, somehow it will get into your experience.* AND WE SAY, IT CANNOT GET INTO YOUR EXPERIENCE IF YOU DO NOT GIVE IT YOUR ATTENTION, BECAUSE YOU INVITE THROUGH THOUGHT. And every time you are inviting through thought, something that you do not

185

want, your Inner Being offers you an emotional response to let you know. You don't feel good about it. And so, that is your indication that this thought is not in harmony with your greater wanting. So don't do that. So stop thinking it. Not an easy thing is it? When we say, don't think about that, what do you do? You think about not thinking about that. But you're still thinking about the thing we told you not to think about. So what do you do? You think about something else. You cannot remove a thought, but you can think another one.

*Law of Attraction won't let you remove a thought. You cannot concentrate upon not thinking about something, hard enough to stop thinking about it. For the more you decide you will not think about it, the more you think about it. Think about that.* (group laughter) But you can change the subject, can you not? And that is truly what the art of pivoting is about. That is truly the way you get focused upon what you are wanting. You are wanting something more?

## IT'S A PAIN IN HER NECK

QUESTION: I realize that, actually, part of it is positive and part of it is, you know, I really do want to do things in a whole new...I mean, I've got all this new Creative Energy that's just boiling in me, and ....I'm still afraid of it. I mean, that old part of me keeps coming in. *I've got this terrible pain in the back of my neck. I don't know if it relates to this...holding back?*

ABRAHAM: It is your resistance.

QUESTION: The thing that just keeps jerking me back like that. You know, it's hard to not think about this...because that hurts so bad.

ABRAHAM: *It is hard not to think about it when you're thinking about it. But, you see, pain is perceptual. Most do not under-*

*stand that, but bite your toe and see how your neck feels.* (group laughter) We are having a bit of fun with you, but give your attention to something else, for you can only focus upon one thing at a time. That is very important to understand. If you have continuous pain and are focused in this world, what is happening is that you are going back and forth, back and forth, back and forth, and you are focused upon the pain enough that you are feeling the pain. But if you can fill your thoughts with other things, the pain will go away.

QUESTION: So it's to keep my thoughts much more focused upon this incredible Energy that's going through me and all these things I want...and just keep pivoting?

ABRAHAM: Feel the power of your Energy. Recognize that Non-physical Energy is coming into you for you to utilize just as your electricity is here for you to utilize. Whatever you plug into the wall usually works, you see. And so, it is a matter of your contouring that powerful Energy with your thought, getting it all going in one direction. "I want a new red car — but it is too expensive." What have you just done with the Energy? You have set it in two directions. And so, where are you going? Nowhere.

And so, as you say, and you have described it very well, "I am excited about all of these things that I can do, but I'm afraid." And so, we say that it isn't a wonder that your neck is hurting a little bit, because you are giving yourself a sort of tug-of-war.

In the early days, as Esther was speaking for us...she would sit very still, allowing it, because there was great wanting, but really, a little bit afraid, also. And so, at the end of ten minutes, she was very tired. She would say, "ABRAHAM is using me up too fast." She felt as if her physical body was being depleted. And at the end of ten minutes, there was not enough Energy in her body for her even to remain seated or standing. She went right to bed. And so, we would speak for ten minutes and she would spend the morning in bed. Not because the Energy was not of value to her. Not because there was detrimental Energy being offered. Not because there was anything bad happening. But because she was going in two directions. She wanted and didn't want, and resistance is very tiring. Once she relaxed and realized that we are good guys, not bad guys, once she realized that this is a glorious, uplifting, beneficial experience to her and to anyone who participated within it, now she is saying "yes" to all of it, and now the Energy comes through and out, through and out, through and out, and she feels wonderful. And so will you. Good. What more?

## CHANGING BEINGS IN CULTURES OF CONFORMITY

**JERRY:** About changes. I told Esther, a while back, that she and I would have never come together in the earlier years because of how I made decisions about who I would date: they had to be under 60 inches tall and under 105 pounds in weight, because as an acrobat I had to throw them up in the air and catch them and stuff, and so I really wasn't interested in any "thinking", but only in their shape. And so, when Esther came in, her height, she is taller than that and she is heavier than that, but she's interested in the things that I have now changed to. I was raised in a culture that believed that you stayed with the same wife and you stayed with the same job and you basically stayed in the same neighborhood and the same political group and so on and so forth, but I've had 18 or 20 different professions through the years, and many changes that I have made, and so I haven't followed what I was raised to believe. *So how does a person live in a culture that believes in staying with whatever your decision originally was, and still be allowed to change as an individual?*

**ABRAHAM:** Very painfully. Most do not deal with it very well because it defies, or goes against, your absolute quest for freedom. And so, as you feel restricted by society's rules and Laws, most of you struggle and squirm within them, most of you resent it, and most of you begin defending or justifying your position, thereby attracting more negative emotion to you.

*What we would like to impart to you is that whether you know it or not, or whether you acknowledge it or not, you live in absolute freedom. You are so free that every thought that you think is represented into what you are living. How much freer than that can you be? You are so free that every thought enters into the balance of what you live.*

*Your laws do not affect you, it is your attention to your laws that affect you.* Your neighbors do not affect you, it is your attention to your neighbors that affect you. It turns out that you are absolute in your freedom if you could acknowledge that.

In a society that wants you to conform, those of you who know and recognize your freedom, from inner perspective, squirm and resist and have great difficulty with that — until finally you acknowledge that you are free. And usually you end up saying, "I just don't care."

*You finally reach the point where you are not trying so hard to please the others because you are finally wise enough to discover you can't please them no matter how hard you try. There are too many of them. There are too many different intentions. Too many different beliefs. So finally you withdraw from that arena where you cannot win, and you step back into the arena of clarity where you always win: The arena of identifying what you are wanting and then, in a disciplined manner, utilizing your discipline to think about what you are wanting.*

## SEAT BELTS, LAWS AND STATISTICS EVALUATION

QUESTION: Along those very lines, regarding seat belts, I have a problem with the fact that it's a requirement to wear a seat belt in my automobile and I've expressed that to a number of people on any number of occasions, and the discussion is, "Well, statistics this, and statistics that," *and I have a problem with statistics, too. I'm an individual — and just because that happened to a million other people doesn't necessarily mean it's going to happen to me.*

ABRAHAM: Good. That is correct, because what the statistics do not factor in is the intentions that the being who went through the windshield, held. In other words, there is much more to do with it than the statistics state.

QUESTION: I even think that an attention to statistics can even create further statistics that might not be there otherwise, like breast cancer, for example.

ABRAHAM: Absolutely. That is absolutely true. The attention to any subject.... Why do you think so many tankers are spilling their oil? Why do you think so much craziness is happening with the airplanes? Why do you think more, not fewer, why do you think *more* are getting cancer in this time of great technology? Why is AIDS spreading rampantly? It is attention to it.

QUESTION: Well, it's always been annoying to me, and we get into these conversations. And I jokingly say, there are people, who if I was to die in a car wreck, not wearing a seat belt, they'd say, "see there." I don't think that's going to happen, do you?

ABRAHAM: It will not.

QUESTION: It's not that I don't believe in seat belts, but I've just never worn them, and, in fact, there actually are cases that have been documented, not as many as those without....

ABRAHAM: Oh, you do not need to justify.

QUESTION: I understand that, now.

ABRAHAM: We've heard of those who drowned because they couldn't get out.

Here is the point that we are wanting you to consider: Every time you buckle your seat belt, *resenting* the idea that they have passed a law that says that you must, *"How are you utilizing the Non-physical Energy on your behalf?"* And so, you are much better off not to buckle it and not to feel the resentment than you are to buckle it and feel the resentment. Either that, or you must pivot yourself into a position of buckling it because you know that you are making the decision to buckle it, not because it's a law, but because you, at this time, are choosing it. Jerry and Esther are driving a little car today that does not allow them the decision. When they open the door, it unbuckles, and when they sit in and close the door it straps them in.

**JERRY:** It's a rental from the airport.

**QUESTION:** That happened to me, too, in fact it was funny, I had a wreck a couple of years ago and the rental car, I had four miles on it, or something, and I thought "of all people" it was hilarious when that sucker just went right across my chest, and I just had to laugh. You're right, you have no choice. My whole point is that if I feel the need to wear it, then I'll put it on and if I don't, then I'm just not concerned about it.

**ABRAHAM:** What we would like to offer to you, from our perspective, is this: You have many laws in your nation that you don't even know about. They do not attract any attention. Nobody really cares about them. They are written, but they affect you, not at all, because you give no attention to them. And then, there are laws that you give tremendous amount of attention to, and so they affect you more. If you would put all of them in one bucket and just say, "We have laws, some of them affect me and some of them don't, and I don't give much attention to any of them," then you would be in a much better emotional state about them.

We have been hearing and discussing, or hearing Jerry discuss, for he is as you are, freedom seeking being. And so, as he hears about the new consideration by the Supreme Court to have the sobriety check-point whether you are drinking or not, whether there is any reason or not to be stopped and examined, and another ruling regarding punishment for flag-burning. As these issues begin to come forth, many of you, who are freedom seekers at your very core, begin to acknowledge, "Where will it all end? If they can begin offering these sorts of legislations to control our behavior on one thing, then where will it end?" And we say to you — *What are you doing with the Non-physical Energy regarding that subject?*

*When you have those sorts of feelings that say "What is it going to lead to?" then we say, you are utilizing the Non-physical Energy against the freedom that you seek. Your resistance to what you think they're doing to you is what is really affecting your experience more than what they are doing to you with their laws.*

See yourselves separate and apart. See yourself attracting unto you by virtue of the thoughts that you offer, not trying to justify. Now, that is the point we are most wanting to make with you regarding this topic: The tendency is to have something affect you negatively, like somebody telling you that when you are in your automobile, you have to buckle up or telling you that you have to stop your automobile to be examined for sobriety. That brings forth very negative feelings within you, and then the next thing that you do is try to justify your negative emotion, by trying to point out all of the reasons why they are wrong and you are right. And that is just furthering this Non-physical avalanche of Energy toward what you do *not* want. You are just helping them create more laws that you will resist and resent and justify again.

AND SO, WE SAY, YOU DON'T HAVE TO JUSTIFY THE WAY YOU FEEL. THE WAY YOU FEEL IS THE WAY YOU FEEL. AND NO MATTER HOW JUSTIFIED YOU ARE IN YOUR NEGATIVE EMOTION YOU ARE STILL MESSING UP YOUR FUTURE. (spoken very loudly, causing group to laugh) We were wanting you to hear that.

We agree. Some things that happen to you are intolerable, and some people are intolerable, and some of them, as they decide that there are things that you ought to do — whether you want to do them or not — that is intolerable. *It is so intolerable that natural law does not allow it.* And so don't worry about it. They can flap their mouths all they want about it. They can tell you that it is law all that they want, but if you do not give your attention to it, it will never, it will never, *IT WILL NEVER* (shouting) it will never be a part of your experience. *ATTENTION IS YOUR INVITATION YOU SEE.*

And so, every time they pass a law that you don't like, throw it in the bucket with all of the others. It will not affect you. Justification of your opposition will attract it to you, however.

*Give your attention to what you are wanting. Withdraw your attention from what you are not wanting — and live in the freedom that is absolutely yours, the freedom that no one, under any conditions, can ever take away from you, no matter how hard they try. If their words can bother you, you are not free. If you allow their words to bother you, it is the words that bind you. MORE OF YOU ARE AFFECTED BY THE WORDS OF OTHERS THAN YOU ARE BY YOUR OWN EXPERIENCE.*

Right now your world, or much of it, is appalled at the recordings, judged inappropriate and obscene, of a new musical group. So much controversy over this subject. And we say, you have the option, do you not, of letting it in your ears or not. You have the option of buying the record or of turning it on. *You have absolute option regarding all of these things.*

*Exercise your option to hear, to speak, to think, to give your attention. Exercise the freedom that is absolutely yours, and live happily ever after.*

## CAN WE TRUST
## OUR CHILDREN'S MUSICAL CHOICES?

QUESTION: What about, upon that very subject on that very issue, people who have adolescent or teenage children who are very much influenced by that obscene music? I don't have children, and so it doesn't affect me personally. But I'm curious, from the standpoint of being the parent of one of these children, whose surrounding influences you are very concerned about. How do you deal with something like that, because it is a very serious issue, I know, with a lot of parents, and the influences that their children are under?

ABRAHAM: It is not easy for parents to release their children. *Parents like the idea of freedom as it relates to them — they just don't like the idea of freedom as it relates to their children.* They say to their children, "I am free in the Universe, but you are not. I am free to think and be as I choose, but you are not because you are too little and not smart enough to figure out what is good for you." It's starts when you're young, and then you wonder why it carries on until there are still those, when you are grown up, that treat you that way, you see. You are either free or you are not — and everyone is either free or everyone is not free.

*And so, we say, a parent must allow their child the freedom to have experience. How else is the child able to do what he came here to do. If the child has someone else making all decisions for him, he will never learn to decide for himself. He will never be the deliberate creator he has come forth to be. And the child resents and resists and rebels from that feeling of not enough freedom.* That is the reason that that music exists to begin with. It is because they want to make a statement that, "We can be or do or have or say anything that we want." "We can be as nasty as we want to be", they say. And we say, *"Be as nasty as you want to be, and we will be as sweet as we want to be, or as nasty as we choose to be." We all are that, anyway, are we not? And no one can stop us from being that, so why don't we stop playing the game. Why don't we stop trying to control one another and be that which we are, and seek our points of harmony?*

We know it is a big order of business, but if we were physical parents in your physical shoes we would say, "How does it make you feel when you hear that song? *IF IT IS UPLIFTING TO YOU, THEN PURSUE IT. IF IT IS NOT UPLIFTING TO YOU, DO NOT.*

*The children are drawn to it in masses because of the negative attention to it. All you have to say to a little one is, "There is something you should not see or do," and they will find a way to see it or do it. For they are not wanting to miss anything. Their eager little minds are seeking growth, you see.*

And so those who believe that they are working against it, are, as we were talking to you about justifying your position — they are the greatest catalyst right now that is fueling this fire regarding this issue. The more of their negative attention they are giving to it, the more famous this record is becoming, and many millions more are hearing it now than ever would have heard it before.

Jerry and Esther would have never heard it, and yet they've heard quite a bit of it, because it has come across the television. Most of it is being bleeped out, but you don't have to be very smart to figure out the parts that are being bleeped out, you see. You are getting the point.

## HE RESENTS MOTORCYCLE BRAIN BUCKET LAWS

QUESTION: I wanted to touch on one thing, that you said earlier, *in relation to, just basically, the laws, of the government that passes those laws, regardless of what we think of the intelligence behind them. For example, the seat belts, as the lady mentioned, is a law. It is Texas law. I ride my motorcycle a lot, and I have to have a brain bucket. They tell me that I have to wear this thing.*

ABRAHAM: Is it a helmet? We think of your head more as your brain bucket.

QUESTION: That's good. Can you imagine what it would be like if I rejected wearing this helmet, going down this beautiful highway and enjoying the Universe, and everything else, through these little towns ...how many tickets I would get for not doing this? How exposed I would be for it. It shows up real bad, even though I don't like wearing a helmet.

ABRAHAM: We are knowing that the current set of beliefs that you hold would assure you a traffic ticket. As you see yourself as not able to go anywhere without attracting tickets, then you surely would. On the other hand, if you can acknowledge yourself as being free, then, just as you are able to drive faster than the speed limit, just as there are all sorts of beings that are doing all sorts of things.... You see, there are not enough persons in the enforcement system to give their attention to all places at once. And really, they are not even wanting to. They are not really interested in enforcing the law, they're interested in justifying their reason for existence. If what we know to be, was believed by all, then they would have to find some other means of employment, and their current set of beliefs does not provide for them that sort of idea. And so, most of what you are seeing, regarding government, is an exercise in self-perpetuation. "We must find this cause to stand for so that we can help these people?" Well, that is what they say, but it is really because that is the way they perpetuate the employment that gives them the dollars that gives them the freedom that they are trying to take away from you with their enforcement. It is a very strange cycle that is taking place. *Our point to you is, that when you acknowledge yourself as the free being that you are, that you will take your helmet, and you will wear it in the appropriate times, and you will remove it in the appropriate times, just as Esther drives 55 in the appropriate times and 75 in the appropriate times.* You are getting the point.

QUESTION: Oh, I got the point a long time before I asked the question. I guess what we've really gotta do is wait for this realignment, then start all over again.

## GAY FREEDOM SEEKER
## IN A SOCIETY OF DISALLOWERS

ABRAHAM: *There will never be a time when there will not be others who oppose you in thought.* The realignment is not going to change that. Let us look at it from this perspective: We talked with a young man, recently, who is a freedom seeker to the very core of his being, in fact he came into this experience seeking freedom, in a passionate way, and has chosen a very unusual avenue, by the standards of most, in that he is of a community that he calls "gay".

Now, it is his freedom seekingness that has brought this forth within him, but he was speaking to us about the way his family treats him as a result of this. They are absolutely opposed to this and do not acknowledge him as a decent human being anymore. They consider him very strange and very odd, and he is very resentful of them, especially of his mother, because she cannot let him be as he wants to be, and we said, "But you must look at yourself, also, and realize that you are also not wanting to let her be as she wants to be. In other words, she is wanting to see you as doing something inappropriate, but you're not willing to allow her to see you as inappropriate. And so, you are accusing her of the very thing that you believe that she is doing to you."

Now the reason that we have used this rather potent issue, it is an issue that is becoming great in this community, and almost always at the basis of it is this desire of freedom to be, even in the faces of a society that wants to say otherwise. *And so, the individual will always be challenged by those beings who, from their feelings of weakness have gathered together in numbers and made some sort of law.*

Your nation's founding fathers, that is a funny way of saying it, since many of you were there then. Those of you who established the beginning foundation for your nation had the tremendous foresight of recognizing that it is man's nature to confine one another, and so you built into the very precepts of your Constitution, Bill of Rights, and all of those wonderful documents that began, words to protect you from each other. And that is what is bothering most of you, regarding this issue, as you see what you think is an erosion of those very important documents. What we say is, *"If you will stop seeing your freedoms as being eroded and instead see your civilization as evolving — so that you do not give your attention to the lack of what you want, but, again, you are giving your attention to what you do want — you will see that these laws that are being passed, one by one, will also be released."*

All it will take is a few people who are going somewhere, who have an important engagement, who have no alcohol in their system or in their automobile, to be detained by these check points, a few of them who are in the places of authority, and that will be reversed immediately. Or, all it may take is a handful of beings, there are enough of you in this room right now, to set forth your *thought* regarding your absolute freedom and your full expectation that these rules that have just been passed that are out of order with your idea of what true freedom is, just see them as non-existent, and you, in this room, this handful of concentrated beings, as a result of this concentrated conversation today, are enough to reverse those laws. And now, we say to you, begin to watch. Watch for it. Watch the debates that will begin to take place. You have launched it very effectively here together today. Now watch what happens. And take delight as you see the evidence coming toward the dissolution of these cumbersome laws. And in the meantime, do not give your attention to anything that gives you any sort of negative emotion. We have launched it together, now, let it go and watch how far and how fast it will go. Truly. And take credit for it if you want. "We did that. We were sitting in a room in Texas and we orchestrated that one." Are you not already seeing much more freedom. Are you not aware of the things that are evolving. Good.

*If you will be beings who predominately focus upon things that make you feel good, you will be of much more value to your Universe and to your society than if you focus upon the problem or trouble spots.* Wear your helmet because it brings you pleasure, and if it doesn't, do not.

## A DEBILITATING DIAGNOSIS

QUESTION: Thank you. I wanted to touch on one other subject to kind of give you a progress report on my physical apparatus. Namely my eyes, that I had talked to you about before. Almost four months ago, I believe it was. You advised me to concentrate on the pill that I was taking rather than on the fact that my eye was in serious trouble. There was a blister on the back of the retina and I was already blind in the one eye and going that way in the other. And everything was working along. I was having considerable difficulty in erasing this thought out of my mind, "What would I do if I did go blind?" Because every time I opened my eye and looked at it, particularly at night on a white wall, I could see this spot there, and it was like an oval face looking at me with eyes and a mouth, and it was horrifying. But I got around that, and of course I was concentrating on the pill, the pill was going to do all the curing, and everything else, and it made my physical body feel absolutely awful. I started experiencing pain every place else but in my eye. Progressively, it was getting better. Very slowly I could see that it was clearing up. And I was concentrating on both of my eyes, and then I got this examination and I clicked the numbers off of the scale, almost 20/20. So then the doctor was elated, when I went back after dilating my eyes, at the fact that I could read so well through this. And I was real happy. I felt so good, because I could do that. Then, he looked into my eye with his scope and discovered blood, and this is most alarming because of the fact that when blood does appear in the retina, if it explodes, why then you've crossed the river pretty well, other than laser. I must have sank through the chair.

ABRAHAM: Doctors can be very helpful in helping you plummet to the depths of despair, rapidly. Can they not?

QUESTION: Took me from up here, down to under the chair, in just a short minute. So they photographed all this stuff, and everything and all, and he's talking to me about doing laser on my eye. The dangers of the laser and so forth, and I just told him, point blank, "No, I don't want the laser. I will get this positively cured myself. We'll just go along with this and I'll get it done." And the next week when I came back, he looked into my eye and he said, "I am absolutely amazed. I haven't seen anything like this in fifteen years. Never have I seen it in my experience."

ABRAHAM: Tell him to make a note of it. Maybe he'll see it more.

**QUESTION:** The blood had gone down a little and then the last visit I had with him, two weeks ago, it was reduced some more and I'm seeing better all the time. *I am also seeing better in my left eye. It is improving. But, one of my main problems is that I sure would like to speed this up.*

**ABRAHAM:** *You are living the balance of your thought, and so as you are saying "It is wonderful how it is occurring, and I want it to happen faster." It will happen faster.* YOU HAVE YOUR HANDS NOT ONLY ON THE STEERING WHEEL BUT YOUR FOOT UPON THE THROTTLE. *Truly. As you give more attention to it, more positive attention, it speeds it up. If you give attention to what you want, and attention to what you don't want, it slows it down. If you give attention to what you want, purely, it speeds it up. If you give attention to what you don't want, it speeds that up. And so you are constantly finding this balance within your experience.*

You have come a very long way, as a physical being in this society, not accepting the doctor as the remedy to what you are about. To say, "No, I will do it."

*We have experienced with Esther the great concern that one statement from a doctor can bring to you. One statement that takes maybe four seconds to utter, took Esther two months to pivot away from, and in the two month interim, she experienced all sorts of physical manifestations that had nothing to do with what she wanted. Just this little bit of powerful stimulation of thought. And all along we would say to her, "All is well. Just relax, it is passing. It is only there because of the stimulation of thought of one who speaks to justify their reason for existence."*

You must understand that those who are trained to look for things wrong with you, when you go to see them, they will look for things wrong with you. And you, as cooperative beings, try very hard to give them something to find. It is the way you think. And so, you are wise enough to say, "No, I am not wanting your laser surgery. I am not really wanting your probing and poking. I am really not even wanting your opinion. *What I am wanting is to feel free and happy and growing. What I am wanting to have is a magnifi-cent, vital, healthy body that feels good in every way. What I am wanti-ng to have...."* And then you will be motivated to the doing that will bring *it about.* When you know what you want to feel and what you want to have....

We say to you that if the laser surgery were the answer, with the set of beliefs and intentions that you hold, when he offered it to you, you would have said, "Yes." You would have had a feeling of relief about it. You would have felt like, "Yes that is the appropri-ate action to take." But as you felt tremendous resistance toward it, it was absolutely not in harmony, as you have already discovered the reason why. The improvement will continue within your expe-rience.

There is not a reason, there is not any reason, that you expe-rience anything, other than the way you have utilized the Energy with the contouring with your thought. That is all. And we say that, not in a way to beat you up, because everything that you think has been introduced to you by someone. *There is much influence that abounds. The idea that you have degenerating bodies as you get older is an idea that has been thrust into your experience, and has been offered to you as influence. You have pondered it enough that that is the balance of your thought. As a society, and as most individuals, you accept, that with your years, you receive declining experience. And we say, does that not make you feel resistance even when you hear the words from us. It should, because at the core of your being you know there is never a rea-son to decline. There is never a reason to experience anything less than peak, ever. Other than taking some thought and send-ing it off in expectation toward less than that.*

We watch the mail that comes in one small mailbox in Boerne, Texas, and we are appalled at the amount of negative influence that is offered as it says to Esther, "Now you are reaching this age, you may expect these things," and as it says to Jerry, "Now you are approaching this age, now you should expect these things." It is a wonder you do not want to be a part of their census. It is no w der you do not want to be a part of their statistics. It is no wonder you do not want to be part of those who want to pigeon-hole you into expected activity, and declining activity, when what you seek is the other. It is glorious to feel your freedom, is it not.

## THE BODY'S NATURAL CELLULAR PROGRESSION

**JERRY:** *So what do you see as the natural progression of the cellular aspect of the physical body, in the second fifty years of life.*

**ABRAHAM:** *Exactly same as first. It responds to your expectation. When you are little, you expect to grow up and get stronger. You expect to get bigger and stronger until you reach that age. The peak, they call it.*

**QUESTION:** Why accept it?

**ABRAHAM:** You need not accept it. You accept it because so many do, and have, that the balance of thought in the society is there. And so, the tendency is for you, as an individual, to get swept up in whatever the balance says, but you do not have to do that.

*When you finally say, "That may be your world, but it is not mine. What I choose is this." And when you can say to anyone and mean it, really know it,* "MY EXPERIENCE IS PURELY A PRODUCT OF MY THOUGHT. AND MY THOUGHT IS PURELY A PRODUCT OF MY DECISION. AND MY DECISION IS PURELY A PRODUCT OF MY WANTING. AND MY WANTING IS PURELY A PRODUCT OF MY KNOWING." *They will go away somewhere in the middle of that.* You will have lost them, long before you finish your statement. But at least you will be standing in your firm position, saying "There is nothing I cannot be, or do, or have, and that includes health, that includes prosperity, that includes good relationships. It does not ᵃclude blindness or cancer or AIDS or poverty or seat belts." You getting it?

# EFFECTS OF SOCIETY'S
# BELIEFS AND EXPECTATIONS

**JERRY:** *Well, we really don't have a chance to not have beliefs and expectations, because we are born into them. We can work around that, or toward working around that, but we are constantly surrounded.*

**ABRAHAM:** *You are here, as examples, to say, "The beliefs and expectations of a society need not affect me. Of course they are strong, and of course they buffeted me around a bit in the beginning, before I caught on, but they need not affect me. Only if I embrace them do they affect me. And so, some of them I embrace:* I embrace the idea of physicalness. I embrace the idea of physical love. I embrace the idea of eating the glorious food. I embrace walking barefoot through the grass. I embrace the idea of immersing my body in the beautiful water. I embrace the beautiful atmosphere and oxygen. There is so much of this place that is believed that I do embrace. And there are some things that are here that I do not embrace. It is a well stocked kitchen with every ingredient imaginable and I may pick from it that which I want and chew upon it and experience it, but I am pretty picky."

Do you go into a restaurant and try everything, or do you peruse the menu and pick things that you know will delight your taste? Do you eat everything that you see, or do you identify what they are? Esther smells everything before she puts it in her mouth. She makes certain that before she puts it in her mouth that it at least passes the test of her nose. And so, that is what we encourage you to do with whatever it is that is coming to you.

*You do not have to embrace any thought until you have weighed it against the other intentions that you hold, and as you weigh it, you know, right away, by the way you feel, whether this is an ingredient you want in your experience or whether it is one you would rather release. And how do you release it? Take your attention from it.* You don't release it by saying, "That is wrong, that is wrong. That should not be. The should be a law against that. Stop it. Get someone to stop t

We need more policemen. We need more laws. We need more legislation. You've got to stop that. Do not let them have that!" That is bringing it right into your experience. The more attention you give to what you do not want, the more you bring it right into your experience.

*There is never a better way of inviting into your experience than getting really, really excited about something. The more excited you are — negatively or positively — the faster, the faster it comes. The more excited you are the faster it comes. And what gets you excited? Talking about it. Or talking to others who are excited about it.*

Esther is the world's best eavesdropper. We hear things far and wide as she sits in the restaurant. She knows what's going on far over there. And what she has observed, and we have observed through her ears, is that the world delights in horror stories. All you have to do is indicate to someone a little bit of difficulty and they will tell you all of their difficulties regarding the same subject and the difficulties of everybody that they know regarding the same subject, until, by Law of Attraction, you begin to foster your expectation regarding these sorts of difficulties. And so, we say, don't open the door a little crack, for as you open the door a little crack, the bigger the crack is opened and the more effort it takes to close the door.

## ADULT DAUGHTER WANTS HER LIFE FIXED

**QUESTION:** *My daughter is past 30 and she is a pure delight, but every so often, if I try to smooth the waters, that's not good.* If I try to be quiet and listen or walk away, she'll say that I don't care. And I say, "Let's sleep on it." And she'll say, "I want to talk about it now." And I'm kind of wrestling with Tar Baby. I haven't found out how to get away. *We're very different, and I wonder why I draw this. I guess because I'm a nurse and I'm basically a fixer, she thinks I can fix her life. And I guess I think I can, too, so she comes to me. I'm basically positive nd optimistic and she tends to be sort of the opposite, and I don't know how andle that?*

**ABRAHAM:**  Within everyone that you know, including your daughter, and even including you, there is the tendency toward the positive and the tendency toward the negative. In other words, none of you are all positive or all negative. You have the probability of either within you because with everything that you want there is the acknowledgment of the lack of it. Every time you think about money, right in there, right in the same thought, is the identification of the lack of money. It must be. Are you following us on this one?  Every time you think of wellness, a thought that comes right along, so closely aligned with it, is sickness. It is very difficult for any of you to think of the subject of wellness without thinking of somebody who is sick. It is very difficult for any of you to think about having lots of money without thinking about not having enough money. In other words the thoughts of the Universe are very well balanced, you see.

*As you acknowledge that within your daughter is the probability of positive offering or negative offering, then if you're getting even some negative offerings from her, or even predominant negative offerings from her, the question to ask yourself is, "What am I putting out that is attracting unto me, this?"* In other words, "Why is she here in my experience? I'm giving thought to lack. I've acknowledged that she is this way. My expectation of her..." There is that word again, talk about a Tar Baby, "Expectation" is one if we've ever seen one. "My expectation of this one has enough of that within it that I get a pretty good dose of it on a regular basis. And so, how might I release myself?" Now first of all, does that mean that she is, even if it is her predominant personality, does that mean she is a bad person?  No, it just means that she is like everything else in the Universe. She has the probability of either, and for now, she is choosing this one. For now, the negative is the predominating factor in her experience. Does that make me a bad person because sometimes I'm attracting something that is bad within my experience?  No, it does not. It just means that, at least for now, I am attracting, or I have given enough focus to, what I am not wanting, that it is in my experience for now. And so here it is. How do I feel about it. Do I like it or don't I?  That's not a hard one, is it? It feels rotten, which means I don't want it. How do I get rid of something I don't want? What is the only way to get rid of something I don't want?

Oh, we like your analogy of the Tar Baby. Some of those negative thoughts are very sticky. Have you ever tried to get rid of a Tar Baby? It only has your finger. Ahh, and then you try to push it away with your foot, but now it has your foot. And then you try to push it away with your hand, and then you try to push it away with your other foot, and then you try to push it away with your head, and then your head is stuck, too. Pretty soon that Tar Baby has got you. And so you say, "Help! Help! Help!" And then your friend comes, or your mother comes, and tries to push it away with her foot. And then with her hands and then with her head and then both of you are stuck in the negative, and then you both say, "Help! Help!" It is very much the way negatives cling, is it not?

*We'll tell you how to get rid of the Tar Baby. Look over here. Give your attention to anything other than the Tar Baby, and in the moment that you give your attention to anything else, it will just release its grip and off it will go. Waiting for the next unsuspecting person to come along and poke at it a little bit.* (Group laughter)

You are complete? (to Jerry) You will never be complete. We are not really wanting you to ever be complete.

## WORDS TO IMPROVE A RELATIONSHIP

JERRY: *What would you suggest as an overall state of mind, or set of words, that we could utilize to improve a relationship with a critical parent, a rebellious child, a negative mate, or a disharmonious associate...?*

ABRAHAM: *...If you heard nothing from us, or if you said nothing to your parent or your child or to your associate other than:* "I think you are wonderful, and I think we're all trying to find our way of being wonderful. I know that inside each of us there is a wonderful being — and I want to see it in you, and I want you to see it in me." *And whether you speak it to their face or*

*just speak it in your mind, they get the message. And you ben-*
*efit — and so do they — from such a message.*

*Carry that Book of Positive Aspects around with you,* (Process given earlier) and put it in obvious places so that you are inspired to pick it up and look through it often. For as you look for the positive aspects in your experience, it is by Law — a Law that you don't need to know, a Law that you don't have to understand, but a Law that exists, nevertheless — It is by Law that you must begin to attract positive things into your experience.

*LIFE IS SUPPOSED TO BE FUN, YOU KNOW.* That was your plan before you emerged. You said: "I will go forth and I will experience the deliciousness of physical." You did not say: "I'll go forth, (flat tones) and I'll bang around. (Group laughter) I'll stub my toes, (bravely) but I'll persevere. (Group laughter) I know it will be miserable, but I am tough. And I know that all of the odds will be against me, but I am strong."

Because, when you decided to emerge, you knew you did not have to explain "nothin to nobody." There was nobody keeping score. Nobody saying to you: "You have to prove yourself."

*You said, "I'm going to go forth into physical, and I am going to have a glorious life experience! And along the way, I'm going to provide an exquisite example to others of how the Laws of the Universe work. Sometimes I'm going to screw up. And through my mistakes, as they look at me and say, "Ha, Ha, Ha, look what you've done!" I will say: "Yip! I thought about this. I worried about this, and I got this. And isn't it wonderful how consistent the Laws are?"*

You're not here to pretend to be, or even to be, perfect for anybody else. You are here to acknowledge the way the Laws work — and to have fun doing it — so that even the most "horrendous" of situations can be funny to you! Because this is the way that you are expressing yourself right now.

*Even when you are creating what you do not want, you are an exquisite example of the Laws of the Universe. And friends, we cannot express to you the value of that. Nobody here is laughing at you. We are applauding.*

Do you remember watching a child, maybe it was yours, maybe it was someone else's, learning to walk? When he fell down and bumped his head, did you say: "You stupid little fool?" (Group laughter) "Get up and walk!" (Laughter) Or did you say: "It's all right. All of us fell down and bumped our heads. It is the way we learned to walk..."

And so, why do you keep beating up on yourself every time, when in a new experience, you don't know just what to do? Why not take the experience and live it, and bask in the knowledge that comes from it — looking for the positive aspects within it? Because they are always there. Do you know how we know? *Because, within everything, there are positive and negative aspects; there is not an exception to that in all of the Universe.* There is not an exception to that in the people you know; they have positive and negative. There is not an exception to that in the GOD that you know, there is positive and negative. There is not an exception to that in all of the Universe. The perfect balance *IS* what you are wanting — and the lack of it. And by your decision to focus, you bring into your experience whatever it is you have chosen.

## A PERSONAL RELATIONSHIP
## WITH THE NON-PHYSICAL

QUESTION: *ABRAHAM, I would like more of a personal relationship with my Non-physical "family."* I understand that my feelings are my link to my life line, my Inner Being.

ABRAHAM: Your feelings, meaning your emotional responses?

QUESTIONER: Yeah...my true feelings. I grew up with a sense that Jesus is a good guy. And if you need Jesus, kind of "Call On Me." You know how that song goes? And I have this romantic sense of having a relationship with my Inner Being where this little boy inside of me is taken care of. And I understand that I get very excited and thrilled about the creative process that we have going on here. And there's a part of me that...ah...still says, "Well, can't we have both of these things?"

ABRAHAM: Both of what things?

QUESTIONER: Ah ...that kind of ...ah ...as a therapist I look at an illusory co-dependent relationship which I had as a child, where God was going to be the Father and I'm the Child of God. You know, that one where my Inner Being is my parent and I'm here.

ABRAHAM: You are not so different from most. It is the least favorite part of our message, to most physical beings. On the one hand you want freedom and on the other hand it is kind of nice to have the feeling that there is someone older and wiser that will guide you and take care of you. And you're right when you recognize you can't have it both ways. And we will take that a little further and say, you can only have it one way, because you have come forth with the intent of being creator. You were feeling your power. Your wanting was very clear at the time that you emerged into this body. Can't change the deal now, you see.

You said, "I will go forth as physical being and through the power of my thoughts I will apply the Laws of the Universe and be magnificent creator." Further, you said, "I will do it in this time because things will happen faster. Energy is higher upon the planet Earth. It is vibrating quicker. Things will be much faster so that it will be much more obvious, and it will be easier to offer examples for the sake of helping others understand."

The reason that you have such strong feeling of identification with the one you know as Jesus is because that Energy exists in the "family" in which your Inner Being exists.

It is a hard thing to understand because from physical perspective you see yourselves as this. And even as you acknowledge that you have been more than this, still the tendency is that old "dead or alive" routine. And so, you think physical or Non-physical — "Here I am and I've been somewhere else," — but somehow you think that this body is just a continuation of other physical-nesses, so to speak. And it is really not that way. Let us see if we can find a way of expressing it without bursting your bubbles and sending you off in directions where you are not hearing our words.

Jerry and Esther and Tracy traveled to the city of Boston. We said to them, "You will like this because it was your last place of physicalness." They were very excited.

"Who was I? Who was I?" they asked.

"When you stand before that statue, the statue that represents you, you will know."

They were very excited that they were famous enough to have statues, you see. It was midnight or one o'clock in the morning, and they were bounding around in the middle of the night, stand-ing in front of statues, seeing if there would be some message offered. And as they stood before the statue of Samuel Adams, all three of them said, "I was Samuel Adams", in great certainty. And then they looked at one another, saying, "Not you, me...Not you, me."

And we said, "All of you."

The Energy that is now expressed through the three was at one time expressed in one. And in like manner that is the reason that so many of you feel strong connectedness to the one known as Jesus. This thought Energy, this intention, is continually being expressed into physicalness for the purpose of fine tuning. And — very important to understand — for the purpose of experiencing joy, you see. And so, as you are able to begin to grasp this concept, sometimes it makes you feel a little bit lost. Suddenly your iden-tity may feel threatened a little bit, just momentarily. "You mean, me has not always been me? I'm not climbing up the rungs of the ladder from worm to GOD?" And we say, "Indeed not." You began as GOD and you are extending your experiences because you want to have more knowing. There is not an ending to growth.

As physical beings, you think so much about some great teacher that knows everything; this is the father that you were talk-ing about that has everything figured out so that you can say, "Tell me what to do, Dad." And we say that he does not know everything forevermore. He is only that which he is now, and you certainly have access to that, but your reason for existence is to go beyond that.

As we are here together, tonight, of course we are wanting to bring you to points of clarity, even though there are not two of you that are in the same place to begin with. This would be some unusual sort of college course, we assure you, for your credentials are all very different. And how you are drawn here has not to do with what you know, it has to do with the power of your wanting, you see.

*So, as you are here wanting to understand who you are, why you are here and how to do it better —we say to you that you are here to experience the deliciousness of physicalness for the purpose of refining thought beyond that which it has ever been refined. You have chosen this physical dimension in order to feel the momentum of it. It gives you a means of measurement which gives you a feeling of momentum.* It is easier for you to find your place because of the consistency of this life experience, you see, so that you're not floating nebulously. You have purpose and function and the feeling of progress and momentum. You choose it because it helps you to fine tune.

Your Inner Being will offer you that feeling of comfort, that feeling of Well-being, that feeling that all is well, much as the way a mother or father would make you feel if they were to hold you in their arms and say, "All is well." Or that powerful feeling as you see them looking into your eyes, saying, "I am so proud of you. I know that you can do this." *You can get all of those feelings that inspire you to greatness from your Inner Being, indeed. But do not expect the direction from your Inner Being, because that is not its place. It is your place;* you are the one that chewed upon the data of this physicalness. You're the one who has immersed yourself in the ideas and beliefs of this time. You are the one. You have the conscious-thinking mechanism, the tool through which you contour the Non-physical Energy into something meaningful to you. And when you are as this one is, (Esther) and many of you are, your Inner Being is observing every part of it, and participating in every part of it, and lying on the beach with you, and savoring the deliciousness of every part of it. Then you feel the power of the connectedness, but you do not seek the step-by-step guidance, because you know you're the one.

We have watched Esther with her daughter. Both of them are very creative. Both of them are very talented. And nothing bothers Tracy more than when her mother says, "Let me do this...let *me* do this." When Tracy recognizes that Esther is not happy with the way she is doing something, so much so that she will elbow Tracy out of the way and slice it up herself, Tracy wants to leave the project altogether.

*It is not very much fun to have someone else dictating to you or telling you what to do, because you, from the inner perspective, know that you're the one. And nobody else can take that place, because nobody else can think for you. Therefore, nobody else can feel for you. Therefore, nobody else can invite or attract for you. Therefore, nobody else is of value to you when they try to do for you that which you have intended to do for yourself.*

As Non-physical teachers we are bombarded with questions, from many who are seeking guidance. And we are happy to offer guidance, but we are always so careful, also, along with any guidance, to give, as clear as we can, an understanding of *how* you get what you get, because we know that there would come a time, that if you allowed us to guide you, that if we were to say to you, "This thing you are thinking about doing, don't do it  That thing, that somebody else suggested, is a good thing to do." We know that there would come a time that you would say to us, as we are sitting on a cloud basking in the sun, "I've been meaning to tell you I didn't appreciate that very much, for I intended to do that for myself. Who did you think you were?"

We would say, "We thought we were the father you were seeking."

We are speaking to each of you. *As you are experiencing your physicalness, you are making decisions in every day about what you are wanti-*

*ng, and it is by virtue of those decisions, literally by virtue of every thought that you set forth, that you attract that which you are attracting. Our emphasis is upon being deliberate and upon making more decisions, and in that way you will guide your experience.*

## CONSIDERING THE "HOLY SPIRIT"

QUESTION: ABRAHAM, I have two questions. Ah...what is the function of the Holy Spirit relative to ABRAHAM'S teachings?

ABRAHAM: "Holy Spirit." Whenever we are utilizing physical terms, it is of value to define them in the way we are generally hearing them from you. *You must remember that every word you hear us speak is a label that you have created in order to describe your block of thought. And you very often describe, with the same label, different blocks of thought.*

*Predominantly, from what we have observed as we hear it being used, and the way we would interpret it through what we are knowing, "Holy Spirit" is your Inner Being and the family that dwells there, in connection with the power of the Universe. In other words, it is this Non-physical current focused to you for the purpose of your taking it and doing what you will do with it.* "Holy Spirit" is not offered to you to guide you. It is offered to you for you to consciously utilize toward your ends. It is very much like electricity that flows through the circuitry of your home. It is there to plug whatever you want into, you see. But when you combine it with your Inner Being that knows that which you have lived before and knows the combination of intentions that you hold, then we would say, for you, and for the others that are hearing here, that this "Holy Spirit" is your Inner Being and your Inner Being's broad perspective as a result of all that has been lived. In other words, you are growth-seeking, joy-seeking, freedom-seeking beings, and those intentions are all woven around that Energy that is offered to you, so that as you utilize the Energy...let us put it this way: As one who comes forth from that source, who has decided, from all that you have lived, that you like to be happy rather than sad, free rather than confined, growing rather than stagnant, uplifter rather than defeater, then as you find yourself, physically, being a defeater, you feel the negative emotion, which is your indication that you are utilizing this Energy in a way that is not in harmony with your greater intent. Literally, the Guidance System, the feeling of emotion that you've heard us speaking about, is the way that you know whether you are moving toward, or away from, that which you are wanting. We are not liking to call it "Holy Spirit" because it gives a picture that is different from the way we really see it.

## CONSIDERING "DIVINE INTERVENTION"

QUESTION: *Would you explain to me the meaning of the concept of the transcendent God, and Divine Intervention?* (reads written question)

ABRAHAM: It is a little bit along the lines of the last question, that if you are truly the creator of your experience and that if you get that which you are setting forth thought about — *then how is it that miracles happen, that suddenly something happens or something that is obviously going to happen is interrupted, and the miracle occurs? And we say, it is the greater intentions that you have set forth, saving you from the lack of intentions in this moment.*

For example, you are getting in your automobile and you are moving off and the only thing that you are thinking about is that you are wanting to be on time. You are leaving later than you should be leaving, and this is very important, and so you just go, and you have one intention and that is to drive as fast as you can to get where you are going. And you don't stop to think in terms of safety or anything like that. And so, as a result of these intentions of just getting there, not thinking in terms of the greater good, which is arriving safely and refreshed, you become swept up in the influence of another who is in the middle of having an automobile accident. Even though your intent, *in the moment,* doesn't seem like it should be powerful enough to save you, your greater intentions have been established for such a long period of time that miraculous things happen. We like to say that the "fairies of the Universe" arrange circumstances and events to save your neck. All of it coming because of the combinations of intentions that you hold.

You see, when we start talking about "Divine Intervention," then those who really want to live, but are dying of cancer, wonder why the Divine is not intervening on their behalf. "What did I do wrong? Why is the miracle not coming to me? I have said my prayers every day of my life... How good does one have to get?"

*We say, there is not really such a thing as Divine Intervention, in the way that most think of it. It is the way many justify the experiences that they get because they can't understand what happened.* EVERYTHING THAT HAPPENS TO YOU, EVERYTHING, WITHOUT EXCEPTION, IS BY VIRTUE OF THE COMBINATION OF INTENTIONS AND BELIEFS THAT YOU HOLD.

If you have been fostered by parents who did not see themselves as worthy and who, as you were born, did not see you as worthy, and who talked to you, every day, about how bad things happen to you, because you were not born in the family of worthiness, and how all the good things happen to others, but that you have to be part of that society, or that whatever, in order to have the good things...And so, all of these years, you believed. You really come to believe as they tell you.... And as you see it in their experience because they attract what they talk about, you say, "Yes, it *is* that way. We are of the unchosen few. Not good things come to us..." Then we say that you are probably one that will attract not-good things coming to you, because that is where your predominant thought is. Whereas, someone else — who has been encouraged to believe that they can be or do or have whatever they are wanting — they attract all the good things, because they are not getting in the way of it.

*Non-physical current flows to all of you, equally. And your thinking mechanism is the way that you contour it, or focus it or funnel it, into your physical manifestation.* And so, as you say, "I want that, and I am worthy of it, or I am capable of it, or I am able," or whatever, so that all of your thought is going in one direction, then there is nothing that is stopping you from getting this.. But if you say, "I am wanting it, but I should not, or I cannot," then you are countering and keeping it from coming unto you. Nothing else! We are wanting to SHOUT as we speak those words to you because there are so many who...when things aren't going right, want to give the credit, or the blame, to somebody else. *And we say that as long as you are giving the credit or the blame to somebody else, you remain powerless — because you can not control what they do.* And the more you try, the more you find that out. The more you try to control what they do, the more you realize that it is hopeless, because there is always another one who is stubborn about what they do.

And so, your freedom comes when you finally recognize, "It is me and only me. I need not let them influence me toward my lack. As they look at me and I see them seeing lack in me, I can change the thought, or, if need be, if it is so powerful, I can remove myself from this one who causes me to continually focus upon lack. And as I do, I am free. Free to have what I am wanting."

We are talking upon a very advanced level of creation. You are aware? For you to understand that your thoughts, the combination of your thoughts — is what equals what you get, sometimes it empowers you and sometimes it frightens you, because sometimes you're surer than others about what you want. And in your uncertainty, what is happening?

Have you ever felt?....You have. Let us remind you: There is a decision for you to make. And you haven't made it yet. You are still exploring the options. You might even have narrowed it down to one or two things. Do you feel how enervated you feel? How tired, even depressed? How you wake up in the morning, and you really don't want to get out of bed? The reason for that is because your Energy is diffused. You don't know what you want, and so this powerful, or potentially powerful, Energy is coming into you — but you are sending it off in so many directions, you feel tired.

And do you remember how, whenever you made a decision about something, how good you felt?

*ONCE YOU MAKE A DECISION, NO MATTER HOW MINOR THE DECISION IS, YOU ARE SUDDENLY EMPOWERED AGAIN — because, suddenly, you are saying "yes" to something.* You're not saying, "yes, no, yes, no, maybe." You're saying, "Yes," and so the Energy flows. That is "Divine Intervention." When you get all of your thoughts going in one direction, then we say "Let it go!" And "everyone" gets behind and offers to you, and that is why you feel this great power of momentum, you see. All of the "fairies of the Universe" get behind you when you're decided. And otherwise, it is sort of, nobody paying much attention to you. There is not much point in sending it off in a thousand directions, is there? You are getting the point?

**QUESTIONER:** I understand. Thank you.

## TEN IDEAS FOR A GOOD WAY OF LIFE

**JERRY:** *If you were a "burning bush"* (group laughter) *and I would like some guidance for my people, do you have "10 commandments" that you would offer?*

**ABRAHAM:** We have 10 good ideas. We would not command anyone to do anything, for a number of reasons. They never listen anyway. (group laughter) Rather than "commandments", what we would offer are examples, in this case, verbal offerings, of that which we have found to be a very good way of life. Commandments are usually offered in action form, are they not?

**JERRY:** "Thou shalt not kill." "Thou shalt not mess around with somebody else's things." (group laughter)
**ABRAHAM:** So a commandment is what NOT to do. Rather than telling you what NOT to do, we will tell you what we do. How's that?

- Seek joy — first and foremost.
- Seek reasons to laugh.
- Seek reasons to offer words of praise — to self and others.
- Seek beauty in nature, beasts, and other humans.
- Seek reasons to love. In every segment of every day — look for something that brings forth within you a feeling of love.
- Seek that which uplifts you.
- Seek opportunity to offer that which uplifts another.
- Seek a feeling of Well-being.
- Know that your value can only be measured in terms of joy.
- Acknowledge your absolute freedom to do any of these things or to not do any of these things — for it is, without exception, your choice in every moment of every day.

*That is the recipe for eternal joy. And it will provide a format for a life of dramatic, magnificent creating, also.* That feels like the "bottom line" to you: "How much success, or how much acclaim...how much value can I offer here and now?" And what we are wanting you to understand is that your value can only be measured in terms of joy.

Once you get upon that path where you are seeking and finding — you are abundant with joy. *You see, the nice thing about this offering is that you cannot seek something without finding it. It cannot be. For that which you are asking for is always that which is coming to you.* And once you've got the first one down, the second one is easier, and once you get the second one, the third one is easier...In other words, they all dovetail into one another.

## EXAMPLE OF LIVING JOYOUSLY

**JERRY:** I was lying on the beach today, or on a rock at the beach at the La Jolla Cove, and just in total ecstasy. Every breath was bringing in fragrances from the ocean and the seaweed, and all. It almost lifted me off the rock. And the sun touching my body was so spectacular and the breeze blowing over my body, I just let it flow to no thoughts, only those marvelous, marvelous feelings. And then I thought, "Gee, I guess a person could stay here forever and do this." And then I thought..."But then I'm not doing any good." And then I thought... "ABRAHAM, said that we're doing good by example more than we are by words." *And then I thought.. "Boy, being happy as I am, must be the best example." But then I said... "But nobody knows I'm happy, 'cause I'm here by myself."*

And then I thought of when I was nine years old and the doctor said that I probably wouldn't live through this winter, although I *had* made it last winter, living in a little chicken house, in Arkansas, and Mother living in another chicken house, because our house had burned down. And I remember saying to GOD, "If you'll let me live through this winter, I'll work for you in the future." And then I remember trying to decide what kind of work, and I couldn't figure which church, because every church that I went into, the rest of them said that that one was wrong. So I couldn't find any church that the other churches would agree was the correct church. So as I went from church to church finding where to do GOD's work, I just couldn't find it. And, I wasn't interested in starting my own. And then I thought, "Maybe I can work for GOD by uplifting mankind, by making them happier and making them feel better about themselves and about their bodies and about their lives...

*But then I come back to you, and you say that we really don't have to do any work, that just to be joyous and happy is doing enough work for all of the...all beings in the Universe. Would you clarify that little moment of confusion I had on the rock today?*

ABRAHAM: You are a physical being, looking through physical eyes, still thinking that *doing* is what makes the difference. Still believing that it is through your action that you accomplish, or offer, while we continue to want to guide you to the understanding that it is through your thought and corresponding feeling that you create, you see.

And so, as you are a physical being, and you are giving your determination, you are giving your discipline, to your thought, aligning your thoughts, getting them all going toward what you are wanting, of course, chewing, in order to determine what you want, but once decided, giving that your full attention — then you come to know that the action part of your experience is not the way you make it happen.

*ACTION IS THE WAY YOU ENJOY WHAT YOU HAVE MADE HAPPEN THROUGH YOUR THOUGHT.*

If we can help you to understand that the benefit that is occurring as a result of your being here in this combined arena of thought, tonight, is of more value to the Universe and All-That-Is than what most physical beings will do with their *actions* in an entire lifetime, then perhaps you get the idea. If you can understand that your willingness to add your thoughts to this kettle of creation, and your willingness to have your corresponding feeling, is accomplishing more in terms of creation than all of the actions that you could ever do, then you get the idea.

As you think, you feel. Always. And as you feel, you ooze. You know that. If you are afraid of the dog, it knows it. It will usually bite you. If you are mad at your child and you are still saying sweet words, your child still knows he's in trouble. All of you are receiving on levels far beyond your language. And so, as you think, you feel. As you feel, you radiate or influence, and that is what is making the difference. That is why when you lay on the rock and bask in the glory of beingness, oozing that fantastic positive Energy, you are uplifting All-That-Is. Everyone who seeks it, now has access to that which you are feeling. You have heard Esther say, "I used to be happy just driving past Jerry's house because I knew there was happiness inside." There are those who are in other parts of the world that see you not, today, and who will not ever see you again, who benefit from the memory of that which they experienced as they were with you while you were radiating your joy. Can you not bring images of people to mind and immediately you feel good or bad? And do you know that it does not have to do with what they said or what they did? It had to do with what they were thinking and feeling, predominantly. And so we say, "Do not underestimate your value."

*Many people will say, "ABRAHAM, you teach laziness."*

*We say, "Not at all, we teach doing it in the way which is powerful."*

*They will say, "Then what you are teaching is selfishness."*

*We say, "Indeed we do. Because if you are not selfish enough to make yourself happy, you have nothing of value to offer the world, as far as we are concerned." Because every time you ooze or radiate that which is less than happy, you are going against your greater intent and certainly working against that which we work for. We are wanting to uplift and to bring joy. Any time you are feeling other than that, you are oozing it.* It is the reason that your animals exist here. One of the predominant reasons that they exist is not because they give you eggs or meat. It is because they are pure essence of inner world and are predominantly, predominantly — your influence gets to them now and again — but, predominantly they are joyful beings oozing good feelings and adding that balance to your Universe, you see.

*We are not saying that action has no value. The point that we are wanting to make is that the majority of the action that we see is not in harmony with the greater intent. More physical beings are acting out of negativity than out of positivity. More action causes you to feel negative than positive. As we listen to the surveys and as we listen to the individuals, the majority are not happy with their work. And their work utilizes the majority of their time. And when they're not at work, they are still thinking and talking and feeling about their work.* FROM WHAT WE ARE SEEING, THE MAJORITY OF BEINGS ARE UTILIZING THEIR ACTION TO COMPENSATE FOR INAPPROPRIATE THOUGHT.

QUESTION: Okay, and...and that may be the majority, but I want to go outside the majority and say, specifically, like Jerry, I consistently feel, from Jerry, his desire to make a contribution, and he kind of continues to ask that question in a lot of different ways, and you continue to say, don't worry about it, just be happy, and all that. And although I can get that on one level, and I certainly don't have the bigger picture to see how one person's happiness affects the whole Universe. But I can see where one person's action can have a powerful effect, and so I just get a little confused there, because it's almost like I hear you saying to Jerry, which he is certainly a big boy and he will do whatever, but I hear you say, "Don't worry about that issue, just sit on the rock and bask in it and enjoy it"....and I like that.

ABRAHAM: As he was sitting on the rock you heard him say, "But then I thought, I am seeking growth." In other words, because you have this triad of intentions: joy and freedom and growth, you do not usually lay on the rock too long before you feel you are wanting to get up and make something happen, for you have this quest for growth.

*What we are wanting to reinforce, or to enhance, or to add power to, is the knowledge that, as you are feeling good, that is when your great inspiration comes that leads you to your greatest happy ending.* And so, we say, "bask." Now if he is asking for us to say, "You've laid there long enough. It is time for you to get up, and here are the things to do," and we could do that, for we have a very clear picture of what is coming, but we are not wanting to step upon his creative toes. How much satisfaction do you get by working for somebody else and performing the tasks that they assign to you in comparison with following out your own inspiration? And so, what we are knowing is that his inspiration will come from his perspective of basking, and it will be inspiration that will satisfy *all* of his intentions. You can jump into action, very easily. Let us say that somebody comes to you and says, "I have it from a very reliable source that there is going to be an earthquake here this weekend. The scientists are reading it on their scales. The psychics are seeing it in the stars. And...ah...Madame Whoever saw it in a crystal ball. All good sources, and we know it is coming." And so you take that little bit of information and because you are worried about your physical neck, you pack up everything you can put into the greatest container and off you go.

You've satisfied one intention. But if you have, from your inner perspective, identified all of the things that you are wanting, and you're utilizing your own Guidance System, you will not find yourself hightailing off into the bushes in a lopsided manner. That is what we are saying.

## I INTEND, I WANT, OR I AM?

QUESTIONER: I got it. *This is just kind of a subtle question about intending. Is there any significant difference in intending, where you say, "I want something" ....let's say, "I want a healthy body. I want a vibrant body" versus "I am becoming vibrant and healthy" versus "I AM healthy and vibrant?"*

ABRAHAM: Good. *The words you say are really not so important as the intent that you hold as you say them — for everyone who uses a word means something a little bit different.*

If we were to define these words on a scale of appropriateness or benefit, we would say *need* should be removed from your experience altogether. The word *need* is purely coming from a position of lack. Not even something you mentioned, of course. The word *want* is on the other side of that. *Want* is thinking about where you are really wanting to go. The word *intend* includes wanting *and* believing. For some of you, wanting does not necessarily mean getting, because you have wanted many things that you didn't get, and so *wanting* is sometimes even a negative word to some of you. So if you say, "Oh, I want to have that...oh, I really want to have that." (pleading) THE WAY YOU ARE FEELING IS WHAT THE UNIVERSE IS HEARING. If you say, *I intend*, then that is stronger than *want* because it includes belief. As you say, *I am*, that is stronger still — *if you believe that you are.* But if you say *I am*, and you look down and say, *I aren't really*, (group laughter) then your attraction and your words are in opposition. You see what we are saying? And so, it is as you *feel. Use the strongest word that describes the way you feel, and keep trying to get yourself to feeling it in its strongest sense.*

**QUESTION:** And so, probably, if I'm not feeling real healthy and I am saying, "I *am* healthy," then there's that problem. But if I can get in touch with "I am becoming," that may be the strongest position I can take at that point. And to find the strongest position that I can get a feeling for?

**ABRAHAM:** That is the way it is. That is the way you utilize your guidance, you see. Let us say that you are very much out of shape and many more pounds than you want to be. And you see something, as a role model of what you are wanting, that stimulates your thought, and so you say "I want that." And then the next time you look into the mirror, your thoughts go the opposite way. And so, your wanting is going one way and your expectation, for that moment, is going the other way, and you say, "Wait a minute. *WHERE I AM IS AS A RESULT OF WHAT I'VE THOUGHT AND FELT BEFORE. BUT WHERE I AM GOING IS AS A RESULT OF MY PERSPECTIVE OF WHERE I NOW STAND.* And so, I can see myself becoming this. I will act, out of my inspired thought, to that which will lead me to that. I am becoming that." And so, then as you are seeing others that are that which you are wanting to be, it uplifts you rather than depresses you.

The feeling of jealousy that you feel, regarding anything, whether it is seeing someone's body or seeing someone's relationship or their home or their lifestyle, *when you feel that thing that you call jealousy, that is your Inner Being saying that you want this, but you are, right now, giving thought to the lack of it.* And so, as you feel yourself doing that, you pivot. Now, what will happen, as you are starting out with the weaker word, "I want", after you pivot on it awhile — it will get stronger, and you sill say, "I want it and it is becoming.... I want it and it is." And when you reach the place that you say, "I want it, therefore it is," you are there. You are at the point of instant, or as instant as you can experience it in the physical, manifestation — because every thought that you define, you take that Non-physical Energy, which is powerful, and you direct it right there, with no detours. When you do detour, pivot.

And eventually it will all come in, and right toward where you are wanting it to be. And then...then that is really when you get down to your real work, which is the deciding and the chewing on the data, and the making the decisions. And, really, the pivoting process is that deciding process, too.

*Your beliefs serve as a backup system, as a sort of ballast, to assist you in your decisions and in your creations. If you had no beliefs, any idea that touched you would carry you away toward that creation.* Stimulated to a new thought, you would take the powerful Energy and, boom, you would go there. You wouldn't like that. It would not be good. We would not like it if you were, here today, so empty-headed and so ready to accept everything that we say, that you would just (clap) go off to it. *We like the fact that you have beliefs within you that you use to temper new ideas.* And that is the way you decide, in every day, and every segment of every day, what it is you most want.

What we are really wanting to guide you to is more decisions, more decisions, more decisions. Because a decision is saying that *all* Energy is going there. Decide what you are going to have for lunch, early in the morning, and let the Universe arrange the circumstances and events so that it will satisfy you. If you have an appointment at three o'clock in the afternoon, and you know about it two weeks ahead, launch some thought out there in advance, and let it get going on it.

USE THE POWER OF YOUR THOUGHT AND THE POWER OF YOUR EXPECTATION TO PREPARE IN ADVANCE THE THING — SO THAT IT DOES NOT TAKE SO MUCH ACTION TO PERFORM.

And now, what is it you are wanting to talk about?


## HE WANTS TO GET RID OF THE BAD GUYS

QUESTION: I have some related questions. I'll give them all to you at once and you can answer them. *How do we get the bad guys? And, is there anything to be afraid of?*

225

ABRAHAM: We really appreciate questions that have been stacked in such a way that they take very long unraveling. For rather than answer the question, "How do you get the bad guys?" Clarify that a little bit. Are you meaning how do you get rid of them, or how do you bring them in?"

QUESTIONER: That is part of the question, "How do we get rid of them?" Am I one of them? If joy is the purpose of creation, these guys don't seem to be spreading much joy around, from my perspective. Yet they're out there creating because they are swishing out in a very directed path. They know exactly what they want.

ABRAHAM: You see, the reason that we are having a difficult time in answering the question, "How do we get the bad guys?" is because it isn't your work. You can't get all of them, even if you could get one of them.

QUESTIONER: I don't want to get them, in the sense of locking them up. How were they created? How did...

ABRAHAM: How did they come to exist?

QUESTIONER: And how did they get off track?

ABRAHAM: *Technically, everyone who has a set of intentions, and sees another who opposes those intentions, classifies the other as the bad guy. We all think that we are the good guy, in those terms.*

When you come to understand that you live in a well-stocked kitchen with every ingredient — or intention — imaginable, and you really come to understand that it is not your work to come here to influence them all to think and speak and be just as you are ...That is one of the greatest misunderstandings that abounds upon your planet, so many believe that there is one truth and then they believe they have it — or they look very hard for it until they find it — and then they want to tell everyone about it. *And they say, "Won't this be a good place when everybody thinks and believes and does as we do." And we say, that is an absolute contradiction to what you know, as creator, because you know there is not ending. And you know that it is your differences that stimulate your thought.*

*IT IS STIMULATION OF THOUGHT THAT LEADS TO FOREVER — WHILE IT IS CONFORMITY THAT LEADS TO ENDEDNESS.*

And so, as you understand that, then you are no longer wanting to squelch those who do not agree with you, because you understand that *they don't get into your experience because they're powerful. They get into your experience because you invite them as you notice them and give thought to them and worry about them and chew upon them.*

*And so, the way you get rid of the bad guys from your* personal *experience is to give them no attention. But you do not have the power, nor the wanting, to eliminate them altogether — because* they *are free to be as they choose, as* you *are free to be. You see?*

QUESTION: So my perspective of the bad guys is somebody who has different intentions than I do?

ABRAHAM: Correct.

## CONSIDERING ADOLPH HITLER

QUESTION: Then, from Adolph Hitler's perspective, he had an intention and everybody went along with him. He was a good guy for that position.

ABRAHAM: Correct. He was also someone who utilized the Laws of the Universe. He gave thought to only one thing. He did not deviate from it. Not until the end. He was very powerful in his thoughts, and that was the reason that he was powerful in his creating.

But what we are wanting you to understand is that those who

became that which you now term the victims were not without decision. They were not without choice.

Many of them created by default; we will agree with that. In other words, when you have something in your experience that you don't want, and we say to you, "You are the creator of your own experience." And you say, "But ABRAHAM, I wouldn't have done this to me. I don't like this. I wouldn't have done it; therefore, somebody else, powerful, outside, must be responsible." And we say, "We didn't say you did it on purpose — but we did say you did it."

*The trouble with going back into history, or even trying to make your decision based upon what somebody else has said about something, is that you don't get a clear reading, because their intentions of what they are trying to get you to believe, get all in there, and it gets a little hazy.*

It is our knowing that if you had been there among those, you would have understood how it was that they received that which they received. There were those who did *not* die at Hitler's hand, who sensed it coming, who were aware of it, who said, "No, not me," and who did not experience it, you see.

## IS THERE NOTHING TO FEAR?

QUESTION: Then, there *is* nothing to be afraid of?

ABRAHAM: Absolutely not. Now, let us talk about this. This is good. *There are only two emotions. One feels good and one feels bad. You call them all sorts of different things depending on what's happening when you're having them. And so, the emotion of fear is nothing more than negative emotion to say to you, "This is an important issue, and what you're thinking about is not in harmony with what you are wanting." And as you give thought to something else — the fear will subside.*

NOTHING BAD WILL EVER HAPPEN TO YOU AS YOU UNDERSTAND THAT IT IS ONLY GIVING THOUGHT TO THOSE THINGS THAT ATTRACTS THEM.

And so, if you find yourself very frightened about something that you are thinking about, and you are able to change the thought and feel better, then you have removed your attraction of that.

*You do not live in a dimension of instant manifestation, and that is a lucky thing for most of you.* For as you say, "I thought I would die laughing," over you would go. (group laughter) "I thought I would break my neck," it is done. It is nice that it is a very long process of offering the thought. In other words, your thoughts would have to get very strong, by Law of Attraction, and the way they become powerful or strong is by your attention to them.

*IF YOU SPEND A LIFETIME WORRYING ABOUT SOMETHING, IT USUALLY HAPPENS TO YOU, SOONER OR LATER. OR IF YOU SPEND A LITTLE BIT OF TIME INTENSELY FOCUSED UPON SOMETHING, YOU CAN BRING IT ABOUT — GOOD OR BAD.*

QUESTION: So my willingness to know what I'm really focusing on, through my feelings, knowing what I'm really feeling, is my key to success or to getting what I want?

ABRAHAM: That is correct. Ordinarily, it falls back to three basic issues: freedom, growth and joy. Ordinarily, when you feel negative emotion, the majority of the time, it is because your freedom is being challenged. Somebody is telling you you can't do something or somebody is not believing you can do something, and you're feeling it. *The majority of the negative emotion that all of you feel has to do with freedom.* And we say that to you as a unique group of very intense wanters of freedom. Everybody doesn't want freedom with the intensity that you do, so everybody doesn't have their feelings squelched as much. That is why it is not possible for you to understand why other people do the things they do. It is why, as you look at a story in history, such as those who were led to Hitler's gas chambers in Germany, you say, "How can that be? It must have been a very powerful situation. They must have had no choice whatsoever." Because you cannot imagine *yourself* being in that sort of position, short of being hog-tied and dragged there, you see. And what we are wanting you to understand is that you can't understand why they allowed it because you can't understand how they *felt.* Some people really, really, really want freedom. So just the slightest little hint that they are not free for a moment sends them off the scale, while others don't care about freedom, so much. So you could lead them around by the nose and they would say, "Okay." And they do not feel negative emotion about it because their power or their desire to be free is not so intense. And one is not better than the other. *There are not greater states of evolution. That is not our point. There are different states of evolution.*

To the majority of questions that we were asked in the early years, from this one, (Jerry) we responded first by saying, "It isn't your work," which was usually to questions such as "How do I get rid of some bad guy?" He was always wanting, not to protect himself, but wanting to protect the innocent ones from the bad guy. It took quite a bit of conversation before we convinced him that there are no bad guys, there are just *different* guys.

## HE WANTS TO KNOW WHAT HE WANTS

QUESTION: I have two questions which are really diverse. One is kind of on a personal level, and one is on a more universal level. On the personal level, I feel like, for the past three to six years, I've been doing things that really made me intently unhappy, and finally, about nine months ago I came to a point where I couldn't do any of those things anymore, and everything got pushed away, mentally, physically, just cleaned it all out, and I've been spending the past nine months kind of getting rid of it all, one way or another, mentally or physically. I still feel, though, like when you talk about your intention of making a decision, I've made a decision. I don't want to do these things or have these things anymore, but I don't feel like I've gotten to a place where I can take that void and fill it up. *I still feel like I'm waiting to find out what I want to do when I grow up. I'm good at a lot of things and I'm not great at anything, and I need some guidance on how to make the decision, "I could do this, I could do this." I'm not doing anything, and I'm becoming more depressed about it.*

*How do you start making those decisions when you don't know what to write, that you do want?*

ABRAHAM: Good. You are not alone in that. It is the most common question we hear as we say to you, *"You are powerful and you can have or be or do anything that you choose."* Sometimes it is exciting if there are things that you already know you want, but if you don't know what you want, then that sort of information is very discouraging because it feels like a waste of all this power and Energy.

The reason you are feeling that way is because you are a typical physical being believing that you must decide what to *do*. In other words, it is exactly what we were talking about earlier, as you believe that your decision to do is what is dominant, and you simply do not have enough data collected for the decision to be clear.

If you would start from the inside out rather than creating backwards: *Most physical beings create backwards. They say, "I will do this, and then I will have this, and then I will be happy. I will go do this work and then I will have money and lifestyle and feeling of purpose — and then I will be happy."* And sometimes it works that way, especially if they have pondered wanting joy, and that sort of thing, for a long time. But, usually, those who are quick to jump into action, find their lives — as you found yours — so jam-packed full of things that are not bringing you joy and things that are not even giving you the lifestyle that you are wanting, that you wonder, *"Why am I doing it?"* And then you feel like you want to "clean house" and throw some of it, or as you said, all of it, out. Instead, create through your thought, and start at the core of your being.

Now you have heard us, all evening, talking about Inner Being. And the reason we call it Inner Being is because it exists within you — and it exists in a state of being. Some have said, "ABRAHAM, where do you live? Tell us about your place." And we say, place is physical, and we are Non-physical. We are in a non-place. And a few have said, "Then you must not be worth anything if you do not have a home planet." And we say, "Guess not, at least from your perspective. But from our perspective, we are very well placed, or non-placed, we should say. We exist in a state of being."

*Because you are eternally connected to your Inner Being, then as you understand that your Inner Being exists, and that it is joyful and growing and free, then it is not so difficult to understand that that is the place for you to begin to come back to. In other words, if the doing is confusing, come back to the being.* You don't know what you want to do, let us say.

You know a lot of things you don't want to do. And so, as you identify something you don't want to do, if you will stop and say to yourself, "Why don't I want to do this?" It will lead you to what is being challenged within you, and usually it will be, "Because I don't feel that I am free as I do it," or "I don't feel that it has enough potential. I feel like I'm stagnant. I'm not growing." Or, "It doesn't make me happy." And sometimes it is a combination of all of those things.

*YOU ARE IN THE VERY BEST POSITION, THAT YOU WILL EVER BE, OF KNOWING WHAT YOU DO WANT WHEN YOU ARE FEELING STRONG EMOTION OF WHAT YOU DON'T WANT.* If somebody is rude or abusive to you, you know what you want. You want something different from that. You are wanting to be appreciated. You are wanting love to come rather than anger to come. And so, if you will stop for a moment, in the moment of the awareness of the negativity, and ponder, "What is at the root of this? What is happening to me? Well, I don't feel free." Don't ask yourself, "Well, what can I do, instead?" Because, immediately, as you try to decide what to *do,* you put up all of these roadblocks, "Well, I *can't* do that. If I could have done that, I would have done that instead of this" And so, as you try to decide what to do, you miscreate in the moment.

Step back from the doing, and say, "I want to be free." And then ponder the *feeling* of freedom. Go back to a time, as Jerry was describing, lying on a beach, and remember the feeling of freedom and the feeling of joy. Ponder that for a little bit. And as you do, ideas will begin to come forth.

You will literally be inspired to what you want to have. If you have a job or a home or a relationship that isn't as you want it to be, in the moment of the negative emotion, stop, and say, "What is it that I am wanting to have? What is missing here? What is this lack pointing out that I want?" *Every time you feel negativity because of the lack of something, you can always figure out what it is that you want. And then, turn your attention to that, until you feel better. That is what pivoting is.*

*PIVOTING, IS UTILIZING THE NEGATIVE THINGS THAT ARE HAP-PENING IN YOUR LIFE TO HELP YOU PINPOINT WHAT YOU WOULD RATHER HAVE.* And that is the reason for the physical life experience. That is the value of the "bad guys." Bad guys help you identify what you would prefer. Interacting with those that make you feel bad, helps you to be aware that you want to feel good. Technically, we see a manifestation of some physical illness in your body as a very helpful thing, because never do you want health more than when you are feeling some negativity regarding your health. That is when you go to the gym. That is when you decide to change your diet. That is when you begin working more deliberately on your own behalf. Is it not?

*And so, as you are feeling negativity, let it do for you that which it is intended to do for you: help you to clarify what you do want. And don't try to figure it out all at once.*

**The most important thing for you to hear is that from a negative place, you cannot find a happy ending. You cannot figure out a happy thing to do when you are in a negative feeling place. You cannot have an unhappy journey to a happy ending; it defies law.** That is the reason for statements such as, "Within every adversity lies the seed of equivalent benefit." Look for what pleases you in this experience, find your joy, so that you are offering your future in a happy way. It is the reason they say, "Look for the pot of gold at the end of the rainbow. Look for the cloud with the silver lining. Look for the good within it. There is always something good within every experience." Now we don't want to get too heavy on that — because we don't really encourage you to go out looking for bad experiences. We don't encourage you to bite your finger just so you can feel how good it feels when you stop.

But we do encourage that you acknowledge the value in every life experience. What is the other question?

## CAN HUMANS DESTROY THIS PLANET?

QUESTION: When you were talking earlier about certain things not being our job and not being responsible for the world, and also, how if you put more attention on something, you create more of it ...What flashed to me was the problem with the environment and the hole in the ozone layer. *Is it not our responsibility to try to educate people to changing things so that we don't destroy our planet and our environment?*

ABRAHAM: You cannot destroy your planet. You cannot, no matter how hard you try. Many, who were more destructive than you, have come before.

*From this level of your creative endeavor, you do not have the ability, nor will you ever have, to destroy your planet. What do you think about that?*

QUESTIONER: What about the 20 hydrogen bombs going off?

ABRAHAM: Oh, we're not saying that you can't mess things up a bit. But *you* cannot destroy this planet. The great volcanos devastate an area and then make it better for that which is to come later. Your Earth is continually growing new skin. All sorts of things are occurring. *Your Earth, itself, is an entity seeking its own balance. You are like fleas on the back of a dog, and there aren't enough of you to cause the dog very much trouble.* (group laughter) Don't worry about it.

QUESTION: I was, personally, brought up in this mental environment that it is part of our duty to do good, to do things to help other people, to protect the innocent. Sounds like Jerry. And you're saying, just leave all that alone....?

ABRAHAM: We are not. *We are saying that, as it is your intent, you will be inspired to the action — but you are stepping on the toes of someone else if you are trying to convince them that they should stop doing anything.*

Now, we are not saying that it is not of value for you to have causes, and for you to have those things you are believing in. Certainly, that is one of the most glorious parts of physical experience. *You have come forth in an environment where there are many others — because you are wanting to exercise your power of influence.* And what is it you are wanting to influence toward? State of joy.

*What we are wanting you to understand is that there are all sorts of things that lead to joy.* AND WHERE PHYSICAL MAN MOST OFTEN GOES ASTRAY IS THAT HE WANTS TO DICTATE TO YOU YOUR BEHAVIOR, IN ORDER TO LEAD YOU TO YOUR STATE OF JOY — *not understanding that in his dictation of your behavior, he is stepping upon your toes of freedom, because you are here to make those decisions for yourself.*

The majority of those who speak out, wanting to improve the ecology, let us say, or the earth environment, do so — and we are going to be very bold here — they do so to support their own intentions. And they include you; they sweep you up in their intentions, because that is the way they are able to gain access to money. If they wanted to be of greatest value to the ecology, they would visualize it as they are wanting it to be rather than spending so much money and so much attention on what is wrong.

If those who want peace would visualize peace, instead of campaigning against war, they would offer much more value to the cause of peace. Most of them work very hard against themselves, you see. Your doctors, who claim to speak for wellness, do more through their advertisements regarding illness, to create illness, than the rest of you, all put together. With the great attention that comes across your television airways, pointing out to you the perils of physicalness and the vulnerability that your apparatuses have, as they flash their statistics at you and give you that strong impending feeling of vulnerability, they are influencing you, through their media warnings, to illness. Now, while most of them would deny it and say, "I am a doctor because I want to help people," we say, the results are in opposition to that. The more you talk about cancer, the more people will experience it. The more publication about AIDS, the more are going to experience it. The more you talk about vulnerability, the more are going to feel, and therefore be, vulnerable.

*And so, if you are wanting to influence the world toward the ultimate ending, what is the ultimate trophy? Is the ultimate trophy a beautiful house? A beautiful car? A beautiful relationship? A beautiful Earth and atmosphere? Or state of Well-being?* THE ULTIMATE TROPHY IS THE FEELING OF JOY. *Certainly all of those things enhance your state of joy, but you cannot get to the state of joy by attacking what is wrong out here on the fringes.* You are following?

QUESTIONER: I am following, but I'm also kind of getting the feeling that you are saying you can make bad things go away by pretending they're not there.

ABRAHAM: You can. Oh, here it comes. "ABRAHAM, you mean, if we put our head in the sand?" Here is the point. And you will like this: *You do not live in one world. You share a dimension and are individually creating in as many separate worlds as there are beings.*

Your physical experience is very much perceptual. Now think about it. How has the deterioration of the ozone layer affected you? Now, we are wanting you to tell us the difference in your experience. Are your tomatoes less red? Is your suntan different? How? We are talking about your personal experience. Not your perceptual experience as it has been carefully influenced and guided by those who have something to gain by your coming along with them. We want to know how has the ozone layer affected your experience?

**QUESTIONER:** It has not.

**ABRAHAM:** Furthermore, we are wanting you to understand that your ozone layer is not "deteriorating." It is like looking at a little girl and saying to her, "Bad things are going to happen to you. You're going to stretch within that skin. You are not going to stay as you are. You are going to get bigger and bigger and bigger. Things in your body are going to change." And as you begin to describe the evolution of a physical being, you could horrify a child, could you not? And so why are you horrifying yourself about the evolution of your earth? Why do you not just let it evolve, let it seek its balance, and why do you not put your mind upon why *you* are here? Which is to create the experience around you through the direction of your thoughts.

It goes back to what you were asking earlier about the bad guys and all of that. Most of you, as you mature, go through stages where, in the beginning, your world is very small and very content because you are pretty much focusing on what is in your toy box, do you see? And then, as you get bigger and you expand out a little more and you get out into the world where they start talking about what things are wrong and begin comparing you, and all of that stuff, then you start feeling less secure and less safe in your own world. And then, as you get a bigger look at the world, as you go to school, and you see that Tommy eats sandwiches that are different than yours, and that this one pulls that one's hair, therefore he must be a bad boy. *As you start comparing behavior and start hearing yourself compared — you begin making judgements about what is good or bad, what is right or wrong.* AND WHAT WE *ARE WANTING YOU TO UNDERSTAND IS THAT EVERYTHING IS RIGHT — BUT THAT DOES NOT MEAN THAT YOU HAVE TO EXPERIENCE IT.*

We see your Universe as a well-stocked kitchen, and let us say that you have decided that you are wanting, in this kitchen, today, to create an apple pie. So you take the apples and the cinnamon and the sugar and the shortening and you put it all together and you make a very delicious pie. Oh, it is so good. Just what you imagined it to be. In fact you have decided it is so good that, from this perspective, you don't ever want to eat anything else. And so, from your perspective, you really don't see the reason for any of the other stuff in the kitchen. And then you see another reaching for Tabasco sauce. "How evil of him," you say. "He is wanting something that has no value at all." And then you organize a group of beings, you send a campaign across your nation, and you decide that you will omit Tabasco sauce from the kitchen because you don't have any use for it, personally, therefore, nobody else must have any use for it, either.

And our point is, now this is the real point....we know we are stretching it a little bit. It is hard for you to equate Tabasco sauce with war, because you believe that everybody should want peace and not war. But what we are saying to you is that you cannot see through their eyes. You cannot understand.

It is our absolute promise to you that the politicians are giving much more attention to war, than they are peace, no matter what they say, because their greatest issue is the economy, because the economy is what keeps them where they are. *And so, do not be mis-guided by what anyone is saying — because you do not understand the intentions that motivate their actions.*

Are we getting a picture across to you at the futility of trying to fix it all? You cannot, in this short lifetime, even identify the causes, let alone be of any value to any of them. All you'll end up doing is being frustrated beings that have seen the things that are wrong here and here and here and here and here, and you will end up being one of those who dies, who says, "I just can't help those people. There are too many of them and they are too messed up in their thinking."

*You can have the most blissful, delightful, delicious physical experience, that uplifts beyond your wildest dreams — as you just focus upon the beauty that is right here in your experience. And as you see something you are wanting to see, as you see the beautiful butterfly, or the wonderful smile on the little child, or as you see the friendship from a friend.... AS YOU FOCUS UPON*

*WHAT YOU WANT TO SEE AND YOU FEEL YOURSELF FEELING GOOD FROM THAT, NOW YOU ARE THAT MAGNET ATTRACTING UNTO YOU MORE GOOD THINGS.* We watch our friends, Jerry & Esther, joyously bounding from place to place. Those from the outside think that they live in "Never-Never-Land," that they are void of reality. And we say, "Good." *WHAT IS REALITY? YOUR REALITY IS ONLY YOUR PERSPECTIVE OF WHAT IS.*

This group of beings, here tonight, is having an experience together. But we promise you it is not anywhere near the same experience, because what we are sharing here, together, has to do with your individual beliefs and intentions. *That which you have lived before tonight, has much more to do with what you are living than what is happening here tonight.*

And so, as you go forth and you write your book of Michael and you write your book of Richard, and so on, each of you will write books so differently, of that which occurred here tonight, that those who observe from the outside would not even know you were at the same place. And as they try to tell it to the next one and to the next one, it becomes different and different and different and different. *And that different perspective is all very good, because if it were all seen as same, only one being would have come forth. If only one perspective was enough, if the goal was to have only one perspective, you would not be here.*

*IT IS THE BALANCE, IT IS THE PERFECT BALANCE, IT IS THE DIFFERENCE IN THIS WONDERFUL DIMENSION, THAT MAKES IT SO WONDERFUL.* Does that not give you a feeling of relief, as you realize you don't have to fix it? Does it not get you off the hook, as we say to you, "It's not your work to fix it?" Does it make you feel all right when we say, "You can try to fix it if you want. Go for it. Give it your all."

Talk about the things that are important. Certainly, give your influence where you are wanting to give it. But give it from point of joy, not from point of frustration.

As you try to fix it all, usually you feel more frustration than you do joy. That is why we say to you (Jerry) that as you lie on the rock and feel joyful, you are doing more positive than the one who is out there handing out flyers trying to convince people that there is a great war that we are involved in, you see, because that one is influencing disharmony while you are feeling your harmony, and therefore influencing that. You are getting the picture?

## CONSIDERING ARTHRITIS

QUESTION: Arthritis is interfering with my lifestyle. I feel very positive that I have control over my body, but I'd like to have some more help.

ABRAHAM: *We will correct your statement. You would like to feel very powerfully about the control of your body. And if you really did, arthritis would not be bothering you. Now, we sounded a little abrupt, but the reason we started there is because that is what lies at the heart of most of your not getting what you want.* That is what makes you look for scapegoats because you can't figure out how you're doing it.

Many will say to us, "ABRAHAM, this must be wrong. You must have left something important out, because I've wanted this for a very long time and it keeps not coming." And we say, sometimes you fool yourself with your words. You say, "I want," when what you are really meaning is, "I want, I want, I want," (pleading) which means, "I don't have it. I need it. It is gone." So much attention, using words, "want," but meaning "need" or feeling lack. Oh, this is a big one for you — the Universe doesn't speak English, you see. The "fairies of the Universe"...We are having fun with that....The Laws of the Universe — by which all things come to you — responds to blocks of thought and the corresponding feeling, but does not understand English, anyway.

*Whether you say "want" or "intend" or "know" or "am" or "be," it is the way that you feel that is being acted upon, you see. And so, as you are saying "I want" but you are feeling otherwise — then you are getting the*

240

*result of the predominant feeling.*

You are doing very well. We are exaggerating this point for the benefit of the subject, because the physical apparatus is something that everyone is interested in, who is physical.

Your Inner Being is aware of your apparatus and is aware of everything you intend or give thought to about it, and you are literally attracting, by virtue of your thought, that which you are experiencing.

And so, if you are now experiencing, by virtue of past thoughts, something that you are now not wanting, all you have to do is change the thought about it and focus upon the Energy that is bringing you the relief that you seek.

It isn't easy to concentrate upon a healthy foot when you have a throbbing toe, for the more you think about it the more it hurts. And you understand, from this experience, that pain is really very much a perceptual thing, because even though you have much pain, it comes and goes. Sometimes it's there and sometimes it isn't. And if you will pay attention, you will notice that at the time that you are thinking about other things most dominantly, that is the time that you are realizing that you are not feeling the pain the most. It is in your times of weaker interest on other subjects that that often comes up, or in your time of physical tiredness, or that sort of thing.

*IF YOU CAN ACCEPT THAT YOUR BODY WILL ABSOLUTELY RESPOND TO YOUR THOUGHT, AND YOU WILL GIVE YOUR THOUGHT NOT TO THE PAIN BUT TO THE FEELING GOOD. IF SOMETHING HURTS, THEN THINK ABOUT WHAT DOESN'T HURT. GIVE YOUR ATTENTION TO THAT, AND YOU WILL NOTICE GREAT RELIEF. AND OVER A PERIOD OF TIME YOU WILL HAVE TOTAL RESTORATION.*

*THERE IS NOT A PHYSICAL APPARATUS, NO MATTER WHAT THE DEGREE OF DETERIORATION, THAT CANNOT BE RESTORED TO FULL FUNCTIONING PERFECT HEALTH. NOT ONE.*

Even if you've lost a part, even if something is missing, your body has great resiliency and ability to compensate, for it is thought that creates the response, not those physical things, anyway. Oh, we agree that there are some major organs that once they are removed you are no longer experiencing, but that is a very extreme case. This is something very simple.

## CONSIDERING TRANSEXUALTIY

**QUESTION:** *The other is a question of what does* ABRAHAM *have to say about a person dealing with transsexuality?*

**ABRAHAM:** There is much to say about that subject. It is a very broad subject. Are you asking in terms of, is it right or is it wrong?

**QUESTION:** No, just how to make a decision, which way to go?

**ABRAHAM:** We would say give your attention, again, from the inside out, seeking joy, seeking freedom, seeking satisfaction, seeking feeling of freedom, seeking feeling of Well-being, and then identify that you are wanting to have a relationship that is satisfying in general ways rather than in the specific ways — and then be inspired to the doing.

*We would encourage anyone, regarding any subject, even this big subject that is so controversial in your time, we would encourage you to not worry about what anyone else's opinion is, for they cannot understand why any of you make the decisions that you make.*

We had a very wonderful example of that. A woman, a very wonderful woman, living here in the state of California, and as many of you, she had heard recordings and had talked with Esther and Jerry and ABRAHAM on the telephone, and she then came to Texas for a visit. And as she first approached Jerry and Esther's home, her feeling was one of disappointment, for their property is one small acre and their house is about 1600 square feet. And her envisonment of those who speak for Abraham, who have access to the power of the Universe, is that they would live in something extraordinary, something that would satisfy all of *her* ideas of what

242

happiness and Well-being are about. And she comes from a very beautiful land and a very beautiful house overlooking the very beautiful ocean. And so, as she said, to Esther, words that let Esther know that she was feeling disappointment, Esther felt them for a moment, as would most of you who are seeking approval of others, you see. But then, as Esther regained her balance, she remembered the set of intentions that she and her mate had established prior to the attraction of this home. This property satisfying all intentions that they held, so much so, that just being there delights them. Esther realized, for the first time, clearly, *"Someone who does not understand one's set of intentions cannot possibly feel the same gratification from the experience.*

Now let us tell you about this business of sexuality. Let us tell you what is underlying, and at the very basis for, the decision that many make to resist what society says is appropriate and rebel and seek their own freedom to be. There are many who are teachers who are understanding so clearly that they are the creators of their experience and that they are not here to conform or to teach conformity, but that they are here to satisfy their own intentions. *There are those of you who are teachers that are here wanting to express, very clearly, that what you do does not need to affect any other — and that if they have the ability to restrict your freedom, then you have the ability to restrict theirs. And who gets to choose what is right?*

What is present, is not working. Look around. You are killing one another, in great numbers, as you are trying to justify your religious and political wars, your wars that say, "These are the rules that are right, and since you are not conforming with these sets of rules, off with your head, or down with your country," you see.

And so, we say, there are many of those who are very powerful from their perspective of Non-physical inner — inner perspective — who are so much wanting to make the point of freedom and wanting to be individual creators under very extraordinary, almost irrational, circumstances, that they choose...we're not saying that they came forth into the physical body with that decision. We are saying that that decision was so strong within them, as they emerged forth into this physical body, that they were inspired to that action, because it was an avenue that would let them find their freedom. Unfortunately, most of them have not found that freedom because they're still looking for approval. And so, they are wanting to speak what they do, openly, and they are wanting the world to say, "We applaud it," or "We agree with it," which is just as much doing to the others what they have been accusing the others of doing to them. You are following?

To ask for others to approve of what you are doing, doesn't get you any further ahead than to feel the negativity of their disapproval of you.

In other words...here it is....we've been beating around the bush long enough: *If all of you, or if any of you, or if you, could reach the point of acknowledging that your work is to find harmony with you, period, and that what anybody else thinks about it, has nothing to do with your experience — you would all have a much happier experience, and you would be of much more value to all.*

As Esther tries to express to her mother her joy of working with ABRAHAM, her offering terrifies her mother. The same experience brings blissful joy to one and tremendous terror to the other, because of the set of beliefs that are currently within each of the two women. As Esther tries to get her mother to understand ABRAHAM, she only makes it worse. And as her mother tries to get Esther to understand how bad ABRAHAM is, it only makes the relationship worse. But as each of them steps back from that issue and focuses upon the fact that what they want is harmony with one another and talk about the safe subjects: "How is the weather, how is the chicken, how is the daughter, how is father, how are you doing, are you happy, I think of you often, I love you very much, I'm so appreciative of all of the time we have had together, what you have offered me has meant a great deal, I think of you every day, for one reason or another. I look around my home and see the beautiful things that you've added, and I'm filled with such love as I think of you,

Mother." As Esther is focused upon what she is *wanting* to see in her mother, she extracts harmony forth. And as her mother focuses upon things she is wanting to see in Esther, she extracts harmony forth. And as either of them focus upon the one thing that drives both of them crazy, they have a terrible experience.

*As you stop trying to get the others to agree with you about everything, and just be, and seek harmony with self, and then let them find their harmony with you as you look for your harmony with them — then you are in a very good place.*

## CONSIDERING BIRTH CONTROL AND SEX

QUESTION: I'm going to go ahead and ask this. I feel funny. It's on the subject of sex. I've always been confused about it. I mean, what's it for? I mean, couldn't we do without it? Is that what causes pregnancy or do they just say that?

ABRAHAM: No, it is really what causes pregnancy. (Group laughter) Now, often the action is inspired from a long train of thought before. In other words, let us say, a woman really wants a baby, and even though she is going through the physical action of sex, she does not find herself with the baby, and so, the sex is part of the physical process that facilitates the greater wanting, but the greater wanting must also be in alignment before the whole thing comes together. What it's for is really for the perpetuation of your species. That is the reason that it is an inherent, very deep seated desire.

QUESTION: *So then, is birth control evil?*

ABRAHAM: We are not saying that it is important that everyone who is a part of the species be interested in it. In other words, certainly there are many who will come forth and...Oh, you are thinking that we are saying that sex is only for the purpose of having babies. We are saying that it is for the purpose of enhancing your experience, and enhancing your experience includes the perpetuation of your species. Certainly, birth control is not evil. Birth control is decision to have sex without having baby.

QUESTION: So then, some people think that's evil.

ABRAHAM: *Some people think a lot of things are evil. We do not think that anything is evil. We think that all things are choice, you see.* In other words, you have continual options. Let us follow this through for a moment.

QUESTION: You were going to ask, "What brings forth the question?" It just seems that sex seems to cause so many problems.

ABRAHAM: It is attention to lack that causes negative emotion, always, and so, sexuality, because it has been distorted, brings forth the attention to lack of worthiness, to lack of righteousness ... It is a very complicated subject.

QUESTION: So it's just another part of our physical experience. And it's not either good or bad, it's just there.

ABRAHAM: That is correct. It is as good as you are expecting it to be, or as bad as you are expecting it to be. As is every other aspect of your experience.

You see, you come together, as two, for the purpose of cocreating. In other words, any time that two minds come together, then there is a greater pool of thought. That is the reason it is so satisfying to come together as a group. And that is the reason that sexuality can be satisfying, or unsatisfying, just as coming together in thought can be satisfying or unsatisfying. You are seeking harmony. And a truly gratifying sexual experience is one where two come together for the purpose of that harmony, for the purpose of each being uplifted by the physical expression, you see. *Anytime two come together for any experience, it is infinitely more satisfying than one, because as uplifters, it is wonderful to be happy, but is it not even more wonderful to be with others who are happy?* Do you not find your joy even more magnified when you are having joy with another? And so, in that sense, sexuality is a way that two physical beings can come together and, in a physical way, experience more than what one can experience singularly. And the reason that there is that climactic point, that point of ecstasy, is because one coming together with one in harmony, one plus one is many times more than two. You are following? The reason that more, most, do not experience sexuality in the exquisite delicious way that it is intended, or that is possible, is because of their attention to lack. Because they believe, in the action, that they are doing something wrong, or that they believe, that in the action, that they are less than they could be, or should be, or because the two, under normal circumstances, are not in harmony. That is the biggest confusion. Two that are out of harmony in every other way come together sexually and are surprised that they cannot find harmony, sexually — when it is more of a psychic thing than it is a physical thing.

*And so, when you have the pleasure of coming together in harmony with one with whom you are in tune with psychically, emotionally, as well as physically — then you have ecstasy.*

QUESTION: Thank you.

ABRAHAM: It would be a good topic for a very long discussion, for there are many facets to it that could be explored. But, primarily, we have covered them. Greatest attention to lack, being the culprit. But then isn't it always?

### THE NIGHT THEY DANCED THE HULA

QUESTION: Margaret Mead found a culture in which there was sexual activity from puberty but there was no pregnancy until the couple got married. Now, they believed so strongly that that wasn't going to occur?
ABRAHAM: Correct. Their beliefs affected their experience.

247

Absolutely. You see, they were not distorted regarding the subject of sex, and so they were so in tune that their desire not to have pregnancy outside of marriage caused them not to be inspired to the interaction at the time that it would cause pregnancy. In other words, that was the night they danced the hula.

JERRY: Esther's body is taking a little beating this evening.

ABRAHAM: Uhmmm....

QUESTIONER: ....a concerned husband?

JERRY: Yeah, well....(group laughter)

ABRAHAM: We have a very strong agreement with Esther. It is what goes on at the beginning of the sessions as her head is spinning around and she is sitting here breathing before she begins speaking. She is saying, "ABRAHAM, I am wanting to speak, clearly, your words. I am wanting this to be an empowering experience for me and for those who are here. I am wanting to be uplifted. I am wanting to have fun. And I'm wanting it to be an experience of Well-being for my physical apparatus." And we say, "Agreed, agreed, agreed, agreed." And so, you need not worry, for our motion with Esther is our way of keeping the Energy flowing through her. That way we don't knock her eyes out of her sockets or blow her socks off, you see. It is a good time for segment of refreshment, however.

JERRY: Yes, it sure is. Yes.

ABRAHAM: We are complete.

(intermission)

ABRAHAM: Now what are you wanting to talk about?
## WORKING WITH KIDS AT RISK

**QUESTION:** I'd like to talk about something ABRAHAM, that I'm confused about. *My focus, from ABRAHAM'S point of view, seems like it's negative. I work with youth at risk, kids that are the bottom one percent of the population and labeled as real troubled kids. So a lot of the Energy is negative, and yet I feel like it's real important work for me.*

**ABRAHAM:** Absolutely. It is important from your perspective; it is important from their perspective; it is important from the perspective of All-That-Is.

Let us tell you something about that. This will help you a great deal. If someone you did not know called you on the telephone and said, "I will never see you again," you would say, "Who cares?" In other words, the lack of them would not bother you, because there was not wanting to begin with. THE POINT WE ARE MAKING IS, WHEN YOU FEEL GREAT NEGATIVE EMOTION, IT IS BECAUSE THIS IS AN IMPORTANT ISSUE TO YOU.

*As you meet those other beings who are acting out, behaviorally, in extreme, negative ways, you may celebrate with us about it, and say, "This is wonderful, for this is a powerful wanter."*

We would far rather see someone acting out in tremendous negativity than saying, "Who cares," because wanting is the beginning of all deliberate creating, you see, while not caring is not deliberate or not powerful. And then we pivot upon it. We say, "We know there is tremendous wanting and they are currently focused upon the lack of it, and that is why they are feeling such exaggerated negativity. What is it that they want?" And then we began to visualize, on their behalf, what it is that we believe that they want. And then we are inspired to words that assist them.

They are very smart, most of them, very powerful beings. They have come forth at this time, in this experience, because they are wanting to make a difference. They have chosen, much of it not deliberate, but they have chosen all sorts of experiences that have given them a very large data base, so they really, really know what they don't want. And we know that from that experience they will be those that, in the years to come, they will be the ones who very clearly are — much more clearly than many — are able to speak what they *do* want, because of the exaggerated experience of what they don't want.

As they hear you, what they are wanting from you is that you will go away and leave them alone. Really, what they want from you is their freedom. And so, your mere existence threatens them a little bit; that is why they resist you so much. They resist any authority that has been thrust upon them to try to straighten them out, because they don't feel there is anything to straighten out. They think they are where they should be, and everything else needs to be straightened out, you see. And, in many ways, we are not so disagreeing with that, because they are more of the attitude of live and let live. Truly, they are more of the attitude of being free and allowing others. They, for the most part, would be much more willing to allow you to do whatever you want than most "respected" citizens of the community would be willing to allow them. So they are in a much better place than most of you see them. And so, if you will look at them through these new eyes, you will be inspired to some words and processes that may assist you a great deal.

We would say to them, things such as you've heard us say to Esther. As Esther was feeling so overwhelmed, even to the point of tears, we said, "What do you want?" And the first thing she stated, or near it, was what she didn't want. That is very common. So you may repeat the question, "Well, it is pretty obvious what you don't want. What I am wanting to talk about is what you *do* want."

And they might be cute with you; they might say, "I want you to go away. I want to get out of here. I want to be left alone."

Then follow them with that. Say, "I don't blame you a bit. I think that is a very wise statement, and I am pleased that you are saying what you mean. So much of the world does not do that. So much of the world says one thing while they mean another. And so, I am appreciating your telling me what you really think, because until we're communicating honestly, we can't be of any value to either one." And then say to them, "Now, what is it that you want?"

And again they will say what they don't want, and listen to them. Listen to them. More of your work is in listening than it is in offering. And as you listen to them, you'll get a very clear picture of what they don't want, which will give you a clear picture of what they *do* want. And then you may say to them, "Now from this position, very clearly stated of what you don't want, I think that you've never been in a better position of stating what you do want. What is it?"

They will say, "Well, what difference does it make? Saying what I do want doesn't make any difference."

"Whether it makes a difference or not I would like to hear it. I would like to know what you want. You've told me what you don't want, and I respect that. Now I would like to hear what you do want," so that you get them talking. Get them talking. Get them in the habit of knowing that whenever they think of what they don't want, that on the other side of that is what they do want.

You will bring them to a position that they will look forward to visiting with you, because they will begin to notice — they can't help it — that when they're talking about what they don't want, they feel rotten. And when they're talking about what they do want, they feel better. And because all of you want to feel good, they will start seeing their interaction with you as something that feels good; therefore, it will be something that is sought after. You will not be a threat any longer, something to be resisted. You will be an ally. Someone that understands.

*You are not trying to get them to stop doing anything. You are wanting to guide them to identifying what they do want so that they can attract what they do want instead of what they don't want.*

You can't stop doing something. Did you know that? No matter how hard you try, you can't stop doing something. You can start doing something else. But you can't stop being. You can't stop offering yourself. You can't stop being.

*And so, all that you are wanting, when you are wanting somebody to stop doing something, is to put their focus upon something else. To begin doing something else. To replace one behavior with another. To replace one thought with another. To replace one feeling with another.* You see? We believe that will be of great help to you.

## WHEN FOCUSING ON UNWANTED WORLD ISSUES

QUESTIONER: Thank you. The second part, ABRAHAM, is ...I do a lot of work with Werner, Earhart and Associates, and I don't know if you know what that is, but basically it's focusing on the same thing you were talking about..., world issues. But I guess, from what I was hearing tonight, so much of that is negative. *I mean, when I'm looking at world hunger, when I'm looking at youth at risk....it really is a lot of negative focus.*

ABRAHAM: Again, any time there is negative *feeling,* it is an indication that there is great wanting. And so, if you immediately take your thought from what is bringing forth a negative feeling, or from focusing upon the problem, and you give your full attention to the solution, then you do not feel negative. *IT IS ONLY WHEN YOU FOCUS ON PROBLEM, THAT YOU FEEL NEGATIVE. WHEN YOU FOCUS ON SOLUTION, YOU FEEL BETTER.*

QUESTIONER: That's great, thank you.

ABRAHAM: And as long as you are feeling good, you're helping yourself and you're helping others. Good.

The Universe is responding to your block of thought, and sometimes you kid yourself; you say words that you don't mean. You say to your child, "I love you," when what you mean is, "I would like to wring your neck, for that which you are doing is making me feel terrible," while the child, no matter what you are saying, is knowing your meaning. And the Universe is responding in the same way.

## PEOPLE PLEASER FEELING A LOSS OF SELF

QUESTION: *I am a people-pleaser. I just work terribly hard to please most of the Universe, and in the process I sense a loss of self.* I can do real well with my oughts, but as far as wants, it's hard to get that. The other day I was at a function and I saw somebody coming, and I knew they were going to ask me to help out with a YMCA campaign, and I told myself, "Say no, say no, say no, say no." and...

ABRAHAM: And you said "Yes."

QUESTION: Within thirty seconds, I said, "yes." How can I change? How can I move out of people-pleasing and operate out of who I am and what I want?

ABRAHAM: Coming from a position, as most of the physical world has come, from a position of acting first, and going about life backwards, it will take a little bit of transition to get it squared away. In other words, you can't fix it from an action standpoint. That is the reason why you said "yes" instead of "no." Your decision to say "no" only happened in that moment. Your decision to say "yes" has been going on for many years.

*Your dominant intent is to please others...Your action always follows your dominant intent, and so, what is required for your action to be altered is that you must change your dominant intent — making your intent, first, to please yourself.* And that is really what the thrust of this gathering together has been about, here, tonight. The majority of what we have talked to you about, has been wanting to bring you to the point of knowing that it is okay to please yourself and to give you a new definition of selfish.

Most of the world sees selfish as something that is bad. You've heard them say to you, "Oh, you are so selfish," as if that is something that you should stop doing. Have you noticed that they call you "selfish" when you are not doing what they selfishly want? And when we say, "Ohhhh, you delightful, magnificent, selfish being," what we mean is, *you cannot see other than through the eyes of self, and if you are not pleasing self, you are oozing negativity, and if you are oozing negativity, you are not uplifting, anyway.*

Now, let us see if we can exaggerate this scenario a little bit, because we speak through the body of a woman who could be your identical twin. Coming from a small town where everyone knew what everyone was doing, and as she heard many talking about the others, she became aware that they talk about you. And so, she became aware that her behavior was important to the conversations that abound, and so she became one who always wanted to please and was unhappy, much of her experience, because she realized she couldn't please even two of them.

Now, you say "yes, yes, yes" out of habit, and then you resent it, then you beat up on them for asking, then you feel like you've gotten pushed into a corner. You say "yes" to the things you really mean "no" to, and then you resent it, and so you are filled with negative emotion. And so, even though you have said "yes" to something that you believe you should do, or you wouldn't have said "yes", it turns out to be a negative thing, because you are filled with negative resentment.

Here is the thing to do about it: As you are going to a gathering where you are interacting with any other, set forth your intention to have a good time. Start from the inside out. Think in terms of how you are wanting to *feel* or *be* : "I want to have a good time; I want to *be* clear; I want to *feel* good; I want to *feel* strong; I want to *feel* sure; I want to..." Talk about the things you are wanting to feel. You can do it in seconds. And then move into the areas of *having* ..."I am wanting to *have* conversations that uplift. I am wanting to have...", whatever. Whatever the occasion is, you would be better at knowing what you are wanting to have. And then, having just set forth that much intention, you have enough momentum going toward the satisfying of you, that when another comes to you and is asking you to do something that you know the action will not have satisfied what is within you, you will feel appreciation for them, and you will say something such as, "I am so pleased that you think enough of me to ask, and I really thank you. It is very much of a compliment that you are asking me to do this, but I have a very full agenda, right now. And I'm so much wanting to take care of these important issues in my experience, right now, that I just feel that doing one more thing might diffuse my Energy enough that I would not do you a good job and I wouldn't do me a good job, either. But thank you so much." Now you have left them feeling very good. Because they have complimented you, you have felt good about it, and you're not feeling like you're running away. You see, when you feel bad about what you're doing, you ooze it. And so, if you are saying things that make you feel good, then you can please you and please them, too. They will walk away, saying, "That is a very nice man and he has a very good reason." They wouldn't walk away saying, "Oh, that lazy bugger. He could do it if he wanted to." They would walk away feeling the power, because you are clear about what you are doing.

*There are only two hindrances to your deliberate creation, only two worth mentioning. One is influence from others, and the other is your own habits.*

You have an old habit of always saying "yes." You have an old habit of saying "yes," even to your own detriment. And you also have a habit of seeking approval from others. And so you have pretty well got both of those hindrances very well adapted into your experience.

Here is the way you get rid of it: by Segment Intending, by doing more deliberate intending of what you want.

Have you ever walked through a busy shopping center, or an airport or any place where there is a crowd of people, and you're undecided where you're going? You're just sort of waltzing through. Do you notice how many people get in your way and how they bump into you? You are buffeted about. But take the same situation, but where you are moving with purpose, do you not notice that they get out of your way?  As you are in the flow of things, it is as if you have the whole place to yourself.  You find yourself really enjoying the challenge of your agility.  You are understanding?

Well, that is what Segment Intending will do for you, *if you will stop, anytime you realize you are going into a new segment — which simply means a block of time when your intentions are different — if you will stop and say, "What am I wanting to feel in this segment?  What am I wanting to have?  What am I wanting to do?" It will come forth to you, very quickly, and then you will not be swept up by the influence of someone else's intentions.*  If you're not deliberate, and they are, they'll over power you every time.  It is Law.  It is momentum.  You are getting the point?

Good.  This powerful Energy that comes forth from Non-physical is there for all of you.  And the way that you utilize it affects your experience.

*When what you want and what you expect are all going in the same direction, you are so powerful that nobody can dissuade you.*  Nobody that is out of harmony.  And that is not a bad thing, for what happens is, you begin attracting those who are in harmony.  In other words you might find yourself at a time in your experience when you are wanting to fill that YMCA post.  And as you walk into the meeting on that night, thinking, "I have some extra time now," that one would come right to you, and you would embrace him with your ideas.  You would say, "I'm glad to see you.  Have you got anything for me to do?"  And he would say, "Funny you would say that.  I was just thinking..."  You are getting the point.  You are wanting to speak?

## TO CHANGE THE NEGATIVE SUBJECT

QUESTION: *What is the best way to change somebody's attention from a subject matter that they are really holding on to strongly?*  Somebody that you are in a relationship with and you can't just ignore them, and they are bringing up a subject, continually.  What's the best way to deal with this?

**ABRAHAM:** You have already discovered that what doesn't work is to oppose them. Because when you oppose them it just brings forth in them that much more resistance, because that is Law of Attraction at work.

Here is what we do: *When someone is upon a subject we are not enjoying and we sense that they are not enjoying it, either, because of the anger that is present, we realize that because they are feeling negative emotion, that their Inner Being is making a very important statement to them.*

You understand that emotion is guidance from your Inner Being letting you know how you are utilizing the Non-physical Energy. When you feel bad, your Inner Being is saying, you are working against what you are wanting. When you feel good, your Inner Being is saying, you are working toward what you are wanting, and so, when you see a friend, or another, feeling anger, you may acknowledge that their Inner Being is saying two very important things to them. The first thing is that this is an important issue to them. Ordinarily it is something stepping upon their toes of freedom or their toes of growth. It is usually one of those two things. And the other thing that their Inner Being is saying to them is, "you are working against what you want. You are faced in the opposing direction of what you are wanting." When you feel your own negative emotion, the way to stop feeling the negative emotion is to say, "I'm focused upon what I do not want. What do I want?" And there is never a better time for you to acknowledge what you *do* want than when you are feeling what you *don't* want.

*And so, you may pivot on behalf of your friend.* You may say, I see his anger, therefore I know that this is important to him. I also know that he is focused in opposition to what he really wants. And then, you do the "balance beam" thing where you step back to your inner point of view. You step back, back, back, and you say, "How is it that he wants to feel? Well I think he wants to feel free, and in this issue he is not feeling free, he is feeling confined." And so, for a moment, visualize him as free. And then try to envision what you think he wants to have. *And as you draw an image toward what you think he wants to have, you are taking the Non-physical Energy of the Universe, and upon his behalf you are focusing it toward what he wants.*

If you are not splitting your Energy by opposing him.... In other words, if you are now feeling better, and you will be, now your momentum is all going in one direction, and you are much more likely to sweep him up in that. Where, if you are opposing him, now you are on that sort of a downhill spiral with him. *The only thing that saves you is that you go your separate ways or that sooner or later you go to sleep, and that stops the trend of thought.* Although very often you wake up and take right off where you left off. But you are getting the point. It is a process of pivoting, you first, and then assisting the other.

A young father called and said, "My little son is wetting the bed. He's too big for that, and I'm at my wits end." We said, "When you come into his bedroom in the morning and you are aware that he has wet the bed, how do you feel?" And the young father said, "I feel disappointed and then angry." We said, "What do you say?" And he said, "I say, you are too big for this. We've talked about this before. Get out of your wet clothes and get in the bathtub." And we said, *"You are perpetuating bed wetting, for you are harmonizing with what he does not want."*

ANYTIME YOU ARE FEELING NEGATIVE EMOTION YOU ARE PER-PETUATING THE VERY THING YOU DO NOT WANT. We said, "Pivoting is in order." "What is pivoting?" Pivoting is the way you change your focus from what you don't want to what you do want — and you know you've pivoted because you feel better.

We said, "When you go in the bedroom in the morning and you see he has wet the bed again, and you feel that negative emotion which tells you what you don't want, stop and see if you can think about what you *do* want. What do you want?" And he said, "I want a little son that wakes up happy and dry and feeling proud of himself, rather than embarrassed and ashamed. I want a room that smells good, and a room that is fresh and a little son that is feeling better and not cranky." We said, "Good, ponder that a little bit, and then after you have gained that perspective, the words that will come out will be more like, 'Oh, this is part of growing up. We have all been through this, and you are growing up very fast. Now get out of those wet clothes and get in the bathtub.' This young father called two weeks later and said the bed wetting had stopped.

*Our point is that you perpetuate "bed wetting" in many of your friends as you see those things that you don't like in them, or that you know that they do not like in themselves, and you give your attention to that.*

*Do you know that even when you do not speak, you ooze. All of you are communicating much more by block of thought than you are through words.* And you have learned to deceive with your words. You deceive not only each other, but yourselves as well. We're not saying that you blatantly lie and that you are trying to deceive one another. We are saying that you use your words to fool yourselves. You say, "I want, I want, I really want," when you what you are saying to the Universe is, "I can't have it, I don't have it, I'm not worthy, I'm not smart enough." Even though you're using the words, "I want," what you are saying isn't the same thing.

Your Inner Being gives you an emotional response to tell you what you are saying to the Universe. YOU CANNOT WANT AND FEEL BAD AT THE SAME TIME. **You can focus upon the lack of what you want and feel bad.** That is Law, you see. Pivoting is the most important process in your experience, because it is the process whereby you chew upon the data of this life and decide, for now, what you want — and when you feel good you are on the path. When you feel bad, you are on the "balance beam", but you're on your way to a broken neck. Good to stop and back up.

Most physical beings go about life backwards. They say, "What should I do, what should I do?" Everything that you consider, "I don't know what to *do.*" We hear it every day, "I don't know what to *do.*" And we say, if you don't know what to do, action is not in order.

THE FACT THAT YOU ARE NOT KNOWING WHAT TO DO MEANS,

"STAND STILL, DON'T DO NOTHING." WHEN YOU ARE INSPIRED TO ACTION, THAT IS THE TIME TO MOVE, OTHERWISE YOUR ACTION IS ABSOLUTELY COUNTER-PRODUCTIVE. *Because it is not your action that is making it happen, anyway. It is your intent.* It is the oozing to the Universe that is making it happen. And so, most of you are so busy, so buried in activity, that you are tired. You are overwhelmed. And so what are you oozing? You are saying, "Not enough time, not enough money, not enough love...." And so, what are you getting back? You are too tired, you don't have enough money. Not enough people love you.... Exactly what you are asking for. Are you getting the point? And so, we say, go on vacation. Get yourself in a place of feeling good. Bring yourself to a point of feeling good. That is the giant pivot in the sky.

When you begin to feel good, then good things begin to come to you. Then and only then can you be inspired to the action that will please and satisfy you, you see. Fighting it out with your friends is certainly not the answer. Good.

## USING ACTION TO VALIDATE ONE'S EXISTENCE

QUESTION: *What I was going to ask about was more in the terms of action. I look, in my entire life, that action validates my existence.*

ABRAHAM: Most physical beings see it as that way.

QUESTION: And in being physical, the action must have been desired, or I wouldn't have become physical.

ABRAHAM: *Indeed. But, you never saw action as the means toward the end. You saw it as the way of enjoying the creation that you have created through thought. You see, physical beings have it all backwards. You think that it is through your action that you make things happen. And now, you are coming to understand that it is through the state of being that you make things happen, and from that state of being you are inspired to action. And the action enhances the state of being.*

When you are in that glorious flow of acting, out of your glorious wanting, that is delicious, but when you are like a little ant, carrying a very heavy load on your back, for the sake of trying to get over some crevasse of lack, then it is not so glorious, and that is the world you have learned from. The world you have learned from, at large, is trying to justify its existence through action. Let us see if we can find a bridge. Let us first assess it clearly.

Physical beings, we are speaking to you, and to many others, tend to validate your experience, or justify your existence, by acting. Thus, philosophies such as "If you want to make something of yourself you must work very hard." And, "Those who don't work, don't get." And, "Without pain there is no gain." Out of your quest for growth, and because you have become conditioned to believe that for you to have growth you must have pain, you look for the justification for your experience. In other words, if you're not hurting, you're not worthy.

Now what we want to help you understand is that regardless of your reason — whether it is your quest for success or your quest for worthiness, or your justification of your physical existence — ANY-TIME YOU ARE HURTING YOU ARE MISCREATING. ANY TIME YOU ARE FEELING PAIN, YOUR MAGNETIC POINT OF ATTRACTION IS ATTRACTING ALL SORTS OF THINGS THAT YOU DO NOT WANT INTO YOUR EXPERIENCE.

What we're talking about here is replacing some old habits that don't work with some new habits that do. Habits such as stopping and saying, as you are recognizing that you are moving into a new segment: "How do I want to feel? What do I want to have? And, what do I want to do in this segment?" Letting the action be inspired from the first. Of course, you have heard all of that from us before. So where are you now? What might we say to you that will dislodge you from this stuck place into new clarity?

# CATAPULTED FROM LACK TO INSIGHT

**QUESTION:** *Well, the correlation you made between my horrendous feeling of lack, many, many years ago, and what it catapulted me into, has given me insight I did not have before.*

**ABRAHAM:** Good, so you're not so ready to beat up on yourself from *this* position of lack, because you now see it as the launching pad to something you want.

**QUESTION:** Yes.

**ABRAHAM:** Picture the man who seeks fortune. And we do not mean to be materialistic, except everything in your environment is, and so it is a good point to start. He seeks fortune, but he does not have a fortune. So how does he get from his position of not having it, to having it? By acknowledging the good fortune in what he has. By looking for reasons to feel good about what he has. By taking the meager one hundred dollars, putting it in his pocket and acknowledging how valuable it is. "I can have that, I can have that, I can have that." Until that one hundred dollars will foster within him a feeling of prosperity. Now, we know that if this man will continue to do this, in very short order he will have 10, or 20, or 30 million dollars that he will be using to foster that feeling of prosperity. And we know, that in a very short time, he will look back upon that time that he had only one hundred dollars, and he will have a hard time remembering why it excited him. But from his position, right now, it will excite him if he will allow himself to focus.

What we are really saying to you is that under any and all conditions, if you will look for your reason to feel good, for it is always there, rather than look for your reason not to feel good, by virtue of some comparison of something outside of you, then you will be in that centered place of positive attraction, and from that centered place of positive attraction, you will move beyond and move beyond and move beyond.

COMPARISON IS YOUR DEATH TRAP. *It is the beginning point, and middle point, and ending point, of most defeat or failure — for it holds you in that position of negative emotion, which holds you in that place of negative attraction. And you simply cannot offer enough action to compensate for that. You just cannot. The way you feel is too powerful. Far, far, far too powerful.*

Let us take the example. You have all witnessed another who wants, very much, to feel good about self. It is innate within you. You want to appreciate yourself, because when you appreciate yourself, that feeling of Well-being that oozes out of you is glorious. And so, out of that wanting to appreciate yourself, sometimes you are fortunate enough, by the power of your wanting, to attract another into your experience who is already appreciating himself, and so he has enough to give you. By his appreciation of himself, he can appreciate you, which, by Law of Attraction, extracts that feeling of appreciation out of you. And so, then you say, "Ah, it feels good to be appreciated." And so, then you still don't understand what happened. You don't understand that this one drew it out of you. And so, now you are running around looking for approval. You seek it, you want it, and then you see another doing something magnificent, which causes you to feel less, because here is one doing something so wonderful or looking so beautiful or having so much, it doesn't matter what the subject is, and by your attention to what he has, that you don't have, you now focus upon your own lack, and thus comes forth the feeling of lack, which, in that case, you would call jealousy. And so, then, the tendency is to be critical of that, "It is improper for that one to want that, or to be that, or to do that," because your way is different. You think if you make this one not so grand, then the feeling of difference between you and that one will subside, and that is a predominant attitude that abounds in your society. It is a very critical society. Looking for reasons not to appreciate another, with the hope, the futile hope, of that bringing you to greater appreciation of self.

When we know, and you are coming to know, that that will never work.

*It is appreciation that begets appreciation. In other words, you must feel some appreciation for something in order to attract more of it, you see.*

And so, what it comes down to, under all circumstances, is looking ..."Look for the seed of equivalent benefit." And with those very few words, your friend Napoleon Hill said — he said it all. He is saying, look at what you've got here, in this sea of probabilities, and focus upon something that makes you feel good, not bad, good. And sometimes you have to look a while, because sometimes your habit is of finding fault. The biggest fault that you find is in yourself, and that is the reason that as you find yourself mad at yourself, you find that it is so contagious, until everybody's mad at themselves too, because you have not inspired or uplifted, and that is the same thing that you are doing to the Universe at large, you see.

The key is, starting from the inside out. Often you say, "I don't know what to do." True, you don't know what to do. There are infinite possibilities. And a bunch of them haven't worked, for you. A lot of them have been tried, and they haven't worked under what you think are the same conditions. *And so, you sort of pace around, you don't know what to do. Sometimes, you don't even know what you want to have. But you always, you always, if you will stop and think about it,* YOU ALWAYS KNOW HOW YOU WANT TO FEEL.

Play the game, "I know I would rather be happy than sad, I know I would rather be rich than poor, I know I would rather be fed than hungry, I know I would rather be uplifted than deflated. I know I would rather be powerful than weak. I know I would rather be focused than diffused. I know I would rather be..." Say it, say the words, say what you know you would rather be, until you are it, you see.

We know that the negative attention that the world offers to you about the subject of health, as they offer cancer and AIDS and emphysema, and diabetes ...they are throwing these things to you, and they are bringing your attention to them, and as you hear all of those things, you say, "No, no, not me." Holding tight and saying, "No, not me." Why do you shout so loud? Why is your outcry so powerful? It is because you do not feel your power to be healthy. They have influenced you to feel vulnerable and so you resist. Well, what happens when you resist? You are playing right into the hands of it. And so, what we are striving for, as a group here tonight, is to find that place of acknowledging your perfection, now. Acknowledge that there is no lack in your experience. Only a distorted, temporary, perception of it here and there. Cancer, no matter how exaggerated it is in a body, is only a distortion of reality brought about by this one's, whoever has it, attention to the subject long enough to have it. The reality of it is that your body is perfection.

Look at your bodies. Are you aware that within every cell of your body is another one of you. Do you not understand that your cells are regenerating, continuously? That you are becoming anew, over and over and over again? This is not the same body that was born 29 short years ago. We are learning well, are we not? (group laughing as ABRAHAM plays Esther's game of being 29 forever)

And so, as you acknowledge your perfection, as you say, "Here I am, healthy," and live with that for a moment. Envision yourself, and try to get to that feeling place. "Here I am, a magnificent mother. Here I am, a most creative artist. Here I am, a generator of thought and new ideas in the world." Find words that will exaggerate the *feeling* to you. "Here I am, here I am."

Friends, your work, your work, your work ...what you are to do has nothing to do with doing. *Your work is to bring yourself, in whatever way you can figure out to do it, to the point of feeling your strength, feeling your perfection, feeling your health, feeling your talent, feeling your wonderfulness. Feeling good about you.* Which means, if we were standing in your physical shoes and there was someone in our experience that was critical of us, we would make ourselves scarce from that one. That one would see very little of us, for you are not needing that sort of negative bolstering. If there was something that we predominantly thought about that always brought us to a feeling of lack, we would make a conscious effort to avoid that subject for a while. In other words, your work is to bring yourself to the point of feeling good, because it is from your point of feeling, that you attract all things.

*When we say, "You are creators," you think we are talking about creating furniture, or creating houses, or creating empires, or creating relationships. That isn't what we talk about when we talk about creating. We are talking about the creating of your state of being. And when you have understood that, and are giving that your dominant attention, then all of the physical trappings of this Universe will fall into alignment in such glorious fashion that you will amaze even yourself.* YOU CANNOT DO IT WITH ACTION. IT IS THROUGH FOCUSING UPON HOW YOU WANT TO FEEL.

## WHEN FEELING OUT OF PLACE HERE

QUESTION: What is it that's holding me back, still.

ABRAHAM: From what?

QUESTION: I don't know. I've been saying, I want to feel like I belong here.

ABRAHAM: On the planet?

QUESTION: On the planet. I wanna feel like it's OK that I'm here.

ABRAHAM: What it is friend ...it is common with our physical cohorts. In other words, those of you who are physical counterparts of the Non-physical family of teachers, in this case, specifically of ABRAHAM, are highly evolved beings who know your power, and so there is this feeling, sometimes, a frustrating one of being trapped in the mundaneness of the physical. It would be like knowing you are an eagle who can soar and then having somebody clip your wings, and say, "You are an eagle, but here, eagles don't fly." And so, you're walking around on the ground, knowing, remembering what it was like to fly, but not being able to get off the ground. And that is the whole point of our discussion with you, here.

*The majority of the world is not ready to hear what we have talked about here tonight. In other words, they are not ready to accept their limitlessness.* They are not ready to acknowledge the Universe, this physical realm, as their play shop. You are ready for it, but you have been fostered, intellectually, mentally, by the world that isn't ready, and so you still struggle back and forth. There is a part of you that is ready to soar and does soar, but it is the feeling of limitation that you are describing to us. And it is that feeling of limitation that we have been addressing all evening, is it not. Just leave the physical part aside, for a minute, while you acknowledge how powerful you are.

Let us say that you are not feeling well, you can't breathe through your nose, your eyes are watering, your entire body aches. You have something that has been diagnosed as the common cold, and you feel miserable. Do you fear for your life under those conditions? *Does this common cold, for which there is no known cure, threaten your life? It does not. And the reason that it does not, is because the evidence produced by others, brings about, within you, an expectation of recovery.* Cancer, on the other hand, a disease for which there is no known certain cure, does threaten your life, because the evidence— produced by others — brings about within you an expectation of doom    Are you understanding why cancer more often takes your life? The word, *cancer,* fills you with the fear, and the *fear* brings you to your physical end.    Now, the reason we brought forth that example is because the belief in cancer, or physical vulnerability, is part of that limitation that you struggle against. In other words, just one of many.

*There are so many physical beliefs that are not in harmony with your greater knowing, and so it is not unusual that from time to time you will just stand there and say, "What am I doing here in this place of madness, when I know that we have the potential of experiencing only joy? Why are we experiencing less than that?" That is what it is.*

## OUR DUTY TO SHARE THE INFORMATION?

QUESTION: Oh, I've really enjoyed being here. This is a first for me, and it's been really exciting. And I know that we're all on our own path and we're all at different levels, and my question is, *"What is our duty in sharing this enlightenment, or this information, with other people?"* I find that often, I kind of call it, people dump on you, telling you all their problems, and they're wanting some guidance, but yet they're not ready for where you are or what you're feeling, and it is such a frustrating place to be at that point. Where do you see our duty? Where does it start? Where does it end?

ABRAHAM: *YOU HAVE NO RESPONSIBILITY TO ANOTHER. YOUR REAL RESPONSIBILITY IS TO YOURSELF.*

Some have said, "ABRAHAM, you teach selfishness." And we say, "That is because unless you are selfish enough, or willing to focus through your own eyes, which is the only perspective that you have, enough, to bring yourself to a place of feeling good, you have nothing to offer the others, anyway."

When your friend is "dumping on you" as you say, of what value is that to you? But, often, when that friend is in that place of negativity, when you are now feeling responsibility, and so, out of your sense of duty, in trying to fix the lack, you try to help them — they just resist it, anyway. And so, what we encourage is not trying to deal with it head on.

*Here is what we do:* We pivot on their behalf. In other words, whenever we see someone feeling negative emotion, we acknowledge that their Inner Being is saying to them, "There is something you want, but that you are focused in opposition to." And then we imagine what it is they want. And it usually boils down to one of three things, or a combination of the three. Freedom and growth and joy. They are usually feeling stifled, like they are not moving forward, and so it is out of that feeling of lack that they are offering their negative emotion. And so, we just stop and acknowledge that they are absolutely free. That they are so free that their every thought and feeling attracts unto them, and then we feel better for them. *We envision them getting what it is we know that they want. We envision them moving through life experience and discovering what we have already come to discover. But we do not see ourselves as responsible to help them discover. We jut see them as discovering it.* AND THEN WE TRY TO BE THE BEST EXAMPLE THAT WE CAN BE FOR THEM TO DISCOVER IT.

Now if you are really wanting to roll up your sleeves and help them, you might help them see the correlation between what they are getting and what they've been thinking and feeling. Or you may say, "I have felt that way, but I noticed that the more I felt that way, the more I got it. And so, I started concentrating on not giving so much attention to that, and then I didn't attract so much of that."

In other words, with each one it will be different. You must be sensitive to where they are. You have hit upon it, perfectly. It is as if, let us say that you are a quantum physics instructor, in very advanced years in college. You would not enjoy, very much, the teaching of this information to the little ones in first grade, nor would the one in first grade enjoy hearing it from you. There would be lots of silence. Nobody saying much of anything, and nobody really communicating, because you are too far apart in your current interests, you see. *Much of the world is not ready for your understanding, but much of the world is ready, also. And by Law of Attraction, those who are ready for you are being drawn to you, just as you are all drawn to one another.*

And so, our encouragement is, keep your ears open. Keep your feelers out there. Tracy said that the dolphins have sonar or radar, or something. And we say, all of you have it. Keep your sensors open, and when you are having a conversation that is making you feel good, and you sense that the other is ready for some of what you know, offer it. As a tennis player you do not look for someone who doesn't play as well as you do. You look for someone who plays as well as you do, if not better, so that you can have fun in your interaction for the purpose of moving forward.

And that is the basic point that we are wanting you to hear. You are not here climbing the rungs of a ladder. This is not a testing ground of worthiness. You are not here trying to prove yourselves worthy of something. *You are here by the power of your wanting and you have come forth into this dimension in order to go beyond that which has been before. But if you are too far beyond that which another is, then you are of no value, but you are of value to those who are ready for you. So just be sensitive and you will recognize them as they will recognize you.*

It is through the clarity of your example that you have the greatest offering, for words don't teach. It is your beingness that offers, you see. And that is really why we interact with you. We have very little value here in your physical society. Oh, we can say the words that stimulate you to thought and offering, but it is your offering that influences and uplifts those who are here, you see. Just be the magnificent being that you are.

## THE ART OF CO-CREATION

QUESTION: I have so many questions. I've been trying to get some clarity and get them distilled down to one or two.

ABRAHAM: This is a good thing. Now this is a new segment of *your* experience. You have this little block of time where you have some time for asking some questions of ABRAHAM. And so your intent is, "I'm wanting to ask that which is most important to me. That which will be most beneficial to my experience." Now what is it?

QUESTION: I'm having problems co-creating with people. It's like I simply don't understand it or I'm not being able to get it. I knew, very early, that I created my own existence. It did not come as a shock to me. As a matter of fact, the first ABRAHAM tape I heard was very emotional for me, because I knew it, very clearly, and could see that everybody was creating their own experience. I thought, when I was young, that they were playing a game and it was like a play. I didn't realize that they were convinced that their actions were out of their hands.

In my life I've created a lot of things for myself, and very quickly, just like that. However, what I found was a lot of jealousy, a lot of misunderstanding and...

**ABRAHAM:** Toward you?

**QUESTION:** Yes, and I felt quite isolated and alone, and I quit doing it. I remember making the conscious decision that I cannot do this anymore. I felt so out of place here in this life. I've gone through several phases. Now, what I'm trying to do is, and probably have been all along, is find a place that was comfortable for me to fit in, because most people I knew did not know this, that I know, and when they saw me create what I wanted, I didn't have good reactions from other people.

In my co-creating, at the present, I've just gone through another big deal where I, in cooperation with my partner, tried to buy a house and pull it all together, and I did my part. He didn't do his, and the deal fell apart. I'm also working with him, and with other people, on doing a TV series. It's just incredibly frustrating for me, because somehow there's not a harmony. It isn't coming together, and I feel held back, pulled back, like I can't go ahead and move this show. And I'm experiencing a lot of frustration. I also can't write now. I'm having horrible blocks and not being able to go ahead with writing. I feel like I'm waiting for other people. I don't seem to understand how to work in cooperation.

**ABRAHAM:** Let us tell you. We are appreciating your words, very much, for that which you've described is something that everyone in the room has experienced.

*Co-creation is the advanced course of creation. In other words, before you can be an effective co-creator you must understand how it is that you create.* And at a very early age, as you say, you had a very clear picture of that. And so, as you were a soloist, as you were setting forth your thought of what you wanted and knowing that you could have it, it came. And what was happening then, was that you were taking this Non-physical Energy, just like the electricity in your home, you were contouring it with your thoughts of desire and belief, and you were getting. As others did not approve of you, because your abundance pointed out their lack, and they felt jealousy. Their jealousy. Because you were not Segment Intending — you did not know that at the time — you were not clear enough about your thought of feeling good under all conditions, and so you were affected by their negative influence towards you and that influence caused you to divert some of your Energy.

In other words, some of that belief about what could be, you began sending in the other direction. You said, "I want to be rich and famous — *but* I also want to have friends — and they don't seem to go together. I want to be powerful, *but* I don't want to be so powerful that others feel ineffective. I want to be powerful, I want to have all the things that I want, *but* don't want to stick out like a sore thumb in a world of those who cannot create, very well." And what began to occur, what happened, is that your lack of belief in the ability of others — because you sensed their jealousy whenever they saw you believing — caused you to believe that you could do it by yourself, but that when you work with somebody else, they're going to mess it up. That is all that it is.

And so, what you are wanting, is very simple. You will feel the relief of it even as we speak it, and you will see the evidence of it as you move forward. As you look within them for things you want to see, you will let them off the hook.

*Let us see if we can find an example that you can see clearly:* The little girl, two or three years old, sees something she wants. She could very well be you. In fact, this is your story. She sees something she wants, and it delights her. And as she looks at it, she takes this Non-physical Energy, and it comes into her thinking mechanism. She contours it toward what she wants, and she has no reason, at this point, to believe that it isn't good or that she can't have it. And so, all of her thought, belief and desire go in the same direction — and she is just radiating. "Oh, I would like to have that," she says to you. And you would find yourself moving heaven and earth to assist her, you see. But now, for whatever reason, because her little friends are jealous of her or because her mother is telling her "no," now this little one sees something she wants, but now she doesn't think she is going to get it. And so, she is whining or crying or throwing a little fit. Now how do you feel? Are you going to help her, or are you going to send her to her room? That is the way the Universe responds to you.

*WHEN ALL OF YOUR THOUGHT IS GOING TOWARD WHAT YOU ARE WANTING, IT IS YOURS.* All that has happened is that by virtue of the influence that has touched you, you have allowed your Energies to be split.

You remember a time when your Energy was not diverted, and now you are describing a time when often it is. And all that is required to round up that renegade Energy and get it going in the direction of what you are wanting is that you pivot, in the moment of feeling it, identify what is wrong, and then identify what is right, and then focus upon that.

You see, there is a stream of thought, a very common thread, that went through all of the things you said, and that was your disappointment in this one, disappointment in that one, this one didn't do his part, or whatever. As you get upon that thought, as powerful as you are — most others are powerless against it. In other words, when you think they're not going to do it, they are pretty much not going to do it — in your experience. But when you believe that they can, then you offer influence, because the other really wants to do it.

**QUESTIONER:** I attract, very easily, what I don't want, as well.

**ABRAHAM:** It is because you are very powerful. You have spent lifetimes coming to this. Oh, Esther is very powerful, too. She went to a hotel, stayed for one night and when the billing came, she was charged for two nights. And so, she made a telephone call and wrote a letter and expressed some dissatisfaction to the one on the telephone, both in writing and over the telephone; even talked to her mate about it, and her mate smiled at her, because he knew she was talking about what she did not want. And then, as she saw that, she justified her position, "It's not my fault. It's their fault. They messed it up." Within a very short time the next hotel did the same thing. And then the next one. And then the car rental agency. We said, "We think you don't like seven or eight hundred dollars in misapplied dollars. Wait until it gets up to about seven or eight thousand." We're not trying to be mean to Esther. We are wanting to point out to her that as she gives her attention to what she does not want, with the amount of Energy that is surging through her, as it is through all of you... You can't get anything other than what you think about.

Our friend talked to us, last evening, about discipline, believing that it is an action thing; that one must, in order to accomplish, make decisions and stick to them doggedly. *Discipline is of value, but discipline yourself to feel good. That is the only discipline you need.* Make a decision that you are going to do that — and speak that, and think that — which makes you feel good. That is the only thing you need to know.

*We could have boiled down all of these hours of babbling to you into one sentence, and that is, "SEEK THAT WHICH MAKES YOU FEEL GOOD AND GIVE YOUR ATTENTION TO THAT."*

Your writing blockage is the identical thing as the other. You are wanting it, but you believe you are blocked. You want it, but it isn't going very well. We were watching Esther and her mate, they were driving to their place of sleep last night, as many of you were. It was very late and they were very tired. Esther was driving the last leg of the journey, and she was feeling so tired that she was not certain that she was safe behind the wheel. Things were getting a little fuzzy, and the car did not feel as if the wheels were on the ground. She felt suspended as if her maneuvering of the car had no effect on the car. And so she said, "I'm too tired to drive," and immediately she felt herself even more enervated. And then she said, "Wait a minute. The Energy of the Universe is available to me. What do I want to use it for, right now? I am wanting to feel refreshed. I'm wanting to feel safe in my body and in this car. I'm wanting to transport us to our bed." Instantly. Instantly, she was alert, she was refreshed, she was smiling, she was looking around the car, a very new car to her; looking for things to play with. What is this? Oh, cruise control. How does that work? Windshield wipers. Now, she was not only driving, she was investigating the car and sailing home in safety. And the important part of the story is, not in drudgery, not just getting there because I don't have a choice other than sleeping on the side of the freeway. Getting there in absolute joy, because the Power of the Universe is available for her if she will but decide how she wants to use it. By the time they got back to the room, she wanted to go out dancing. Instant manifestation is it not?

Decide what you want as it regards your physical apparatus, and the way you feel. You feel bad? All you have to say is, "I want to feel good, I want to feel good, I want to feel good, I want to feel good, I want to feel good." And before you have said it ten times, you'll be feeling good. "I want to be inspired. I want to work. I want to put it upon the paper. I want to inspire the world. I want to do this. I want. I want. I want." Make your statements.

Make your statements of what you want, and utilize the Power of the Universe to have what you want. And any time you do the opposite, your Inner Being will give you a little nudge. And if you keep doing it, it will give you a little bigger nudge. And if you keep doing it, it will give you a little bigger nudge. Not because it is beating up on you. But because that is your bargain. *Your Inner Being said, "Any time your thoughts are out of harmony with one another, we will give you a nudge to let you know which is the one thought that is the most out of order so that you can alter it.*

You are in a much better place than you know, because never are you at a place of greater creation than when you are in intense emotion. And you have been at a very high emotional pitch. And so, we say, you have accomplished your pivoting as you have been here tonight.

Do not judge the way any of you feel, right now. You are tired. We have been talking too long, and you are ready to seek your refreshment. But it is our promise to you that as you awaken in the morning, you will awaken with greater clarity than you have had in a very long time.

*And if you will begin your day with this process:* Take three pieces of paper, set a timer for 15 minutes, write at the top of the first sheet: *To Be.* And write for one minute, only one minute, how you are wanting to *feel.* "I want to feel joyful. I want to feel free. I want to feel inspired. I want to feel prosperous. I want to feel...whatever." One minute only. Then go to the second sheet and for seven or eight minutes write: *To Have.* "I am wanting to have this relationship. I am wanting to have this house. I'm wanting to have these shoes, this car...whatever, this body." It doesn't matter. Tangible or not tangible, write what are you wanting to have. And then, on the third sheet, these things, for seven or eight minutes: *What I Will Do Today.* Once you have utilized this process for twenty or thirty, or so, days, you will discover that what is in your doing will harmonize with your state of being.

THIS IS THE PROCESS WHERE YOU GET IN HARMONY WITH YOU, AND THAT IS THE ONLY THING THAT MATTERS.

You receive thought from the Universe. You receive thought from those who surround you. You receive thought from your physical friends. You receive thought from your Non-physical friends. But the way that you respond to it by the way you feel tells you whether it is valuable or not.

*Don't try to figure so much out. Just concentrate on feeling good. As you receive the Non-physical flow of Energy, "current" is a very good way of describing it, as you receive this current of Energy — make more decisions about what you will do with it.*

It is as Esther was in the car last evening; that was such a valuable point of pivot for her, to realize that the power of the Universe was at her fingertips, or at her thinking-tips. In that moment, she didn't have to decide what she wanted forevermore — she didn't have to decide what would be a more effective plan for the next event, or whether we should alter these ABRAHAM sessions in some way. She didn't have to decide anything beyond that moment — all she had to say was, *"What do I want right now?"* And she said, "I want to feel happy and uplifted." That's all you need. And once you get in that place, everything else will come from there.

We have enjoyed, very much, this interaction. There has been tremendous value received by us, not only by you, for All-That-Is has benefited, and there are thousands, even though it is a small gathering here, thousands are sitting upon the Non-physical sidelines who are delighted with the clarity that has come forth as a result of your offering here this evening. This gathering has never been before unto all of the Universe. It is an absolutely unique experience, and your participation within it is tremendously appreciated.

*AS YOU GO FORTH, IN THE DAYS THAT FOLLOW, OUR GREATEST ENCOURAGEMENT FOR YOU IS THAT YOU SEEK JOY — AND ALL OF THE OTHER WILL BE INSPIRED FROM THAT PLACE.*

You will not be inspired to joyful action if you are feeling negative. It cannot be; it defies Law. So do whatever it takes to get yourself feeling good, and then watch, more deliberately. Be in more control of your thoughts so that you are feeling good more of the time. And develop a new habit of feeling good. You're very quick to develop habits, have you noticed? And this one will come very easily to you, because your Inner Being is in that place. Your Inner Being absolutely adores you. Your Inner Being is aware of your power and your strength and your worthiness. Your Inner Being knows that you have the ability to be or do or have anything that you want.

*There is great love here for you.  We are complete.*

# Notes

# Notes

*DIALOGUES WITH ABRAHAM*
*Abraham/Hicks*

# CATALOG ADDENDUM
# November, 1996

*The basis of life is Freedom*
*The objective of life is Joy*
*The result of life is Growth*

*Abraham,* 1989

*Abraham-Hicks Publications*
*P.O. Box 690070, San Antonio, TX 78269*
*Tel. (210) 755-2299 (area code subject to change)*
© Copyright 1996

# 1996-97 GENERAL WORKSHOP SCHEDULE

*For details, call Abraham-Hicks Publications at (210) 755-2299.*

| | |
|---|---|
| 11/16&17/96 .........El Paso, TX | 5/17/97 ...................San Antonio, TX |
| 11/30/96 .................San Antonio, TX | 5/29/97 ...................Cincinnati, OH |
| 12/7&8/96 ..............Los Angeles, CA | 5/31&6/1/97 ..........Detroit, MI |
| 12/14&15/96 ..........Maui, Hawaii | 6/7&8/97 ...............Seattle, WA |
| 1/11&12/97 ............Boca Raton, FL | 6/10/97 ...................Portland, OR |
| 1/18&19/97 ............Key West, FL | 6/14&15/97 ............Spokane, WA |
| 1/25/97 ..................Dallas, TX | 7/4&5/97 ...............Boulder, CO |
| 2/1&2/97 ................Los Angeles, CA | 7/6/97 .....................Fort Collins, CO |
| 2/8&9/97 ................San Diego, CA | 7/19&20/97 ............Chicago, IL |
| 2/15&16/97 ............Orlando, FL | 7/26&27/97 ............Los Angeles, CA |
| 2/18/97 ..................Melbourne, FL | 8/2&3/97 ...............San Diego, CA |
| 2/27&28/97 ............San Francisco, CA | 8/30&31/97 ............Larkspur, CA |
| 3/1&2/97 ................San Francisco, CA | 9/6&7/97 ...............Foster City, CA |
| 3/8&9/97 ................Sacramento, CA | 9/13&14/97 ............Columbia, SC |
| 3/15/97 ..................Austin, TX | 9/20&21/97 ............Asheville, NC |
| 3/16/97 ..................Houston, TX | 10/4&5/97 ..............Boston, MA |
| 3/29&30/97 ............Tallahassee, FL | 10/11&12/97 ..........Rye, NY |
| 4/5&6/97 ................Phoenix, AZ | 10/14/97 .................Syracuse, NY |
| 4/12&13/97 ............VA Beach, VA | 10/16/97 .................Philadelphia, PA |
| 4/15/97 ..................Philadelphia, PA | 10/18&19/97 .........Rye, NY |
| 4/19&20/97 ............Silver Spring, MD | 11/1&2/97 .............Chicago, IL |
| 4/26&27/97 ............Albuquerque, NM | 11/15&16/97 ..........El Paso, TX |
| 5/3&4/97 ...............Rye, NY | 12/6&7/97 .............Los Angeles, CA |
| 5/6/97 ....................Albany, NY | 12/13&14/97 ..........Maui, HI |

COMMENT FROM WORKSHOP PARTICIPANT:
...Thank you for scheduling the extra workshop in Dallas. We really appreciated it! It was even nicer this time because at least a dozen of my friends were there, too. I am always convinced that each seminar is better than the last — but maybe I/we are just a bit more receptive each time. Love, SD — Dallas

*From time to time there are changes in our scheduling, so please reserve with our San Antonio office at (210) 755-2299, before attending any function. Pre-paid reservations required.*

# 90 DAY EVENT SCHEDULE DETAILS

*From time to time there are changes in our scheduling, so please reserve with our San Antonio office at (210) 755-2299.*
*Prepaid reservations are required.*

11/16&17/96 — El Paso, TX — Held at Embassy Suites, 6100 Gateway East, El Paso, TX 79905. For directions c (915) 779-6222. Saturday 10 am to 4:15 pm. Sunday 10 am to 12:45pm. $170.00 per person.

11/30/96 — San Antonio, TX — Held at Jerry & Esther's home at Fair Oaks Ranch. Session is from 2pm to 5:45pm. $75.00 per person. (SOLD OUT)

12/7&8/96 — Los Angeles, CA — Held at Courtyard Marriott, 13480 Maxella Avenue, Marina Del Rey, CA 90292. For directions call (310) 822-8555. Saturday 10 am to 4:15 pm. Sunday 10 am to 12:45 pm. $170.00 per person.

12/14&15/96 — Maui, Hawaii — Held at Maui Marriott on Kaanapali Beach, 100 Nohoea Kai Drive, Lahaina, Maui, HI 96761. For Directions or to book your sleeping room call (808) 667-1200. When booking sleeping rooms tell them you are with Abraham-Hicks Publications group and they will give you the group rate. Saturday 10 am to 4:15 pm. Sunday 10 am to 12:45 pm. $170.00 per person.

1/11&12/97 — Boca Raton, FL — Held at Embassy Suites, 661 N.W. 53rd St., Boca Raton, FL. For directions call (407) 994-8200. Saturday 10 am to 4:15 pm. Sunday 10 am to 12:45 pm. $170.00 per person.

1/18&19/97 — Key West, FL — Held at Ocean Key House, Zero Duval Street, Key West, FL 33040. For directions call (305) 296-7701. Saturday 10 am to 4:15 pm. Sunday 10 am to 12:45 pm. $170.00 per person.

1/25/96 — Dallas, TX — Held at Courtyard Marriott, Northpark, 10325 N. Central Expressway, Dallas, TX 75231. For directions call (214) 739-2500. Saturday 10 am to 4:15 pm. $110 per person.

2/1&2/97 — Los Angeles, CA — Held at Courtyard Marriott, 13480 Maxella Avenue, Marina Del Rey, CA 90292. For directions call (310) 822-8555. Saturday 10 am to 4:15 pm. Sunday 10 am to 12:45 pm. $170.00 per person.

2/8&9/96 — San Diego/La Jolla, CA — Held at Embassy Suites, 4550 La Jolla Village Drive, San Diego, CA 92122. For directions call (619) 453-0400. For sleeping rooms call 1 800 EMBASSY. Tell them you are with Abraham-Hicks Publications group. We have blocked rooms for Friday 2/8 and Saturday 2/9. Saturday 10 am to 4:15 pm. Sunday 10 am to 12:45 pm. $170.00 per person.

2/15/&16/97 — Orlando, FL — Held at Renaissance Orlando Hotel, 5445 Forbes Place, Orlando, FL 32812. Saturday 10 am to 4:15 pm. Sunday 10 am to 12:45 pm. $170.00 per person. (Daytona 500 is in Orlando this weekend and Renaissance has no more sleeping rooms. We have blocked some sleeping rooms for Friday and Saturday night across the street at Courtyard Marriott. Call Sam at (407) 240-7200 and tell him you are with Abraham-Hicks Publications. Cut off for these rooms is 1/30/96.

# Discover Your Vibrational Matches!
## San Diego, CA — G-2/24/96

The formula for Deliberate Creation says, *"I will identify that which I am wanting,"* which means make a decision, *"and then I will achieve vibrational harmony with my own decision."*

*In every moment that you are awake or conscious, you are radiating a signal, not so different from a radio signal, and the entire Universe is accepting that electronic vibration as your point of attraction and is matching it with other things that are like it.* Often, even though you are saying, "I want more money," your signal is not in vibrational harmony with that. So your words are empty and hollow, while your signal is actually often in direct opposition to the very thing you are saying you are wanting.

*Over the next few days, hold in your mind a phrase, "Vibrational Match." In other words, that which is like unto itself is drawn."* So when I vibrationally match the vibration of my own desire, then there is no contradiction. There is no resistance. The Energy is pure. And when that happens, the Universe must deliver to me that which is in vibrational harmony with my desire, my decision and my point of attraction. Because, in every moment, everything that is coming to me is coming in response to my vibrational output — every single thing.

*No one, nothing, can deny you your desire. Only you can deny your own desire, through contradictory vibration. No one has ever kept you from anything. Nobody's keeping you from being rich and famous. Nobody's keeping you from being well. No one but you. And the reason that you do it is because you observe things that cause you to offer a vibrational outpouring that doesn't match the vibration of your own desire.*

*One who is predominantly an observer, thrives in good times but suffers in bad times,* because what you observe is reflected in your vibration. The Universe accepts that vibration as your point of attraction and then matches it with other things like it, and then you have more to observe which causes you to offer more of a vibrational offering which the Universe accepts as your point of attraction and gives you more like it... So the good gets gooder and the bad gets badder. *But a visionary thrives in all times* — because a visionary is one who learns to flow Energy because of decision, not because of what-is.

Do you ever get to a place where you just cannot stand what is happening? That's a very powerful place to be. It won't get you what you want, but it's the beginning of the process, because when you reach that place, always within that contrasting experience erupts clarity of what you want. And so, then you say "I don't want that. What I do want is this. I don't want that. What I do want is this." And even though your words, or our words here, sound negative, it is the beginning of Deliberate Creating.

Now, this is the part that begins to go wrong for almost everyone. In that place of decision, you know what you want, but you are still in a very contradicted Energy position because your statement of desire is coming out of the keen awareness of what you do not want. So you are not in a place of purely attracting what you want. You are in the beginning of your creation. Now your work begins and it usually takes two to three weeks. Now that you know what you want, your work is to find thought and words and actions — most of all the feeling place — that matches the decision that you have just made.

Here is the cycle that we see most of you — once you really get the hang of this — living: You live some contrast. You know what you don't want. You reach that place of shouting "No" at it. Out of the "No," erupts clarity of what "Yes" is. You feel your strong decision. You're still very contradicted in your Energy. Then you spend two to three weeks getting the Energy lined up. When it lines up, you feel it. You can feel it click into place. It feels like relief. And when the Energy lines up, then almost instantly there is physical evidence of the alignment. And at the same moment, you are now standing in a new perspective with a new set of contrasting elements in your experience. Then the process begins again. In this now different level of achieving and wanting, you now are examining contrast again, and again you are saying "No" to some things, which brings you to the conclusion of "Yes." And again your Energy is contradicted, and again now you must find the vibrational alignment.

In every moment, you can feel whether you are matching or mismatching. When Esther was a little girl, she played a game with her sister. They called it "Memory". They would lay a deck of cards face down all over the table, and when it was your turn, you turned over two cards looking for two that matched. That's the thing we're wanting you to hold in your mind. *You are looking for Vibrational Matches — and you can tell by the way you feel when you've achieved that Vibrational Match. What you are getting always matches what you are vibrating, and what you are vibrating always matches what you are getting, without exception. They are always the same.*

Now sometimes, especially once you begin this Deliberate Creating Process, we see you feeling guarded and tentative in your offering, afraid that you might miscreate, afraid that you might get a manifestation that does not please you. And what we want to say to you, in a way that you can hear it, is that that is what physical manifestation is for. It helps you in the learning of the flowing of the Energy. So, if you have something in your experience that feels a little out of whack, no problem. Just offer your thought in a little bit more consistent vibration.

When Esther makes candy, her recipe book says, put these ingredients in the pot and cook it on your stove, and it doesn't say for how many minutes because the recipe book doesn't know how hot her fire is or how well her pan conducts the heat. Instead, her recipe book says, cook this substance to a soft ball or to a medium ball or to a hard ball. So as Esther is cooking this mixture, frequently she takes a little spoon full of the boiling candy and she dribbles it into a clear glass of cold water. If it is nowhere near ready, it just dissipates into the water. It makes the water cloudy. If it is getting closer to be ready, it forms a little clump in the bottom and as Esther pinches it, she can feel if it's soft or if it's medium or if it's firm. She can tell by doing and testing, when it is right where she wants it. And that's the way we want you to use your physical manifestation. Don't stand guarded and afraid that you might make a mistake. Instead,

(cont'd page 289)

**NEW !!!**
**G-SERIES TAPES**
**SPRING, 1996**

# *Discover Your Vibrational Matches!*

*There is hardly a day that goes by that I don't hear Esther speaking for Abraham and it really does make my day. I have found that the fastest way to get my valve open is to just pop in a tape, any Abraham tape, and bounce back up to 100%.*

*A friend came over to borrow some of my tapes and my husband said, "Be careful, these things are addictive!" And that's true. When I am making dinner , I automatically put a tape on to keep me company. I used to listen to music. Now, I revel in hearing Abraham's glorious answers...always uplifting, always kind and considerate. I listen to some tapes several times, and each time I hear something new.*

*Thank you over and over again for the wonderful window you have opened up to us. We all feel so good knowing that now we understand what this is all about and how to be deliberate creators. The big stuff is still a little scary. We're working on one now that would have been terrifying several years ago. We are both amazed that we can be so calm. We look forward to see you in Orlando. Love, G.M. — FL*

G-1/7/96 — To spiritually invest her material dollars? Eastern religions, meditation and the Non-physical Energy. The ultimate objective of a physical entity? Abraham would choose passion over fear, anytime. You can influence only as per vibrational matching. "Focus Wheeling" to purify his prosperity vibrations. What Abraham wants for each of us.

G-1/13/96 — Being a most effective Teacher of Well-Being. Should we ignore the unwanted in another? When fearing the fear of thought control. How vulnerable are we to Mass Consciousness? Do our cells remember from other lifetimes? Why is a "desperate" wanting counterproductive? When to take action on your vision.

G-1/27/96 — Difficulty in helping those who "need" you? Wanting a specific vs. general business growth. Her negative family conditions are positively shifting. They have created a fun specialty business. Some characteristics of the "Family of Teachers." Wanting "positive boundaries" for their first child. Why birds often serve as Non-physical messengers.

# G-SERIES TAPES SPRING, 1996
## (CONTINUED)

G-2/24/96 — Managing in midst of a heated argument. You can't defy the "forces of fat." When we can't get there from here. Resolving the dilemma of criticism of obesity. Can we simultaneously exist in another place? Does their different opinion make them wrong? A potty training and bottle wanting conflict.

G-2/25/96 — Discipline, can only net a mediocre experience. Her daughter is taking crashing Karate falls. Incapacitated mother existing in nursing home. Family of Teachers is finding each other. Daughter is caught up in parent's divorce. Painlessly observing the pleasure of diversity. A perspective of the evolution of physical.

G-3/2/96 — Shyness, critics and music conductors. Conscious cells, dead bodies and ghastly apparitions. Parent/Educator questions allowing children their freedom. When humans create the illusion of scarcity. Attorney choosing to publish "spiritual," technical works. To travel backward and forward through time? High points of new Deliberate Creation perspectives.

G-3/17/96 — "The 'imp' in me contradicts my desires." "Is the deck stacked against reality observers?" Focus Wheel, Prosperity and Parade of Processes. Benefits from friends who re-emerge early. A bisexual in love with a married man. Understanding school skipping, lawbreaking troublesome teenagers. Mandating legal adventure illegal, creates illegal adventurers.

G-3/30/96 — Contrast, decisions and contradicted Energy. Considering an infringement on the copyright laws. A pre-intended relationship as a co-creation. Wanting evidence of being a Master Creator. Mental health worker discusses "belief system" effects. "Vibrational Matching", in childlike terms. Infants, manifestations and "vibrational vocabularies".

G-3/31/96 — "Tithing of talents, treasures and time?" Feeling vulnerable to mate's "frivolous" legal decisions. Fearing her daughter will abandon her again. That vital feeling of lined up Energy. "I really like my political opponent." The evolution of a street gang member. To personally empower your governmental leaders.

G-4/13/96 — Trying to exclude exclusion is still including. You are individual perspectives of a greater whole. Deciphering a leaf-bearing dream of driving. High school "dropout" considers value of education. How do you feel about dollars without work? To attract an "Abraham" into my thoughts. The American Dream in process of achievement.

Here is a delicious, new adventure into a study of Spiritual Practicality. This is a one year experiential study of twelve evolving segments, of increasing intensity, of imagining and planning and manifesting.

There may be Study Groups that would prefer to experience these materials in as little as a twelve week period — and those decisions are for each individual or group facilitator to make relative to their cocreational desires.

Habits are usually created slowly. And since a major aspect of the value to you of using this material is the changing — often slowly — from unwanted habits of thought to habits of thought that are more appropriate to your current conscious desires — the most common use of this calendar will be as a joyous 365 day journey into a world of leading edge thought and experience.

You can begin experiencing the power of this calendar at any time throughout the year. You don't have to wait until the first of next year. However, in order to get into time sequence with the calendar it is best to start at the beginning of any month. Just let the first day of your first month be day one (page three) of this calendar.

After over 30 years of studying and teaching and enjoying the art of personal fulfillment, I have long understood the power of clarifying and writing out my decisions in appointment books, journals, organizers, etc. But as the years passed, I became aware that at the most joyous and highly productive segments of my life — I simply carried, daily, a fresh, updated sheet of paper in my pocket. This works!

The second sides of the pages are designed to accommodate your daily list of things to do — but as the course progresses, you will discover that they will be offering processes and techniques to fit the advancing stages of your progression within these materials.

Your only power to create your life is in this moment, and the Abraham-Hicks Daily Planning Calendar is designed to focus the purest of your intentions to your todays, the time in which you have your power.

- The Abraham-Hicks Calendar/Workbook is a tool. Utilize it to create, and to teach others to create, the perfect (by your ever changing standards) adventure in living.

- Use it as a medium of exchange: Exchange any habits of thought, word or action that no longer serve your best interests. Exchange them for bright fresh habits that are more appropriate to who you are in the current moment.

- Exchange any patterns of interaction that are not allowing of each individual's freedom, growth and joy — for ever changing cocreational interactions that allow the very best from every life you touch.

- Exchange any restrictions to your flow of health, relationships, abundance...Exchange them for an open flow — to and through you — of all that you will come to see as your perfect state of Well-being.

One day at a time you will be giving your attention to that which feels best to you, and you will, thereby, be creating for yourself the most progressively wonderful life that you can imagine.

From our hearts,

Jerry and Esther

---

(cont'd from page 285)

just keep saying "What I'm getting is what I'm vibrating. Hum. What I'm getting isn't pleasing me in every way. I think I could use a little more visualization and a little less observation. *The key for most of you will be to goose up your visualization and play down your observation.*

As far as your observation goes, we would like you to become very good selective sifters, because there's so much that you can observe that does match your own desire. But most people are not looking for those things, purposefully, because you have not known the power of thought. *Sometimes you're careful about what you say or sometimes you're careful about what you do — but few of you are really deliberate about what you think.* You sort of offer your thoughts as if they don't matter, and then you watch your words as if your words do matter. And what we want you to hear from us is that what matters is what you are radiating which means what matters is what you are feeling. If you're feeling fearful about something, you are sending contradictory Energy. If you're feeling angry about something, you're sending contradictory Energy. It is really as simple as that.

*The Universe does not know if your vibrational offering is because of what you are observing or visualizing. In either case, the Universe is matching it with things like it. So your work is to deliberately offer vibrations that are a Vibrational Match to what you want.*

— Abraham-Hicks, 6-2/24/96

# G-SERIES TAPES WINTER, 1995
## *YOUR MAGICAL CREATION BOX!*

G-10/8/95 — Using jelly beans as "Cosmic healing symbols." Very old souls inhabit crack baby's fetus. At each religion's heart was a connected individual. Your economy as a Stream of Energy. Beatles nightmare and a seductive guru. On starting a group of learning thinkers. In reality, every death is a suicide.

G-10/14/95 — Is this moment of negative judgment justified? The etiology of a schizophrenic scenario. Points to ponder when considering helping another. Feels blamed for her son's schizophrenic symptoms. When fear of wakefulness equals sleeplessness. Butterflies understand the joy of the journey. Are they uncomfortable in your "unrealistic" joy?

G-10/21/95 — "They need my help," a counterproductive belief. Why success begets success that begets success. To do about negatives in the workplace. Is this worth disconnecting your Life Force? On living each moment as a new beginning. Why his fear of being totally alive? When a murderer receives financial justice.

G-10/28/95 — The "yes" on other side of every "no." A new game: "My Magical Creation Box." Any way to understand our original Source? Smoking and drinking reduced on 120th birthday. Let your pleasurable vision be more dominant. Battered and bruised mom's 90th birthday. Allowing family members their contrasting diversity.

G-10/29/95 — Chronic back pain in doctor's thriving office. The rhythmic stream of Non-physical consciousness. Brother dogs are biting each other. Your Non-physical friends love you anyway. Children diagnosed with Attention Deficit Disorder. Bickering human brothers are biting each other. "Survival of the fittest," dogs and humans?

G-11/11/95 — Matchmaker, matchmaker make you a match. Resistance free contrast at cookie counter. Are fruits and vegetables healthier than Twinkies? Missing link in teaching broader Non-physical wisdom. Nurse disturbed by media's attention to mistakes. Treating a zinc oxide allergy with zinc oxide. Commit to work or to split pea soup?

G-11/12/95 — She fears her pure erotic stream of Energy. Sexual transmutation and "Think and Grow Rich." Considering "DNA scattering at a molecular level." Jerry and Esther and the Seth synthesizers. Your big dreams attract their vibrational essence. Everyone on the planet can be wealthy. Can we create Universally without taking action?

G-12/6/95 — Achieve a vibrational match to your desire. A question about vision, the eyesight kind. What a Focus Wheel can do for you. Paradox of a singular ego vs. All-That-Is. Is the "subconscious mind" a valid concept? Evaluating the match of wellness and herbs. The "Sara" book eased their pang of "death".

G-12/9/95 — What is the order of the Universe? Easing grief and terror of widowed mother. Contented choices in cookie counter contrast. Widening crevasse between the haves and have nots. She craves the intimacy of a sexual experience. Abraham study group dynamics of co-creating. The Universe will always match your vision.

G-12/10/95 — How Esther received and transcribed "Sara" book. The success secrets of Sudbury Valley School. Trusting home schooled child to choose appropriately. Their multi-media Life Force game boomed. She doesn't coddle her ailing husband. What is Abraham's view on abortion? A dynamic, comprehensive, practical summary.

G-7/9/95 — Geratologist's body is showing signs of deterioration. Why weight gain can influence physical decline. Why to never speak your negative symptoms. As Jane Roberts resisted utilizing Seth's suggestions. Defensiveness and a debilitating live-in critic. Relationship took a nose-dive after child birth. Why the laborious "C-section"?

G-7/22/95 — Example of a beneficial use of contrast. Relieving an electro-magnet from it's metal burden. Why he fears trusting in the Universe. Self critique of her process for acting. Brief process to augment your Place Mat Process. A mother's greatest empowerment for her child. She still smokes and enjoys doing it.

G-8/5/95 — How much "doing" to leave to Universe? Efforts required when your recipe contains resistance. Mother's role between father and prodigal daughter. An assignment from a loving Inner Being. Can A Spiritual journey be extraordinarily painful? When new friends face your old reality. Your similarity to an attracting electromagnet.

G-9/9/95A — Nothing is ever worth disallowing Life Force. To harmonize with her eighth grade teacher. Significance of the O.J. Simpson murder trial. Musician ponders a harmonic European band tour. Why he can't comfortably let her go. "Social responsibility" in a fear driven society. Even "lowly" bacteria naturally immunize themselves.

G-9/9/95B — What is Abraham's opinion on smoking marijuana? Since early childhood she's never slept well. You can appreciate your way to success. When "abnormal" mid-life physical sensations become frightening. Preparing for a catastrophe with health insurance. Dark thoughts intrude into her happiest moments. Varieties of definitions of synchronistic events.

G-9/10/95 — Why so many people talk about negatives. You are an extension of a Nonphysical "we". Dealing with the issue of personal bisexuality. A perspective of a Down's Syndrome scenario. Do human beings share other's Inner Beings? It's not about dollars; it's about abundance. Anything to do for a dead friend?

G-9/16/95 — Venting her MT M and Place Mat contrasts. A butterfly as baby chicken's chicken hawk. From whence comes Abraham's leading edge thought? She still isn't keeping her bedroom cleaned. Why sell home you want to keep. Teaching the children that all is well. Increasing an income on airline's pay scale.

G-9/24/95 — Public defender seeking truest justice for all. Esther's translation process relative to her vocabulary. Video producer in a collaborative quandary. Feels a personal slave to clinging children. Trading her "prosperity cup" for a hose. The economy, a simple exchange of Energy. How Jerry attracted his two ideal businesses.

G-9/30/95 — "In this world but not of it"? Abraham's perspective of a "schizophrenic personality". "Realty", as only the majority's agreed perception. A "cloned" mother resists mood modifying medications. To joyously render Caesar's levied revenues. Consider our contradictory beliefs about law-keeping. So "sovereign" that we can choose bondage.

G-10/7/95 — Three statements for living happily ever after. Sculpting one's body in contrast to beliefs. Fred, our flying friend of a feather. Psychologist wanting to integrate Abraham's teachings. She very much wants to get pregnant. Adopted Korean son and Scripting a birth mother. Relationships are either getting better or worse.

# SPECIAL SUBJECT TAPES — VOL I

Focused into our now — the only point in which we have the power to create — neither speculating into the future nor reminiscing into the historical past — ABRAHAM speaks, primarily, toward that practical information which we can personally learn to deliberately apply to our current experience and thereby gain beneficial results....From their broader perspective — unemcumbered by your cultural beliefs — ABRAHAM reaches into a place, within you, of clear primal acknowledgement, from which you will repeatedly hear that enthused inner "voice" reminding you, "I knew that!"

As you experience these Special Subject tapes, expect a fresh state of joyous becoming—for ABRAHAM'S words will stimulate you to a new beginning. Retain the beliefs that are of value to you, and learn to become unaffected by any acquired beliefs or influences that have been a hindrance. ABRAHAM guides us, first, to harmony with our Inner Being, and then all else falls into perfect alignment.

In order to build a foundation of an understanding of Abraham's teachings, begin with the tapes AB-1, Free Introduction To Abraham, through AB-6, Great Awakening and Blending, and then progress through the Special Subject Tapes Series—as per the order of your interest. Each tape addresses different levels of awareness, and as you repeatedly listen to them, as you are moving forward, you will continually be achieving new insights and experiences.

*Order a single at $9.95, 3 or more at $7.75, or order 5 or more,*
*and receive a complimentary (while available) 10 space cassette album.*
*Order any complete set of 10 tapes for only $77.50 (plus S/H)*

**AB-2  LAW OF ATTRACTION \*** — The most powerful Law in the universe. It affects every aspect of your daily life. A Law which is, whether you understand that it is or not. Specific processes are offered here to help you learn how to harness this Law — to get what you want.

**AB-3  LAW OF DELIBERATE CREATION \*** — Discover the ecstasy of understanding universal Laws which are absolute -- no matter what the circumstances. Without an understanding of this universal Law, it is as if you are playing in a game where the rules are not understood, so it is not only impossible to know if what you are doing is appropriate, but you do not know how to win the game. The rules of the game of life are clearly offered here.

**AB-4  LAW OF ALLOWING \*** — Of all things that you will come to understand through this physical life experience, nothing is more important than to become an allower. In becoming an allower, you are free of the negativity that binds you. Learn the joyful difference between tolerating and allowing — and experience the blissful difference in every relationship you have.

# SPECIAL SUBJECT TAPES — VOL I

**AB-5  SEGMENT INTENDING** — Our futures are individually paved by the steady stream of thoughts we set forth. We are literally creating our future life as we direct our thoughts of this moment into the future. Discover the magnificent power you hold in this moment — and learn how to use that power always to your advantage.

**AB-6  GREAT AWAKENING, BLENDING** — You have deliberately and excitedly chosen this time to be physical beings upon this planet, because you knew in advance that this would be the time when many — not all — physical beings would recognize the broadness and great value of their being. Follow this step-by-step process for awakening.

**AB-7  RELATIONSHIPS, AGREEMENTS** — We are all creators as we individually think and plan, but we are also often co-creators as we interact with others. Most relationships with others are far less than we want them to be. Find out why. Discover how to rejuvenate unhealthy relationships and attract new harmonious ones.

**AB-8  BODILY CONDITIONS** — Nothing is more important to us than the way we feel and look, and yet so many do not look or feel as they would like to. There is not a physical apparatus, no matter what the state of disrepair, that cannot have perfect health. Discover the powerful processes to bring your body to the state of being that pleases you.

**AB-9  CHRIST CONSCIOUSNESS** — While it can be satisfying to read and remember the teachings of the great ones who have gone before us, it is ever more joyous to discover the power of that knowledge within our own being. Learn the process to go within — as Christ encouraged — to experience the blissful oneness with Christ.

**AB-10  ADDICTIONS** — Habits, or compulsions, or addictions can range from annoying to destroying. Often, long after they are no longer wanted, they can bind and control your life. As you listen to this recording — you will for the first time understand exactly what the addiction is, and the simple process offered here will free you from it.

**AB-11  JOYOUS SURVIVAL** — While there are seemingly earth shattering events occurring in greater frequency upon your planet, you need not be affected by them. Discover how to create and control your experience in this seemingly unstable environment.

# SPECIAL SUBJECTS TAPES — VOL II

**AB-12 PIVOTING & POSITIVE ASPECTS *** — If I am the "Creator of my own experience", why don't I have more of what I want? Fostered by an action oriented world, most of you do not understand your true nature of attraction, thus the confusion in why you are getting what you are getting. These processes of pivoting and the book of positive aspects will assist you in the self-discovery of what is important to you, and will put you in the strong, clear place of well-being, so that you can allow what you want into your experience.

**AB-13 SEXUALITY** — Love, sensuality and the perfect sexual experience -- pleasure vs. shame. This misunderstood issue lies at the heart of more disruption in the lives of physical beings than any other issue. Discover the true nature of your being, and release yourself from the negative turmoil that surrounds the subject of sexuality.

**AB-14 DEATH** — Aging, deterioration and the perfect death experience — choices vs. chances. The gathering of years is a natural experience. However, deterioration of your physical body is neither natural nor necessary. Be healthy and productive and active and happy until the very day of your chosen re-emergence into the nonphysical.

**AB-15 DOLLARS** — Abundance, in perfect flow -- gaining the freedom that dollars can bring vs. losing your freedom while gaining your dollars. As there is an abundance of the air you breathe, so there is an abundance of the dollars you seek. Listen and learn how to relax and breathe in the fresh air of freedom offered to you through the abundant flow of dollars.

**AB-16 HEALTH, WEIGHT & MIND** — The perfect states of weight, health and mind -- how can I get there and stay there? Diet plans abound and research continues and yet the number of those unsuccessful at maintenance of satisfactory bodily and mental conditions increases steadily. Understand how your body functions and why you are as you are -- and then begin your swift and steady progress toward that which you desire.

**AB-17 MATING** — The perfect mate: getting one, being one, evoking one -- Attracting vs. attacking. While it is your natural endeavor to co-create with others, there are few who have discovered the bliss of magnificent relationships. Find out how you can experience the joy of a perfect union.

**AB-18 PARENTING** — Perfect harmony between my children and me -- and me and my parents. Harmonizing vs. traumatizing. While often disconnected from parents, either by death or by distance, your parent/child relationships often have great influence in your experience with your children or with your current life experience. Learn how to perceive what has been in a way that is beneficial to your now rather than destructive. Let that which you have lived be of value.

# SPECIAL SUBJECT TAPES — VOL II

**AB-19  CAREER** — The perfect career.  What, where and when is it -- and what can I do about it now?  With so many exterior standards or rules regarding the appropriateness of your behavior or choices -- in most cases more confusion than clarity abounds.  Use this process to discover and attract that which is perfect for you.  Stop the futile backwards approach -- and begin creating from the inside out.

**AB-20  SELF APPRECIATION** — If I am so "Perfect as I am" -- then why don't I feel better about me than I do?  Selfishness vs. selflessness.  Your awareness of your perfection was intact as you emerged into this physical body, but it was soon sabotaged by the critical, comparing, judgmental world that surrounded you.  Rediscover your true sense of value and well-being and perfection.

**AB-21  INNER GUIDANCE** — Tell me more about my Inner Voice?  Because you have thought in terms of being dead or alive, you forget that you are, simultaneously, physically focused while another part of you remains focused from nonphysical perspective.  Once remembering that the inner you exists, you may begin to listen to what your Inner Voice is offering.  Here is the process for re-establishing that important conscious connection.

---

## FREE 90 MINUTE
## INTRODUCTION TO ABRAHAM TAPE

A stimulating overview of Abraham's basic message:  How to consciously harmonize and interact with your pure, positive Inner Being...How to realize who you are and why you have chosen to be physical in this time...How to joyously and deliberately utilize the Laws of the Universe to Attract all that you are wanting to be or have or do....Also, Jerry & Esther summarize the process of their introduction to Abraham.  This cassette is a comfortable means to share Abraham with those who seek a new way of realizing a successful life experience.  (Order AB-1. *  Include $3.45 S/H)

---

...I am a medical doctor and have not, before, run across material that has this much potential to create health...Have enjoyed Abraham's books and tapes beyond any expectations I had when my mother originally sent them...I would like to subscribe to your"Weekly Tape Program"...Thanks.  — MAINE

# G-SERIES TAPES SUMMER, 1995
## UTILIZING THE VALUE OF CONTRAST

G-4/29/95   Should evil be resisted or not resisted?   How would Abraham handle a bomber's punishment?   Bombed, broken babies of Baghdad and Oklahoma.   How banks of anger fuel future disasters.   The case for banning potential killer cars.   To positively observe all the baby killing bombers.   Consideration of our moral and ethical positions.

G-5/13/95   When your creating is out of balance.   When noticing a case of background anxiety.   You were trained to respond to conditions.   Feeling guilty about living her leisurely life.   Have you asked "What is my work?"   Abraham's teachings considered as a unifying force.   Why so "hard for her to tap in"?

G-5/14/95   When one declines while moving through time.   When doing the unwanted to please another.   Why most have a hard time empowering others.   On saying "yes" when we mean "no."   To live in harmony with your government.   Nothing is "greater," because it is all one!   Is Non--physical only pure positive Energy?

G-6/1/95   The killer earthquake versus the killer military.   To understand the bombing of the children.   How can she help her chemotherapied sister.   Inspired teenager saves friend by his belt loop.   Role of Appreciation in Process of Creation.   Depressed over daughter doing 90 days for DUI.   What is your Vibratonal Point of Attraction?

G-6/3/95   Could she have been her own grandmother?   "Home alone" child felt no bitterness.   Allowing the passion for whatever you want.   What would the perfect lover FEEL like?   Value of a state of impatient patience.   Positive aspects of a state of procrastination.   Getting a grip on the Karma Koncept.

G-6/4/95   How do you decide what is appropriate?   Dreaming of silver dollars and homelessness.   To do if suddenly engulfed by grief.   Real estate broker experiencing competitive trainee.   In Eternal Becoming we find eternal joy.   Effect on fetus of smoking and drugging?   Children, limitations, agreements and cocreative decisions.

G-6/17/95A   Planetary depletion thesis vs. "All is well"?   Your Economy as an exchange of Energy.   Pot smoking, acid tripping disconnected granddaughter.   Creator, as an orchestrator of conditions.   Have fun on the way to your happiness.   Suffering, is not essential to your growth.   "All is so well in my world!"

G-6/17/95B   Time, is not the income producing factor.   Naught more normal than woman's changing body.   On keeping her husband and her lover.   Religion, worthiness and creating one's own reality.   His daughter is failing "scissors" in kindergarten.   Some advantages and disadvantages of home schooling.   Natural childbirth, menstrual cycles and menopause.

G-6/18/95   Another enlightening session at Unity of Ft. Collins.   The Principles of Spiritual Living Made Practical.   Wanting a mosquito-free gardening experience.   Is your relationship ripe enough to pick?   Catch the spirit of collecting the data.   When a school attempts motivation through humiliation.   A Scripting example for mother of teens.

G-7/6/95   Here is what is normal for you.   When all the desirable ones seem taken.   Can't remember where she hid her jewelry.   When Jerry drank some discombobulating wine.   Why has she lost her sexual drive?   A question about a credit card debt.   The vibrations of appreciation will get you anything!

# A Synopsis
# of Abraham-Hicks' Teachings

- *You are a Physical Extension of that which is Non-physical.*

- *You are here in this body because you chose to be here.*

- *The basis of your life is Freedom; the purpose of your life is Joy.*

- *You are a creator; you create with your every thought.*

- *Anything that you can imagine is yours to be or do or have.*

- *You are choosing your creations as you are choosing your thoughts.*

- *The Universe adores you; for it knows your broadest intentions.*

- *Relax into your natural Well-being. All is well. (Really it is!)*

- *You are a creator of thoughtways on your unique path of joy.*

- *Actions to be taken and money to be exchanged are by-products of your focus on joy.*

- *You may appropriately depart your body without illness or pain.*

- *You can not die; you are Everlasting Life.*

P.O. It is not necessary for even one other person to understand the Laws of the Universe or the processes that we are offering here in order for you to have a wonderful, happy, productive Life Experience — for you are the attractor of your experience. Just you!

*Jerry & Esther Hicks — 11/95*

# BOOK: A NEW BEGINNING I

This extraordinary book is powerfully offered by a group of teachers who call themselves Abraham. They express clearly and simply the laws of the universe, explaining in detail how we can deliberately flow with these laws for the joyful creation of whatever we desire. Abraham describes this as the time of awakening, explaining that each of us chose, with very deliberate intent, this specific  time of great change to participate in this physical experience. An empowering, life-changing book that will assist you in seeing your personal life experience as you have never seen it before.

COMMENTS:

- Thank you for a delightful book—A NEW BEGINNING I— a life changing book...a joyous do-it-yourself book...I have always known this was an "inside job", but I've not known, before, how to communicate well with the "inside." — Germany

- We are thrilled with the data. Everyone we have sent the book to thinks it is the best book they have ever read. — California

- The feedback I've gotten on the many ABRAHAM books that I have distributed has been phenomenal and it has come from all over the world. — California

- The first edition of A NEW BEGINNING I sold out because readers love the practical ideas of Abraham. In the tradition of Jane Roberts, this refreshing new book reveals a unique blend of new-age thought with the Western desire for "more." An inspiring self-help classic that gets results.

Softcover. $15.00. 218 pages. ISBN 0-9621219-3-2.

# BOOK: A NEW BEGINNING II

An uplifting book that strikes a chord with the very core of your being. Written by Abraham to assist you in understanding the absolute connection between your physical self and your inner self. Abraham puts this physical life experience into perspective as they explain and define who we really are and why we have come forth as physical beings. This book is filled with processes and  examples to assist you in making a deliberate conscious connection with your own Inner Being, that you might find the awesome satisfaction with this physical life experience that can only come once this connection is made.

COMMENTS:

- Your book, A NEW BEGINNING II, has been my constant companion, now marked and circled on page after page...So— UP with the "Fairies of the Universe" and beautiful music and laughter! — France

- ..I hugged the book; I couldn't put it down for two days....You should see my metaphysical library—and of every book I have, this is the clearest! — Germany

- Thank you so much for the book—it is the best yet. I like to open it at random and see what the good word is for the day. — California

- Like the book before it, A NEW BEGINNING II is clear, practical, inspiring and empowering with more focus on how to realign with your Inner Being. The bottom line for Abraham-Hicks is to choose to feel good in every moment. From that base of joy you will naturally and easily create what you want for yourself and the world.

Softcover. $15.00. 258 pages. ISBN 0-9621219-1-6

Sara and the Foreverness of Friends of a Feather

Esther and Jerry Hicks
Illustrations by Caroline Garrett

# A Review of Sara and the Foreverness of Friends of a Feather,

*by Denise Tarsitano in the "Rising Star Series, Summer 1996" catalog:*

Here is an inspiring as well as inspired book about a child's experiential journey into unlimited joyousness. Sara is a shy, withdrawn ten year old girl who is not very happy with her life. She has an obnoxious brother who constantly teases her, cruel and unfeeling classmates, and an apathetic attitude towards her schoolwork. In short, she represents a lot of kids in our society today. When I first read this book, I was struck by the similarities between Sara and my ten year old. Sara is really a composite of all children.

Sara wants to feel good and happy and loving but as she looks around, she doesn't find much to feel that way about. This all changes when she meets Solomon, a wise old owl, who shows her how to see things differently through the eyes of unconditional love. He teaches Sara how to always be in an atmosphere of pure, positive energy. Sara sees for the first time who she really is and her unlimited potential. You, as the reader, will realize this is so much more than a children's story but a blueprint for attaining the joy and happiness that are your birthright.

*My whole family read this book and we haven't been the same since. My husband, perhaps, was the most moved by it. He actually said that it had such a tremendous impact on him that he looks at life with new eyes. It's like being nearsighted your whole life and then finally getting glasses. Everything becomes crystal clear.*

I cannot say enough good things about this life-transforming book. You will share in Sara's ups and downs on the way to greater heights of fulfillment and know that there is a Sara in all of us. If there is only one book you ever buy, make sure it is this one. You won't regret it! (all ages).

Softcover. $15.00 ISBN 0-9621219-3-2

G-1/28/95  An introduction to Little Miss Sticky Fingers. You were born into a state of absolute Grace. On islands of freedom for trespassing homelessites. Trespassing dogs are defacing her flowers. His neighbors shot his trespassing dogs. Teaching our children the magical balance. When the deceased dog reappeared in a dream.

G-1/29//95  Your broader view and mass upliftment. Augmenting the value of public school systems. When you're taught that resistance is normal. On allowing a child their own experiences. Empowering the Universe to deliver to you. To replace her skills in her husband's practice. Role playing disaster as a counterproductive act.

G-2/11/95  A whole new orientation for life. He wants to understand those intermittent seizures. "Former" rebel is "controlling" ten teen rebels. Why would anyone ever want to die? Conscious croaking, as a doable undertaking. Ideal physical life and fulfilling one's purpose. Life is not like a football game.

G-2/18/95  Looking at the problem resists the solution. Does Abraham observe us only through Esther? The productive response to "How's it going?" A positive beast and a toothless cowboy. To be able to comfortably kill beasts. When waitresses workplace deteriorates to dissension. To have your cigarettes and well-being too.

G-2/25/95-B  Perspectives of "3rd World" birth conditions. What becomes of "bad guys" in Nonphysical? To create less resistance around sexuality. Gained a lover but lost some freedom. Perusing your history will repeat your history. His girlfriend's pregnancy is closing his valve. Cocreating with critical fundamentalist daughter.

G-2/25/95-C  Clients who remember a forgotten negative past. As a gay man, I write this scenario. Do we have prebirth choices of sexuality? Are there sexuality options in Nonphysical? I'm the gay one who wrote that note. A homosexual is expelled from the Ashram. Take no delight in another's dethronement.

G-3/10/95  On learning to appreciate your diversity. The Power of the Place Mat Process. Five young videoed vandals express their freedom. The vandalee's role in the vandal's vandalism. Reducing your resistance to a horrific event. "Forgiveness," as counterproductive to well-being. One has different sexual passion than another.

G-3/25/95  A perspective of welfare reform and homelessness. You can not not get what you want. Is there form or self in Nonphysical? To help our children continually evolve. Why children rebel in these "better" times. Avoiding contrast isn't fulfilling your purpose. Three teens who love drugs and lawlessness.

G-4/2/95  A butterfly's three generational joyous journey. She's being plagued by irrational relationship thoughts. Why quantum leaps can feel too painful. Reality, as how we feel in the moment. After we croak, then what happens? Nonphysical behavior in a physical body. Will the real Nicole please speak up?

G-4/8/95  Abraham becomes a bit more blunt. Place Matting from resistance to prosperity. When inheritances and trusts equate with resistance. Shortage is a fallacy; there is enough. To give up the counterproductive financial struggle. Benefits and detriments of facing financial deadlines. Knowing when you are fulfilling your purpose.

# VARIOUS SERVICES AND PRODUCTS

## WORKSHOPS & WEEKENDS

*Discuss whatever you are wanting to more clearly understand, ie: Your state of becoming. Finances. Bodily conditions. Relationships. Business/Career. Metaphysicality. Your state of being/having/doing....* To participate in an open group conference with ABRAHAM, contact Abraham-Hicks Publications at (210) 755-2299 for dates, locations, reservations, etc. Conference fees vary with location, duration and materials.

• *...My experience with* ABRAHAM *has provided me with hours and hours of feeling good.* ABRAHAM is so patient and loving—with no hint of judgement...I feel so safe and cared about when speaking to ABRAHAM....It is a message of hope and self-empowerment...such a small cost to me for the service you have so lovingly provided.— *Montana*

• ...Since receiving ABRAHAM'S Free Introductory Tape, I've listened to it 3 or 4 times. It is concise and very recreatable both in my life and in my work as a consultant...*I wanted to thank you for so much value in this one small tape. I am impressed and moved...Enclosed is my first "real" order.—Texas*

## WEEKLY TAPE PROGRAM

For those who want to learn as much as they can "to be and have and do" as fast as they can— and are not in the position to personally attend ABRAHAM'S ever evolving gatherings—we offer this Weekly Tape Program: We choose, each week, what we consider to be, the 3 hour session with the most stimulating, practical new ideas—or significant ideas presented from a new perspective—and we form a 90 minute composite tape and ship it to our subscribers. Four cassettes equal one month's billing. *Fill your spare moments with upliftment, flow and forward motion. Subscription fee: $41.00 per month (or $10.25 per week).*

• ...Enjoy your tapes and appreciate all that is coming through. I have an ABRAHAM tape playing whenever I drive in my car, and it sets a positive state of emotion for the day. Thank you. ES

## MONTHLY TAPE PROGRAM

We select and edit, from as many as 20 new Group Session Tapes that ABRAHAM produces in a month, a 90 minute cassette—of what we feel contains the most new, inspiring and thought provoking material—and we ship that 90 minute composite tape to the subscribers to the Monthly Tape Program. *A gift that keeps on giving. Subscription fee: $12.00 per month.*

• ...I'm getting thirsty for more of ABRAHAM, so, enclosed, please find a check for a one-year subscription to the Monthly Tape Program. One of these days I hope to make it out to Texas again to re-experience the exuberance and exhilaration in person—in the meantime, I find the tapes of endless value...*Every time I replay any one of those tapes I have, I realize that it has a whole new meaning for me and offers ever changing insights. What a great way to start the day!* My profound gratitude to you for sharing this wonderful way of life. — *New Jersey*

# HOW TO ORDER

## ORDERING

Our order forms are for your convenience, and we will send a replacement order form back to you with each shipment. In order to assist in our efficient process of your order, please:

- Print all information clearly, or type.
- List each item, its stock number (i.e. AB-1) and its price.
- Pay with your personal check, money order, or use your MasterCard, Visa, or American Express credit card.

## INTERNATIONAL ORDERS

Orders outside of the continental U.S. will be shipped US Postal Service (unless UPS is specified) and the additional shipping cost will be charged. Send U.S. funds only.

## WE SHIP UPS OR US POSTAL

On larger orders of multiple tapes or books, UPS is usually the fastest, safest, most economical way, but we ship most smaller orders by U.S. Postal. Your order is normally packaged and shipped within 2 working days after we receive it.

## PRICE CHANGES

Our posted prices may vary without notice as those who supply us with services or materials may change their prices to us without notice.

## TELEPHONE CONSULTATIONS

Currently this service has been discontinued. Any further change will be announced in our publications.

## DEFECTIVE OR DAMAGED TAPES OR BOOKS

Should you ever receive, from us, a book that is damaged or a tape that is garbled, blank, bound or broken, please call or write and tell us the title or the series date, and we will replace the item — or refund your cost. Due to the spontaneous group interaction with Abraham, the G-Series, or W.T.P. or M.T.P. tapes can sometimes be varied in volume, so we just take the best — and ignore the rest. (We are experiencing continual tape quality improvement as we move forward.)

---

### ADD THESE SHIPPING COSTS

The following shipping and handling rates apply within the continental U.S.
Additional for International Orders

| | |
|---|---|
| Up to $10 | Add $3.45 |
| $10 to $30 | Add $4.95 |
| $30 to $50 | Add $6.80 |
| Over $50 | Add $8.45 |

---

We are most appreciative of the many suppliers of services and materials who make it possible for Abraham's words to reach you so efficiently. As costs of doing business are increased, or decreased (taxes, inflation, etc.) to any of our suppliers and passed on to us, we, in turn, through our varied business transactions, reflect those changes back into the international economy.

# PRICE LIST

CASSETTE TAPES — $9.95 each. Order 3 or more at $7.75 each — or order 5 or more (in same "Volume" or "Season") and they will be shipped to you in a complimentary, (a limited offer) convenient 10 space cassette album. Abraham's Special Subjects 90 minutes, "AB Series" and their "G-Series" 90 minute group session composites are all priced the same: $77.50 for the album sets of 10, $9.95 singles or $7.75 each when ordering 3 or more. (Plus shipping and handling.)

BOOKS — $15.00 each. Pay $11.25 when ordering 3 or more. (Plus shipping and handling) Study groups, teachers or dealers, call for discount when ordering 9, or more, books.

TELEPHONE CONSULTATIONS WITH ABRAHAM — Currently this service has been discontinued. Any further change will be announced in our publications.

MONTHLY TAPE PROGRAM (M.T.P.) — $12 per month. One 90 minute composite, each month, that presents the most new practical material from Abraham, is selected and mailed to a group of subscribers.

WEEKLY TAPE PROGRAM (W.T.P.) — $41 per month. Composites of 180 minute group sessions. You will receive four tapes each month.

WORKSHOPS, WEEKENDS, SEMINARS — Fees vary with times, lengths, & locations. Posted in our newsletter, when booked far enough in advance, or call for activities in your area.

VIDEO CASSETTES — For prices and details of offerings see catalog. From $23.77 to $29.77.

NEWSLETTER, "The Leading Edge" — Published 4 times a year by Jerry and Esther Hicks. A one year subscription: $14.00.

CATALOG — A complimentary 44 page compendium of Abraham-Hicks published teachings from 1988 to 1995. Over 200 cassettes, books and videos.

* TRANSCRIPTIONS — As per numerous requests, twenty-two 90 minute Abraham recordings have been transcribed and are now available for $10 (plus S/H). Identify them by the asterisk (*) next to their titles.

DAILY PLANNING CALENDAR/STUDY GROUP WORKBOOK — A 772 page planning, envisioning, implementing and manifesting calendar to utilize for your personal creation or for a 12 month Study Group Workbook. $25.00 (plus S/H).

*Please make all checks payable to: J & E Hicks*
*U.S. Funds only*

# ORDER FORM

**TO ORDER BY TELEPHONE: 755-2299 (210) area code is subject to change**
**Abraham-Hicks Publications — P.O. Box 690070, San Antonio, TX 78269**

NAME _____

ADDRESS _____

CITY _____ STATE _____ ZIP _____

TELE: (HOME) _____ (WORK) _____ (FAX) _____

REFERRED BY: _____

(TO SHIP BY UPS, WE NEED YOUR STREET OR RR NUMBER — NOT A P.O. BOX)

| QUAN | STOCK# | ITEM DESCRIPTION | PRICE |
|------|--------|------------------|-------|
| | AB-1 | Tape: Free Introduction To Abraham (S/H only) | $3.45 |
| | ANBI | Book: A New Beginning I @ $15.00 | |
| | ANBII | Book: A New Beginning II @ $15.00 | |
| | SARA | Book: Sara and the Foreverness of...@$15.00 | |
| | ABVONE | Tape Album: 10 Special Subjects @ $77.50 | |
| | ABVTWO | Tape Album: 10 Special Subjects @ $77.50 | |
| | G SERIES | Tape Album: 10 Group Series Tapes @ $77.50 (specify which) | |
| | EACHES | Individual Tapes ($9.95 each or $7.75 if 3 or more) | |
| | CALEND. | Abraham-Hicks Daily Planning Calendar @ $25.00 | |
| Individual Spec. Sub Tapes AB: | | | |
| Individual Videos – AV: | | | |
| Individual Group Series: G: | | | |
| | | | |

| Shipping & Handling Continental USA Additional for International Orders | |
|---|---|
| Up to $10 . . . . . . . . . . . Add $3.45 | |
| $10 to $30 . . . . . . . . . . Add $4.95 | |
| $30 to $50 . . . . . . . . . . Add $6.80 | |
| ~~$50 to $50~~ . . . . . . . . . . ~~Add $0.00~~ | |

ADD TOTAL OF ITEMS _____

ADD SHIPPING AND HANDLING _____

(SUBTRACT ANY QUANTITY DISCOUNTS) _____

TX DELIVERY, ADD 6.25% SALES TAX _____

TOTAL AMOUNT ENCLOSED _____

❏ Personal Check: (Make payable to J & E Hicks — US Funds only)

❏ MasterCard  ❏ VISA  ❏ American Express  ❏ Discover

Card # _____ Exp Date _____

Cardholder's Signature _____

Print Name _____

# THANK YOU!

*Our thanks to you for your role in this joyous cocreation. Your thoughts as we interact, your pondering, questioning, recognizing, knowing, wanting...your thoughts add to our forward motion and to the fulfillment of our purpose.*

*We intend to allow ABRAHAM'S words of perspective, positive guidance, and stimulation of thought, to go as far and as fast as they are wanted, and at the same time, we intend to continue our abundant positive mental and material and spiritual experience — and we do appreciate your contribution of "thoughts, words and deeds."*

---

Do you have a friend who would enjoy our newsletter?

Name (Please print) _____

Address _____

City/State/Zip _____

Your name _____

---

## * EDUCATORS—TEACHERS—STUDENTS *

Are you involved in education and interested in an uplifting perspective? We can mail to you (at no cost) a copy of Daniel Greenberg's *Free At Last*, highlights of the first 20 years of the remarkable Sudbury Valley School experience. We have a few remaining copies (not for sale) just let us know if you would like one and we'll get it off to you as soon as it is practical.. *This book will make your heart sing!*

---

## YOUR UNCONDITIONAL
## GUARANTEE OF SATISFACTION

We are aware that due to technical or personal idiosyncrasies you may receive a damaged or defective item from us — but we will replace it or refund your money (whichever you prefer) just as soon as you call or write and give us the details. Please don't bother with shipping the item back to us. Just toss it away. We want you to be completely satisfied with our products and our service.

Jerry & Esther

Excited about the clarity and practicality of the translated word from ABRAHAM, Jerry and Esther Hicks began, in 1986, disclosing their ABRAHAM experience to a handful of close business associates. Then, recognizing the practical results being received by those persons who began plying ABRAHAM with meaningful personal questions regarding their finances, bodily conditions, and relationships...the Hickses made a conscious decision to allow ABRAHAM'S teachings to

*Esther & Jerry Hicks*

become available to an ever widening circle of seekers. And that circle continues to expand — even as you read this page.

Jerry and Esther have now published more than 150 *Abraham-Hicks* books, cassettes and videos, and have been presenting open group interactive workshops in about 40 cities a year to those who gather to participate in this progressive stream of thought.

Although worldwide attention has been given by leading edge thinkers to this *Science of Deliberate Creation* who, in turn, incorporate many of ABRAHAM'S concepts into their books, lectures, sermons, screenplays, scripts...the primary spread of this material has been from person to person — as individuals begin to discover the value of these materials in their practical, personal experience.

ABRAHAM, a group of obviously evolved teachers, speak their broader Non-physical perspective through the physical apparatus of Esther. *Speaking to our level of comprehension, from their present moment to our now, through a series of loving, allowing, brilliant yet comprehensively simple, recordings in print and in sound — they guide us to a clear connection with our Inner Being — they guide us to self-upliftment from our total self.*

## COMMENTS FROM READERS & LISTENERS:

*...It's hard to believe that life could be so simple and so joyous and that it could take me so many years to find out how to do it...So, thank you, so much, for making an already good life even better! (With lots of good feelings) SC — PA*

*...I've been a "searcher," "seeker," "sharer" since I was a teen. My middle name was purported to be "Why?" The information from Abraham is so down-to-earth, useful, compelling, exciting, sensible, practical, empowering, clear, usable. I'm a marvelous deliberate creator now. Thanks for putting the "fun" back into physical life. JS — AZ*

*...Am so delighted to be reading your books, listening to your tapes, attending your seminars and talking to each of you on the phone. I am so happy and getting happier and clearer every day. My life has been leading to this point, and it feels like the icing on the cake. I know everything will just get better, although it's hard to know how. What a powerful gift you've given us — the recognition of our ability to create the life we want, and the tools to carry out the plan. Thank you for sharing. — CA*

# FOUR INDIAN POETS

Edited by
John R. Milton

*Dakota Press*
*1974*

University of South Dakota, Vermillion, South Dakota 57069

Copyright © 1974, by Dakota Press
Library of Congress Catalog No. 73-76244
ISBN 0-88249-015-X

Grateful acknowledgement for assistance in producing this volume is extended to the Hill Family Foundation of St. Paul, Minnesota, and to the National Endowment for the Arts, Literature Program.

4

# Contents

## TODD HAYCOCK (Navajo)

## JEFF SAUNDERS (Navajo)

Cover design by Elijah Sitting Crow (Sioux)

# Introduction

In general terms, there are two kinds of Indian poetry. The first is traditional, composed orally in the native languages and transcribed and translated and sometimes re-written by anthropologists and linguists. These poems were the songs, chants, and prayers which served a functional purpose within religious rites, celebrations, and various festivities at different times of the year. Recently, poets have been writing new translations which are, in effect, new poems, although the spirit is adhered to as closely as possible. Most of the collections and anthologies which have been published in the past forty years have been made up of this kind of traditional, or oral, poetry.

Very recently, really in the past ten years, and with a noticeable growth in only the past five years, contemporary Indians have been writing poetry in English, so that there is no need for translation and rewriting. Perhaps, for this reason, the poetry is purer. In any case, no one stands between the poet and the reader. The communication is direct.

The reason for the late upsurge in Indian writing is a simple one. Most Indians of the present generation learn English early; for many of them English is their first language, and their native language is learned later. Historically, we have finally reached that point at which the native language is known primarily by the grandparents. European immigrants went through a similar process of language assimilation, some of them only half a century ago. Then, too, the past decade or so has seen a new interest in ethnic minority groups, partly because these groups finally tired of being treated as outsiders and began to demand certain equalities in the areas of politics, education, and social justice, as well as legal justice. The Negro was the first to vocalize

9

his discontent, and he has been followed by the Spanish-American and the Indian. Curiously, perhaps, only the Indian has retained his old name; the others are now blacks and chicanos.

Indian history goes back further than any other cultural history in America, and it is not surprising that even in contemporary times there is a tendency on the part of Indian writers to emphasize traditions, the grandfathers, the longhouses, the continuity of the relationship between Indian and the land, a relationship much closer within the life of the Indian than in any of the other cultures on this continent—European, Scandinavian, African, Spanish, French, English, Chinese, and so on. Therefore, even if the traditions are underplayed, or only implied, the land-relationship remains strong in contemporary poetry. Sometimes this relationship is violated by modern towns, by technology, by saloon-society, and even by modern education. In this case, the poems will show the irony of the juxtaposition of landed values with non-landed values.

The contemporary Indian poet, of course, is free to take any subject for his poetry, and on some occasions it may be difficult to tell whether the poem was written by Indian or non-Indian. Yet, there is almost always an attitude implicit in the poems which establishes them as the insight and thought of a non-white. Even the percentage of "Indian blood" in a poet does not always alter the unique Indian perception of the world and the universe or, more specifically, of his own piece of land, his region of birth. It is the attitude that counts, and the attitude comes from experience, from exposure to the cultural values of the tribe. There are cases of one-eighth or one-fourth or one-half Indians being more Indian oriented than full bloods. The same holds true, of course, of any mixture of blood in any society. The important thing is the "way" a person (or in this case a writer) sees himself, his world, and the relationship between them.

10

The poems in this volume will make their own way, will reveal themselves without any outside commentary.

I have met two of the poets whose work is in this volume; the other two I know only through a mutual friend. John Barsness, son of a friend of mine who was active in the Western Literature Association before his premature death, is part Tuscarora and is married to a Sioux woman. At age twenty-one, John lives in Lander, Wyoming, performing his two years of alternate service as a conscientious objector by working at the Wyoming State Training School. About his poety he has written:

> I can't feel that my poetry is anything more than perhaps a continuing examination of my own life, for what that is worth; it has ranged, possibly, from self-fantasy to parody to homegrown self-analysis over the past few years, but that doesn't mean much, except to me; if it touches anybody else in any way it's only because I'm human (I hope) and anything human simply can't help but be part of everything else. I don't feel any great moral purpose in writing poetry; in fact, I hope that it doesn't change anyone's view of himself or me; putting words together in nice ways is merely my way of making myself appear at least slightly functional in the world.

The most educated of the four poets, in the school sense, is Paula Gunn Allen, who is Laguna (Pueblo)-Dakota-Lebanese, a native New Mexican who is completing work on a Ph.D. at the University of New Mexico. She says that she has been writing, looking, living, believing and disbelieving for a long time. At age thirty-four she is older and more experienced in the two-culture world than the three male poets in this volume, all of whom are in their early twenties. Paula describes her life as a journey in and out of universities, on and off the streets, in and out of marriage, on and off her homelands. She is currently teaching Native American Studies at San Francisco State University and the College of San Mateo, helping to organize programs in Indian

11

literature and culture, and doing considerable writing of her own. About her poetry she says:

> It seems to me that the problem of writing poetry is one of how to contain and, at the same time, transmit the force which is the "message," the form-content vehicle of articulation, the song. I try to create something that is neither mechanical (sequential) nor organic (because a poem can't reproduce itself or grow itself) but that is capable of continuous movement, transmission of force, embodiment of experiential meaning.
>
> But language, at least in its Indo-European forms, makes the composition problematical: how does the poet (in English) transform the essentially repetitive (as in the infinite monkeys and their machines) into the endlessly dynamic, the pattern of universal existence? She must turn from absorbing and assimilating to shaping, putting out, in a sharpness that is widely evocative yet distinct, whatever is most real for herself and those who share her existence and experience. I don't think of the poem as a "being" but perhaps as a shaping, a weapon, a transmutation.
>
> My own poetry speaks to my own experiences, my "history," my perceptions; these in turn are created in concert with where I come from and who I go with. It is seldom happy, it tends to be intense, it is often brief. I try to keep it as close to the springs of my being as I can, toward my own center, because I can only articulate what is a known / part of me, my people, my life.

Todd Haycock and Jeff Saunders seem less articulate than the first two poets, but this is an illusion based upon our usual insistence that all "good Americans" speak and write "good English." These two young Navajo men have not had extensive schooling, although Jeff attended the Institute of American Indian Arts in Santa Fe, and both men took creative writing classes from James White at the Intermountain Indian School in Brigham City, Utah. Todd speaks English as a second language, and in both of these poets the attentive reader will find language mannerisms which reflect a strong influence of the complicated and difficult Navajo language.

Jeff Saunders was born in Flagstaff and speaks English as his first language and Navajo as his second. Some poems of his have appeared in *Nimrod* and he admits that he has been influenced by James Welch, the Blackfeet poet from Montana. Todd Haycock was brought up in Kayenta, Arizona and is also a painter. He has not published his poetry until now.

When Jeff and Todd were writing these poems in school in 1970-71, they went on a reading tour of the Southwest. Since that time they have also read at the Walker Art Center in Minneapolis. In some ways their poetry is, by virtue of its unsophisticated language, closer to the daily reality of the reservation Indian. There is an immediacy of experience sometimes lacking in the schooled poet. However, it should be obvious that all four of the poets in this volume shun the clever, the superficial, and the purely entertaining language and images of much contemporary non-Indian poetry. It is an honest poetry, whatever its faults, and it is therefore a true poetry coming directly from the soul of the poet. Perhaps this characteristic is its major distinction, and it is one worth preserving.

John Milton
Vermillion, 1974

# *JOHN BARSNESS*

# There's A Man
# That Lives Alone in the Hills
# Above the Yellowstone River

up there in the icesharp winter
the snowdrifts, frozen sixpointed dunes,
come hard and final as the wind roars:
he could always listen in the dark
of the deadnight roaring, thinking
that a herd of a thousand grizzly bears
was flying roaring growling through the sky,
and the silence afterward would fill
his hills with the bleached hides
of a thousand dead frostytip bears,
covering the stiff grass with crystal fur
with the sagebrush and spruce trees
sticking up dark through the eyeholes.

he kept busy feeding his horses
refusing to go crazy in the emptiness
and riding through the snow,
sometimes shouting at it
fog riding the air bucking from his mouth
shouting at this huge awkward white horse
that he was trying to break. he also killed
frosted deer and antelope, his old winchester
kicking holes in the dead calm of the heavy air
and was kept busy skinning and butchering.
he apologized for killing them,
speaking to their staringeyed heads
as he tossed them through the air
into the dogpen, not with pity
but with a hardgutted sadness
that let their meat roll down his throat
more easily, greased in his faith.

he had an old radio
that spoke to him in the only voice
that he knew; it frizzled and cracked
a high thin electric singsong
that late at night sometimes
with grizzly bears roaring outside
came to him as the piercing voice of god.
after the spring floods
and the thin flights of returning ducks
black against the sky and the spring rain
the summer would sneak into his life,
suddenly grabbing him like a dull urge
to go into town and get drunk;
with a sweating dirtstreak sun
it came with a slowness that rubbed his joints
and fooled the deerflies
feeding on his horses
catching them in late killing frosts
that came like claps of cold thunder
after bonehot summer ovens of days.

the summer nights were long
and blackhot with wind breathing
the breath of summer grizzly bears
and he'd lie awake on moondry nights
his back to the buffalograss hillside
and imagine the shadowed treetopped hills
as the blacknippled breasts of an antelope woman
holding him peacefully warm and sweating
in the dark coulees of her thighs.

# HILINE/ U.S. Interstate Two

driving between shelby and wolf point
(at eighty miles an hour
in ninety degree flat bright heat
in the grasshopper month of august)
there's nothing, only sometimes
the missouri river, muddy and brown:
a deadly earthworm.
the land is gray & green & tan
and the sky is big, all right, a bucket,
and blue, blue as satan's forge.
it all adds up to a huge aching beautiful
nothing.
the people fill the nothing up
with cold beer from blue & silver cans,
high twanging countrywestern music,
big chevrolets and other things
all drunk and played and driven
at eighty miles an hour
in the bright heat
along u.s. interestate highway two.

# Deer Hunt 1971

grassy cold october sageland.
small birds in the sky,
black maybe: so far away: geese
honking fogwarnings up there
of gray clouds coming
and looking down over
the land veined with gullies and coulees
and spotted with dark bare stubblefields;
spots and veins
over the back of an old man's hand.

up above along the high ridge
old deserted telephone poles
far and apart in their line
the wires long gone from between
the single crosstimbers
rotting held with rusting spikes
lonesome and black, thin against
the graygreen roughshod plain.

below in the poplar blind coulee
the buck lies dead
and hidden. the wind is cold
and dry whistling through the rusted hayrake
a quiet flute in an empty building
so quiet after the thundering
summer storms and thundering
gunshots and thundering
harvest trucks loaded with grain.

# Crazy Woman Rode a Dead Horse

crazy woman rode a dead horse up the creek
like she knew maybe where she was going
and like a dog eating grass to kill
the sharp twist of rotten meat in his stomach
she whipped the dead horse with an alder branch.
maybe she did know; the horse was dead anyway
and she rode him like the same devil that rode her.
at the top the horse fell and kicked on its side.
blood was running like a crazy woman
from the alder cuts on its dead ribs,
as red as the blood from a live horse dying.
crazy woman kicked the dead horse
but he was dead and wouldn't move.
she knew she was crazy then
and didn't want to go back down.

# Crazy Woman

say, crazy woman, i'm glad
that i'm your only man.

oh, i know that crazy woman.
she comes here all the time, for me
and the good times that we have.

once we were all lined along the hot
street, in pickups and on curbstones,
in front of the august postoffice
feeling bored like slow noonday cattle
along a drying dead creek, waiting
for something good to come.
she had cold beer, and gave me enough
to sweat some more. she drank
only a couple of times herself.

of course i gave my cigarettes to her.
they were lucky strikes, had been
a day or two in the dashboard sun.
she gave them back one by one
as i asked, like candy. by the time
the sun went they were gone.
we left to buy scme more, still hot,
and bought more beer, again and again.

hell, by that time the old
postoffice was closed anyway.

# Walking in a Bear's Tracks

the tracks smell warm in the snow
near stinking with the life of the bear
flying fast in the blizzard
as clawtipped ghosts on the ground.
the bear leads through black canyons
and around cold deadfalls and the iron
jaws of human traps. i try not
to come up to him as he leads me
and i try not to let the snow
come up on me and float my feet
and the hopes for a campground
away into the white. the bear
takes me home like a small bird.

in the morning the young man
shot him and took his massive head
wishing for the wisdom of his feet,
holding the snout by the bloody teeth
and spitting into the dead eyes
with the gall of the living.

# Branding Spring

the mornings come in darkness
and cold, hours before the gray
clings to the blackcloud sky.

the horses are as dark and nervous
as the scampering fresh rain.
the cattle run squat and redbrown
in front of them, moaning
whitefaced in the mud.
they mill with the sagewind,
bounded by the barbedwire and line
of jagged blackslickered horsemen.

in the brown intestines of the corral
the calves bawl, sputtering blood
and confusion from their slashed genitals,
held by the slick riders now on the earth.

after the hairsmoke and cattle are gone
its home for the tired muddy workers
and the land is returned to the rain.

# Bearskin Wood

a pineboard sign says:
this way to the source
of crosstop creek
up along the old road
the trail marked by drying bones
and bright red indian paintbrush.

old jones' cabin is empty,
door open. he's gone
but on the gray outside
of the logs he's nailed bearskin,
spikeheads brownrusted
in each shrivelled paw.
the skull, long white and broken,
sits on the chopping block
giving prayers on old jones' head,
dead teeth smiling again.

he shot that bear to keep
the winter away, black fur
to hide him from the cold.
but the icewind came again,
howling for his head.
he couldn't keep it off,
not just with a bearskull
and an empty drystretched skin.

# Coor's Beer and the Rusty Canopener:

Encounter at the crossroads of Montana

tall elk and sam and sam's sister bobbi
drove down in the smooth darkness
across the 45th parallel to sheridan wyo,
sometimes riding happy earthwaves
hard and high around the curves,
windows rolled down to let the smoke out.
they bought three cases of coor's beer
and started back, unthirsty and laughing,
and hit a rusty canopener
coming across the imaginary border.
there was no spare and they slept
curled like gypsies in the car,
sam in front under the steering wheel
tall elk and bobbi holding each other
in the back, all three with nothing
but their coats and a case
of coor's beer apiece for blankets.

# Missouri River

I

the open crown of the blue
holds over the hard earth
the days before, the memory
and time of evening smallness.
the three forks come within
merging to one, threefold
water flowing and holding
the diminishing silt future
of the country and days.
the valley under the space—
that can empty itself of human
worth and scratching steel
on summer flat pounding days
and can hold deer in the shade
and protection of narrow gullies—
is wide and barren, sucking
things into the opaque water.
people in the artificial shade
of garage aprons and storefronts
standing, sitting still and dormant
threaten the sandy blue vortex
with empty color, using the vanity
of worthless blaming stasis.

## II

the river eats the land
and rules the beings standing
beside in their dusty houses.
people try to catch
its strength and hold the guts
of the current that rides
under the muddy roiled
debrisflecked surface, with songs
of the catchall river channel
running. the wet world's dawn
and conceptions of fleetingness
file over the circled riffles,
processions of early light,
the fresh smell of deserts
dampborn with cool dew.
              the morning
reflects the wholeness
and length, small swirled
watercones of disturbance
following the turns of depth,
bridges cutting the strength
but giving no substance
or seeming subreal influence.
riverdawn comes with the rippling
of existing rhythms.

# III

like his brother the snake
he dances with the sun
his scintillating diamondback
crackling with the stretch
for new parts of warmth.
             orange
holds no more beauty for him
than the fish he carries
womblike in his watergut.
the simplicity of easy flowing
rides him high, a rattler goaded,
the warm tongue threetined
at the tail, or three rattles
warning of the length and time
and then assimilation in toward
the other part, the shedding
of his skin into the clear river,
running sibilant into the mississippi
with his freshborn skin
crying widemouthed into the sea—
blood of the dawn weeping again
whitefaced and tenuous after scarring
but feeding the land with his corpse.

# PAULA GUNN ALLEN

# Deep Deep City Blues: Elegy for the Man Who Owned the Rain

On such a day
troubled waters gargle in my chest:
*pericarditis* I suppose they'd say,
though the clouds probably
see it otherwise as they twist and stammer in the sky.
Cold wind kicks up dust, smells of rain.
Inevitably the mesas (aloof) call to me.
Invariably, I can't go to them—such
is the nature of our understanding—
like high pressure zones and cool air flows
twist and stutter in my chest, unmeditated,
unturned: the dead from broken jars remain, unreborn.
No name I say can find its object here: trouble
needs no name. The sandy plateaus speak
their own-way language, and dry gullies
gargle emptiness on to the barren plains.
(Coyote caverns haunt the mounds and
Thunder-hollows curve around the mind
to bend it to their will)

It will rain again tonight.
Then the clouds will be able to be still.

# Hoop Dancer

It's hard to enter
circling clockwise and counter
clockwise moving no
regard for time, metrics
irrelevant to this dance where pain
is the prime counter and soft
stepping feet praise water from the skies:

I have seen the face of triumph
the winding line stare down all moves to desecration
guts not cut from arms, fingers joined to minds,
together Sky and Water one dancing one
circle of a thousand turning lines beyond the march of years—
out of time, out of
time, out
of time.

# Ikce Wichasha

Elusive, sense of you after years; noise
around you I remember, no eagle on your god-side
shoulder, no peace, a stunted
vision.
Today, message: hope gotten
into you somehow, ceremony,
time. I wonder at your face, the
silence around your chair. What
ever is said, you said
"Black Elk,"
"the ghosts of old Wounded Knee stand
in the moonlight,"
"Inipi" you said: close and smoke-dark,
sweet sage I guess is what contains you,
fragrant waka*n* smoke now: and
moonlight spirits walking under five eagles,
Black Elk still praying, still
making things happen out there.

# *Medicine Song*

I add my breath to your breath
That our days may be long on the Earth;
That the days of our people may be long;
That we shall be one person;
That we may finish our roads together.
May my father bless you with life;
May our Life Paths be fulfilled.

—Laguna

# 1 (Shadow Way)

In this room where voices spin the light
making webs to catch forbidden visions (center
that cannot be grasped) climb
ladders that do not reach the Sky, hands
do not meet, glances unmet rise, fall
gracelessly against shadows that hold the song inside,
tongueless celebration of what is absurd.
Light follows dark (helpless voices climb)
as though precious life could be so stilled,
as though a flicker of mind could turn hurt
or terror into this night's entertainment.
The woman next to me clutches knees to chest,
shrinks into a corner of the room, as though she could
disappear, gracefully evade the web that grows around us.
The wall becomes a solid past, no unexpecteds here
her shoulders seem to say, and hurt that is not hers feels
out the room, voices climb, circle, spin toward finity, sing
obstinately.

# 2 (The Duck-Billed God)

On the webbed finger of a water dream swims
One who is named Child of the Lake,
foolish emblem on the bare surface of the dream.
(Finger of time pointed at my face,
as though some unheard shame had dowsed my mind)
and this is unexpected. I have known my shadow lurked
just out of reach, but that it should confront my sight
in crystal clarity, turning into a shadowed burial place,
making of dream absurdity—ah, but I saw the duck-billed face
of Macibol turn toward me, I
heard his words, misunderstood their sounding and became,
as swift as waters bearing him from me,
plaything of a mind half-gone.

# 3 (Lament)

Long (as song so stricken goes)
I've worn the crown of penitence on my tongue,
a layering of cloud familiar to my eyes
(that is the sign of Macibol)
and long have told the songs and tales of Ka-waik
how I might make of wanderings a reason,
an image of a sacred ladder I might climb
as earth and water climb to help the wingless fish upstream.
But in a room of solid sounds, where shame is emblem
and fear its hopeless twin, the voices that climb upsong
can only make blank utterance that grows too blind to dream.

## 4 (The Dead Spider)

Child of water, desert mind
webbed and broken on the surface of the lake
body so small the damage barely shows
small thing, unable to spin, turn
in your death, shadow too stricken to flow,
find a place among some clutching reeds to rest.
Blow your dead breath over the surface of the lake,
dream in your silent shadow, celebrate.

# Rain for Ke-waik Bu-ne-ya

Out the back window the sky is dead. Rain
promises the garden its grave relief, its
promise buried in furrowed hearts:

    Shiwanna

        Shiwanna

old footsteps echo on the southern hills.
To the west, the sky is bright:

Paitamo, set us at rest.

Last night under the yellow light
we told of bright things, spoke of sleep
tried to renew old firelight dreams
like the old ones we sat
gathering fragments of long since broken hearts:

bring tomorrow.

Today the rain comes. It gleans power
of light on a slant, releases blossoms
in the shape of pity and ancient grace:

Grandfather, give us yesterday.

Rain today coming from the east. Tomorrow
from another hill the Shiwanna will send again
a token for our hearts to drink:

a wakening.

# Mountain Song

Let
me sprinkle pollen over your head
tell
the tales that hold the rocks to life.

I
will walk
nobly to Bush Mountain
lost to the redstone gate
of dawn.

The treacherous pot-holes
are drunk with clouds.

The enemy has many wiles.

# Crow Ambush
(Song for '76)


crow
circling overhead
stands on a broken branch
to consider his reflection
in the pool


moon
riding herd on utility poles
wonders
when the converging lines
will surround him


wind
lulling grass into submission
mutters to the drying hills
(eating pemmican)


nothing obvious
a natural sort of understanding
elusive as half-meant charity as
singing a mix-breed song from
INDIAN '49: Hi-ya Hi-ya Hi-ya Hi
I'd rather be a drunkard than a fool.

# Snowgoose

North of here where
water marries ice,
meaning is other than what
I understand.

I have seen in picture how
white the bulge of the glacier
overshadows the sea,
frozen Pentecostal presence,
brilliant in the sun—
way I have never been.

I heard the snowgoose cry today
long-wheeled wings overhead,
sky calling untroubled blue
song to her and morning
(North wind blowing.)

# Sandia Crest, May, 1973

Perilous
cloud-shrouded day—
haze waits over the city in shreds,
what I have retraced in the half-buried rocks
are letters from the trilobites
not yet translated. The sign of
Thunder holds the air still as Crow
demands my attention: he sails
just below the peak I sit on, flies around the mountain
curve to land just out of my sight: another message
the wind and I may read, free for the noticing, today.
South the trail winds up along the crest
five thousand feet above Albuquerque, and along my mind
into yesterday's dream, tomorrow's meaning. Fragile
as it is, that note, undiscovered yet inscribed
in stone, reminds me of a message I laid out for me
and Crow in half-spoken conversation years ago: Idly,
as sun strokes my reverie, I
wonder where mountain stood when trilobite's letter was
    transcribed,
and then I fall asleep, resting uneasily on the edge of the peak.

# Jet Plane (Dhla-nuwa)

This lumbering. A thing
inevitably seen as Dinosaur,
flying somehow programmed into Denver—
49 minutes. (Why not name the numbers
instead of numbering the names?) Make them part
of power. (Clicking brain-studs turn, bearings
east
ward north
ward
click) kin to the center
point, counter
I tell myself not
to feel the fear that rides my gut, it's
only as far down as death, deep
canyons hold no power like flute-song, butterfly—but
heart clings to breath beside the Sandias: I do
not wish to lose to the rising cliff (barely outside of right
wing-tip) yet. (49 is as good as 33, and somehow
significant, as though named.) That
matters someway, this morning.

This place becoming precious, now I'm going;
as my love of spelling right, now I spell so wrong,
love of aborted embryo, now he's gone: the Mountain
knows that this is what I think, and the Center,
white on Two Gray Hills you bring: light
shines up the rivers and codes pools deep below—
bright-shiny talismans
limbering still flight
(who could say in the dark caves of yesterday
that smokedark choking fire could lead
to 30,000 feet in the air and rising?)

# TODD HAYCOCK

# Lited a Smoke To Grind Some Sorrow

Lited a smoke to grind some sorrow,
been walking in hate too long.
Haven't seen those brown eyes I once knew.
See mountains ain't enough.
Sing song helps a little.
Wishing ought to take me back,
but dreaming of endless future
makes me drown forever.
Facing cold isn't hard.
Rivers flow from my eyes.
Makes my eyes red.
Takes summers to winters.
On to this day I feel
sadness surrounding me.

# Above Alkali Spring

Lovable mutton puncher.
Closed day again.
Scrolled himself by alkali spring.
Black coal crow leaped softly,
Landed on death.
Dead skull soaked its head
Near shallow shore
With alkali brain.
Salt weed edged waterhole,
Burst dirt, drew a beard on its face.
Alkali weed meets its need
When sheep are on the run.
Old age cottonwood casts
Stillness on noonday.
Sand canyons steeped high
Above low alkali spring.

# Time Flew in a Manner of Birds

Time flew in a manner of birds.
Me, got up being poor.
Many moons past.
Me, gone like a clear day
thinking of tomorrow's wealth.
Rain left me rich
but wind makes it nothing.
At times, me, felt heaven
falling down on me.
Seeing became dreams
that joy of smiled
no other could replace.
Shouting without reach hands.
Long I waited to find.

# Rain

War-painted arrows
struck heaven's heart.
Crude silver ore poured
when thirst drove deep.
Cries of pain roared.

Crystal glittering strings
hit hard in hunger,
doze off, search peace.

# Wild Flowers

By day light returning
when mother earth touched your kind
you bloom

You
'fresher than winter morning breeze
spouting out your love
as you wave across golden fields

Devil eye orange ball admired your beauty—
it's a shame—rain cries with jealous eyes
gets you wet

Dawn came still, your sunrise
for rest you forgot
while others brought silence

Stars lit their sword,
fought your loneliness

Big mighty moon stood guard
only for your sake

For you, slave with beauty,
yesterday being flowers of light

This coming time
shall you dance in watery tears

# Days Came Through as White Dust Arrives

Days came through as white dust arrives.
Blank, blurry skies massed open air.
White dust coming and going.

Birds flew my direction in gangs.
They came only specks
marking in cotton worlds.

The sun hides itself on the other side,
afraid to appear against the gods of cold
that set foot in this place.

# Navajoland

Land of my people which is old and faded and rugged.
Mountains are grayish mixed with brownish and old
with cedar mixed with pine makes the scene. Mesas
and rocks which stand tall and proud which seems
like sculptured objects. Dry hot sands by burning
suns. Tumbleweed, yucca wild, combined with the color
of the land. The blue sky seems the coolest of them
all. Clouds which seem to smile at the hot buried
land. The rain water and the spring which seems
to retreat at the break of light.

# JEFF SAUNDERS

# I Came Far Today

I came far today
from where winds are white.

Four rising now, west to east
to eat the land, lie with it,
letting it soak into our eyes,
flowing in there were earth houses
rich brown in land.

Our fat faces shone, stared
down the walls.

We came circus
trying to crawl down streets.

I left . . .

I felt like a tourist.

# Poles of Smoke

poles of smoke rose everywhere
makeshift houses leaned against nights
droning voices were higher than canyons
where eagles ricocheted through them

there were doors with trees on them
flashing in orange green shadows
an old hogan sits dark
the ol' one eyed ford made its rounds

we sat with brushes
no sound except the running of the wind
that night we rode the land
down to the canyons

## Summer Came Lightly

Summer came lightly
and into little minds
who took upon the strings.

They made patterns to amuse
when the sun was forgiving.

Until winter they wove
lines into abstract patterns.

Cold brought spiders out
and they entwined their sleep
eyes in strands of darkness.

# The Weekend

the afternoon coldness
falling upon nervous teachers
cars not moving
it is the earth rolling
4 mins. to 3:45
soon to be released
from photographic cells
to the crawling routine
of the weekend
25¢ happiness in the reels
of fantasy

# Black Wind

Ravens grace violent
updrafts, along rims.

Tiny sparrow hawks
fall upon her silent.

Cold afternoons stay
when west mountains hide the sun.

Naked trees fall slow
brown lines on the sand.

Shadows falling from the west
are sleeping children.

Darkness comes early
to our canyon home.

Mountains melt away
high gold cottonwood flame.

Black wind blows evening way.

# Snow Came Easy

Snow came easy in December
to your window.
Serious winds blew laughing
flakes from us,
and wails came from your
dead side.
First day out I was frost-bitten
and put fires out.
Activities and winter
were stopped cold.
Leather is stiff and water is
hard to haul.

# Painted Land

Across painted sands
down to the sleeping canyons
we cling to the land.

My love of our land
stands out with the red rocks
to cool burning sands.

The golden fleece sheep
and the painted rocks are turquoise
when the rain passes.

The earth, golden squash,
hand painted kernels of corn
grown in the heart land.

The earth house alone
stands in the gray brown darkness
and the blue dogs bark.